Canada: The State of the Federation 1991

Edited by

Douglas M. Brown

Institute of Intergovernmental Relations

Institut des relations intergouvernementales

Canadian Cataloguing in Publication Data

The National Library of Canada has catalogued this publication as follows:

Main entry under title:

Canada, the state of the federation

1985-
Annual.

ISSN 0827-0708
ISBN 0-88911-588-5 (1991)

1. Federal-provincial relations - Canada - Periodicals.* 2. Federal government - Canada - Periodicals. I. Queen's University (Kingston, Ont.). Institute of Intergovernmental Relations.

JL27.F42 /991 321.02'3'0971   C86-030713-1

70 565

The Institute of Intergovernmental Relations

The Institute is the only organization in Canada whose mandate is solely to promote research and communication on the challenges facing the federal system.

Current research interests include fiscal federalism, constitutional reform, the reform of federal political institutions and the machinery of federal-provincial relations, Canadian federalism and the global economy, and comparative federalism.

The Institute pursues these objectives through research conducted by its own staff and other scholars through its publication program, seminars and conferences.

The Institute links academics and practitioners of federalism in federal and provincial governments and the private sector.

L'Institut des relations intergouvernementales

L'Institut est le seul organisme canadien à se consacrer exclusivement à la recherche et aux échanges sur les questions du fédéralisme.

Les priorités de recherche de l'Institut portent présentement sur le fédéralisme fiscal, la réforme constitutionnelle, la modification éventuelle des institutions politiques fédérales, les nouveaux mécanismes de relations fédérales-provinciales, le fédéralisme canadien au regard de l'économie globale et le fédéralisme comparatif.

L'Institut réalise ses objectifs par le biais de recherches effectuées par son personnel et par des universitaires de l'Université Queen's et d'ailleurs, de même que par des conférences et des colloques.

L'Institut sert de lien entre les universitaires, les fonctionnaires fédéraux et provinciaux et le secteur privé.

CONTENTS

PREFACE

This is the sixth volume in the annual series of the Institute of Intergovernmental Relations, *Canada: The State of the Federation*. This volume maintains the pattern of including sections with a focus on the issues and a focus on provinces. It is the intent of the Institute to be able to cover, over several years, a cumulative and comprehensive treatment of provinces, regions and a wide variety of issues related to policy matters. This year, as we did in 1990, the first few chapters dealing exclusively with constitutional issues are set aside in a separate section. We also continue with past practice to include a chronological listing, with an index, of the most significant developments in intergovernmetal relations in Canada over the year from July through to June. For the second year in a row we have included as an appendix a select bibliography related to constitutional issues.

The editor would like to thank all of the authors for their contributions, especially those who delivered within a very tight schedule. Each chapter was reviewed by two external referees, and we are most grateful to them for their prompt assessments. Special thanks to Ron Watts for his contribution to the initial design of this year's volume, with our regrets that he was unable to stay with the project due to his leave to work with the Government of Canada. Our thanks also to Bob Young for his helpful reading and suggestions on the section on constitutional issues.

The volume as a whole is the result of a team effort at the Institute. I would like to thank Daniel Bonin, Marilyn Banting, Margaret Day, Patti Candido, and Mary Kennedy for their assistance. However, special thanks goes to Valerie Jarus for her diligent devotion to the desk-top publishing process.

Douglas M. Brown
September 1991

CONTRIBUTORS

Daniel Bonin is Research Associate, Institute of Intergovernmental Relations, Queen's University.

Kathy L. Brock is Assistant Professor of Political Studies at the University of Manitoba. She served as Research Director of the Manitoba Task Force on the Meech Lake Accord, 1989-90.

Douglas M. Brown is Acting Director, Institute of Intergovernmental Relations, Queen's University.

Graham Fraser is Bureau Chief of the Ottawa Bureau of the *Globe and Mail*. He is the author of several books, including: *Playing For Keeps: The Making of the Prime Minister, 1988,* and *PQ: René Lévesque and the Parti Québécois.*

Dwight Herperger is Research Associate, Institute of Intergovernmental Relations, Queen's University.

Terrance Hunsley is a visiting fellow with the School of Policy Studies, Queen's University, and the former Director of the Canadian Council on Social Development.

Darrel R. Reid is Information Officer, Institute of Intergovernmental Relations, Queen's University.

Norman J. Ruff is Professor of Political Science at the University of Victoria and a frequent commentator on British Columbia politics.

Donald J. Savoie is Executive Director of the Canadian Institute for Research on Regional Development at l'Université de Moncton. His most recent book is *The Politics of Public Spending in Canada.*

Donna Tingley is Executive Director of the Environmental Law Centre in Edmonton, and is the editor of *Into the Future: Environmental Law and Policy for the 1990s.*

I

Introduction

1

An Overview

Douglas M. Brown

La fédération canadienne est présentement en proie à une crise rendue plus complexe encore par les nombreux défis auxquels doit répondre notre société sur les plans économique et politique. Si pour l'instant la question constitutionnelle semble être au beau fixe, les prochains mois devraient en revanche faire l'objet, à cet égard, d'un débat intense et mouvementé. Par ailleurs, on a pu observer au chapitre des relations intergouvernementales certains développements nouveaux, notamment en ce qui concerne la politique économique, le dossier autochtone et le contentieux fiscal fédéral-provincial. Cette introduction passe en revue les points précédents et s'emploie ensuite à dégager les idées force des articles du présent volume. Certains chapitres abordent les principaux traits qui, cette dernière année, ont marqué la problématique constitutionnelle, ainsi que les politiques sociale et environnementale. Deux autres articles ont pour thème l'intégration des Maritimes et le rôle de la Colombie-Britannique au sein de la fédération. L'auteur conclut en examinant divers types de scénarios évoquant un déblocage possible de l'impasse constitutionnelle actuelle. Autant, selon l'auteur, ne doit-on pas écarter complètement l'hypothèse d'un règlement fructueux de l'épineux contentieux constitutionnel, autant, par contre, doit-on envisager sérieusement la possibilité qu'on assiste à des ratés successifs pouvant conduire in extremis à un effondrement total du système fédéral.

INTRODUCTION

As this edition of *Canada: The State of the Federation* goes to print, the federation is in a crisis. Unfortunately, crisis is an overused word in some circles, and Canadians are growing weary of the apparent continuation, year after year, of a crisis in their federation. Some see these as a sign that the system cannot work; some see them as symptoms of incompetence. Still others may see them as manufactured for partisan ends. It is nonetheless true that Canada's very existence as a federation has clearly been at issue in the past year, and has been discussed in places far removed from academic and political meeting rooms. Canadians may be facing the banality of crisis, but crisis it is, nonetheless.

This edition is the sixth in the Institute's annual series of commissioned articles on current aspects of Canadian federalism and intergovernmental relations. The pattern of the volume follows that of four of the previous editions, with sections focusing in turn on broad constitutional issues, policy issues and individual provinces or regions. Therefore this volume does not attempt to provide a comprehensive set of constitutional options or analyses for the reader's consideration.[1] The intent of the coverage of the constitutional issue as such has been to survey the major events and issues of the past year and to provide summary analysis. The intent of the remaining chapters is to convey the details of how contemporary Canadian federalism and intergovernmental relations work in specific policy fields, and in specific parts of the federation. Throughout the volume, however, there is a continuing reference to the prevailing constitutional dilemma and to related problems in fiscal, economic and political arenas.

SUSPENDED ANIMATION OR BUSINESS AS USUAL?

The state of the federation at the constitutional level is in effect a state of suspended animation. There have been a number of significant developments, but there is still a sense that the main event is yet to begin and that late 1991 and 1992 will bring more dramatic movement that will set the course of the federation (or successor arrangements) for years to come. The reasons for the suspension of the debate are clear enough. Most of the major constitutional players simply did not have a fall-back position to last year's failure of the Meech Lake Accord. As Graham Fraser outlines in his chapter, Ottawa in particular went through "ten months of shock" before a clear constitutional strategy emerged. The fruits of that strategy will be tested as this volume appears, after Joe Clark, federal Minister for Constitutional Affairs releases a discussion paper in late September 1991.

The political community in Quebec was, of course, much quicker off the mark. The remarkable solidarity of the submissions to and report of the Parliamentary Commission on the Political and Constitutional Future of Quebec (better known as the Bélanger-Campeau Commission), and the bold initiative of the Quebec Liberal Party's constitutional committee in its report, *A Québec Free to Choose* (better known as the Allaire Report), have set out in clear and unmistakable terms that the status quo is untenable, and that what Meech Lake offerred may not now be enough. However, if the intent of these processes was to engage the rest of Canada in a dialogue on the constitutional future, the result, at least until the spring of 1991, has largely been a monologue. The rest of the country has been more concerned with the process of constitutional reform and has only slowly come to formulate its own substantive demands for constitutional change. There have been many signals from several quarters of the nature of these demands — discussed at greater length below — but as this volume goes to print the debate has not been fully engaged.

While suspension characterized the constitutional front in 1991, developments in economic conditions, social trends, and political fortunes continue to affect the system of intergovernmental relations as a whole. Here one might be tempted to conclude that it has been business as usual, or at least the continuation of trends established before 1991. The "Chronology of Events, July 1990 – June 1991" by Darrel Reid provides the highlights of the past year's developments, and several of the chapters dwell on specific aspects. From these, however, there emerge a number of key departures which suggest that business has not been quite as usual in 1990-91.

On the economic front, federal and provincial governments have had to face a recession without recourse to the countercyclical spending practices used to soften the blow of previous recessions. The significant exception was Ontario where the newly elected New Democratic government produced its first budget, with a $9 billion deficit and the promise of similarly large deficits over the medium term. Ontario's apparent lack of restraint was vociferously denounced by Ottawa and most of the other provinces. They did so because the macroeconomic impact of the budget undermined their own restraint budgets, but also because Ontario's lead in responding to the victims of the recession encouraged demands for a similar response in the other provinces. In the longer term the effect of such deficit financing in Ontario could be to restrict even further the ability of Ontario taxpayers to contribute to fiscal redistribution through their contribution to federal transfers (which would add to the fiscal decentralization discussed below).[2] The recession nonetheless hit Ontario the hardest, especially in those sectors where the 1980s boom had been most exaggerated. Recovery from the recession is uneven, with the west poised for more rapid recovery than central Canada — although not perhaps in a total reversion to the 1970s during the resource prices boom. The slowdown in Quebec in particular has had the effect of cooling the momentum and pace of constitutional developments, if not support for sovereignty.

The presence of government deficits at the federal level and the problems they create in federal-provincial fiscal relations is hardly a new departure. During the past year, however, the political realization of the consequences of these fiscal trends grew considerably. Canadians — in particular social policy interest groups — woke up to the fact that the cash transfers to provinces for health and post-secondary education were slowly but surely declining to zero (by one estimate this point would be reached in 1997 for Quebec and 2007 for the other provinces).[3] This has fuelled the debate over whether the federal government will maintain any leverage on national standards in social

programs, which in turn will be a significant theme in constitutional negotiations. Other developments that only served to emphasize the trend to fiscal
decentralization were: the western provinces' advocacy of a regional income
tax collection system and greater freedom in terms of provincial income tax
structure; the Ottawa-Quebec agreement to harmonize the provincial sales tax
base with the federal Goods and Services Tax and to have Quebec collect both
taxes; and the Supreme Court of Canada's 15 August 1991 decision confirming
the ability of the federal government to unilaterally impose a ceiling on Canada
Assistance Plan payments to the wealthier provinces. The systemic outcome of
all of these developments will be unclear until negotiations are completed on
the renewal of the current five-year fiscal arrangements in 1992. However, these
events guarantee the spillover of fiscal issues into the constitutional arena in
the coming year.

Perhaps the most significant departures in 1990-91 have concerned the status
of aboriginal peoples. The violent standoff at Kanewake and Kanesatake in
Quebec in the summer of 1990 (more popularly called the "Oka crisis")
heightened the visibility of aboriginal rights, land claims and treaties, and
native self-government and sovereignty. The role and place of aboriginal
peoples in the federation has become an urgent national priority. Indeed few
issues have gained as much media prominence over the past year, except
perhaps for Quebec's increased support for sovereignty. The two issues are
intertwined in a potentially explosive way, with a high degree of sympathy for
aboriginal demands among Canadians outside Quebec, and a general animosity
within Quebec, caused in part by resentment of the aboriginal role in killing the
Meech Lake Accord.[4] The potential flashpoint is the hydroelectric developments in northern Quebec known as James Bay II, which has pitted environmental interest groups and the Cree and Inuit against the Bourassa government
and much of public opinion in Quebec.

In the meantime the momentum gained from the aftermath of the Oka crisis
continues. The aboriginal leadership, itself undergoing considerable turnover,
was highly sceptical of the various federal initiatives promised in September
1990 by Prime Minster Mulroney. However, progress has been marked at the
federal level, as witnessed by an acceleration of the land claims process, the
review underway by chiefs of the Assembly of First Nations to propose a total
overhaul of the *Indian Act*, the appointment of the Royal Commission on
Aboriginal Peoples with Georges Erasmus as co-chairman, and the initiation
(with federal government support) of a parallel consultative process to determine aboriginal proposals for constitutional reform. As well, the Ontario
government recognized the principle of native self-government, and, apparently at the insistence of Premier Bob Rae, aboriginal leaders participated in
the Annual Premiers' Conference at Whistler, B.C., in August 1991. It is much
too early to predict the cumulative impact of all of these initiatives. However,

the aboriginal cause is clearly the benefactor, and a political momentum is building which will make resolution of long-standing grievances impossible to forestall.[5]

Apart from these developments, the pace of intergovernmental relations continued in 1990-91 with the usual pattern of meetings of ministers and senior officials. While the subject matters of these relations appears to have been as comprehensive as ever, discussions related to the environment, agriculture, health and interprovincial trade barriers were among the most salient in the public eye. The greatest change was in the meetings that did not take place. Shortly after the clock ran out on the Meech Lake Accord, Quebec Premier Bourassa declared that Quebec as a government would never again negotiate as one-of-ten with all of the other provinces, in effect commencing a boycott of all intergovernmental meetings except bilateral meetings with the federal government. This position has since been moderated to exclude meetings that Quebec deems are in its interests to attend (for example, meetings related to trade negotiations, finance and financial institutions). If not complete, the boycott has nonetheless been effective, and according to one account, Quebec stayed away from as many as 70 percent of all intergovernmental meetings to which it was invited.[6]

Quebec's boycott will probably be only as significant as its duration. In the past 12 months it has prevented the convening of meetings of all first ministers, as Prime Minister Mulroney could not afford to call a First Ministers' Conference knowing that Quebec would not attend; to do so would lend his weight to Quebec's isolation, self-imposed as it is. In any event, Mulroney may have also had his fill of first ministerial diplomacy, and its temporary eclipse has made a virtue of the necessity of bilateral meetings with individual premiers. The longer term effect of Quebec's absence from most intergovernmental meetings will be to drive a further wedge between Quebec and the other provinces, and ultimately also to further undermine the legitimacy of executive federalism. The conjunction of Quebec's absence and the aboriginal presence at the Annual Premiers' Conference may be only coincidental, but the symbolism nonetheless speaks volumes about the current state of intergovernmental relations in Canada.

In summary, there are obviously signs of both suspended animation — or perhaps a phony war — on the constitutional front, and also some significant movement away from business as usual in the operation of intergovernmental relations and the federal system as a whole. Canada is at a clear crossroads and many patterns of activity and relations that have long characterized our federal system are coming unstuck, probably forever.

To delve more deeply into these developments is the purpose of this volume, and the focus of the three main parts of the text summarized below.

FOCUS ON THE CONSTITUTIONAL DEBATE:
PREPARING FOR THE "CANADA ROUND"

The current debate over the constitutional future of Quebec began with the demise of the Meech Lake Accord in June 1990, but it turns around issues unresolved since at least the 1960s. The debate is driven by political developments in Quebec but is by no means confined to them. There are movements in the western provinces, but also in the Atlantic and the north for greater decentralization in some cases and for a more effective regional voice in federal institutions in others. Aboriginal peoples also want to see a more secure constitutional status for their rights to self-determination and self-government. Other groups in Canadian society, most notably those implicated by the Charter of Rights and Freedoms, are highly sensitive to constitutional reform and may seek an extension of rights into social and economic fields. Those who assume that this broad constitutional agenda will result in one large set of negotiations have referred to this process as the "Canada Round" (in contrast to the depiction of the negotiations leading to the Meech Lake Accord as the "Quebec Round"). While galling to Quebecers, it nonetheless seems inescapable that Quebec's constitutional status can now only be resolved by a Canada Round.

As already noted, Quebec was the first off the mark in the current debate. In the aftermath of the Meech Lake fiasco, the province has prepared its ground with a remarkable solidarity. Daniel Bonin chronicles these developments in chapter 2: "Le Quebec de l'après-Meech: entre le beau risque nouvelle manière et la souveraineté." While the rest of Canada seemed paralysed, Quebec Premier Bourassa launched the Bélanger-Campeau Commission. The Commission served to maintain a bipartisan front of elected politicians as well as a substantial number of non-parliamentarians in its membership. The maintenance of solidarity ultimately had its price in the form of a final report short on substantive recommendations for reform, but long on the process for deciding the future of Quebec, i.e., a process moving through two parliamentary committees and ending in a possible referendum by October 1992. In the meantime, the public hearings of the Commission in November and December of 1990 electrified Canadians by demonstrating the overwhelming support of interveners for Quebec sovereignty and the paucity of support for federalism (except as a defensive posture in reaction to the perceived costs of sovereignty). Partly to regain the political initiative from the Commission, the Quebec Liberal Party released the Allaire Report in late January 1991. The report called for radical surgery to the federal constitution. It made a set of proposals for extensive decentralization, which were adopted as party policy in March 1991. Bonin's analysis examines carefully the content of both the Bélanger-Campeau and Allaire Reports. He demonstrates how Bourassa, by endorsing the Allaire proposals, bought more time for his government, and the rest-of-Canada, to deliver renewed federalism, and to delay the date of a proposed referendum. At the same time, according to Bonin, he has maintained a delicate balance between the quasisovereigntists and the federalists within his own party. This chapter also reviews the response in Ottawa to the events in Quebec, with the ruling Conservatives managing to minimize defections to the *indépendantiste* Bloc Québécois while struggling to put together a set of proposals before the referendum deadline in Quebec.

Throughout Canada, although more so outside Quebec, the focus of much of the emerging constitutional debate has been on the "Politics of Process." This is the title of chapter 3 by Kathy Brock. The widespread dissatisfaction with the Meech Lake process has set the stage for a broad debate about the role of the public in constitutional reform. Brock's analysis finds the roots for this upswelling of demand for public participation in the specific circumstances of the 1981-82 and 1987-90 constitutional processes. In the former period, constitutional politics went beyond governments to embrace various citizen groups, but in the latter years these same groups felt shut out. She also finds more general roots of discontent in the increased questioning of the legitimacy of representative democratic institutions. The response by the federal and provincial governments to the rising demands for public participation has been to establish a variety of fora for public expression. Brock reviews the context and relative achievements of the Spicer Citizen's Forum, the Special Joint Committee on the Process for Amending the Constitution of Canada (Beaudoin-Edwards) and the consultative processes in six provinces, and compares these to the Bélanger-Campeau process in Quebec. The author's assessment of the feasibility of various forms of broadened public input led her to reject the Spicer recommendation for a constituent assembly and referenda, as these would only exacerbate the dilemma of direct representation. However, the author does endorse the Beaudoin-Edwards recommendations for a "super" parliamentary committee, and makes some further suggestions about how to improve the legitimacy and effectiveness of the process while leaving the final decisions with elected parliamentarians.

The third perspective on the constitutional issue is provided by Graham Fraser in chapter 4, "Slouching Towards Ottawa." Fraser's analysis focuses on the political realities that will shape constitutional outcomes. Canada outside Quebec is rapidly heading in new directions that may not accommodate or even include Quebec. Three key political leaders to be reckoned with owe none of their authority or influence to support from Quebec: Ontario Premier Bob Rae, Newfoundland Premier Clyde Wells and Reform Party leader Preston Manning. Other potential leaders outside Ottawa have been relatively silent, while federal politicians in Ottawa took several months to get over the shock of Meech Lake and, in the interim, were preoccupied by other events (Oka, the Gulf war, the GST battle, etc.). Fraser notes that the Mulroney government finally seemed to resume control over the pace of constitutional events by May 1991, when Joe Clark was appointed the minister in charge, and by grace of a "reflective pause" in Quebec. Fraser is nonetheless cautious in his assessments of the prospects for success in the emergent federal strategy. He cites Robert Normand's indictment of the "bitter confusion" in the country as capturing the prevailing national mood. There are many hurdles to get over, not least of which for the Mulroney government is keeping its caucus intact and avoiding an early election that could signal the final denouement. At the same time, the government must attempt to separate its own unpopularity from its constitutional proposals.

FOCUS ON ISSUES: WHITHER NATIONAL STANDARDS?

There is no clean break from the constitutional debate when we turn to examine the effects of the federal system and ongoing intergovernmental relations on specific policy issues. Chapter 5 by Terrance Hunsley, "Constitutional Change and National Social Programs" and Chapter 6 by Donna Tingley, " The Environment: Conflict and Cooperation" demonstrate clearly the direct consequences of specific constitutional arrangements in policy areas that are very important to most Canadians.

One objective of Hunsley's chapter is to show that while national standards in social policy are not explicitly or exhaustively codified in constitutional or even ordinary statutes, a national social infrastructure nonetheless exists. The author reviews how the federal system, and especially the intricacies of executive federalism, has shaped the current network of programs that collectively provide the social entitlements of national citizenship. These arrangements have been under strain from two directions. The first is fiscal restraint, especially federal cutbacks in payments to the provinces. The second is Charter litigation which is gradually changing social policy from the outcome of negotiated intergovernmental compromises to court-mandated entitlements. The trend to fiscal decentralization is being reinforced, in Hunsley's view, by proposals for more fundamental constitutional decentralization. He suggests heading off the first of these trends by giving constitutional status to national social objectives, and providing concurrent federal power over national standards. If, however, certain social rights were entrenched in the constitution the result would be to reinforce the second trend towards social policy defined as individual rights. Nonetheless, in his view, such change would also allow greater flexibility in program delivery at the provincial level, including a more distinctive approach in Quebec.

National standards are also the focus of the chapter by Tingley on intergovernmental relations and the environment. This chapter begins by outlining some of the reasons why the field of environmental policy was so relatively free of jurisdictional dispute until recently. Cooperative intergovernmental mechanisms covered over any jurisdictional gaps, as Tingley demonstrates with the cases of inland fisheries and safe drinking water. Three recent events have challenged the comfortable cooperative relationship. The rising public concern over the environment has forced a more proactive federal role; environmental interest groups have become disillusioned with the intergovernmental process as a result of their experience with the drafting of the *Canadian Environmental Protection Act* in 1988; and court actions since 1988 have forced the federal government's hand in environmental assessment. In the author's view, federal and provincial governments have no choice but to permit greater openness and public involvement in intergovernmental policy processes if these processes are to continue to deliver effective responses to environmental problems. Thus the public will tolerate having national standards emerge from the mechanisms of executive federalism, only if these mechanisms also provide acceptable due process including public input. Obviously this parallels the general public stance towards constitutional reform: the legitimacy of outcomes depends on the adequacy of public input.

FOCUS ON THE PROVINCES: COPING WITH CHANGE

A closer look at the state of the federation from the perspective of individual provinces provides a deeper understanding of the dynamics of the system. Chapters 7 and 8 do so by providing analyses of the Maritime provinces and British Columbia respectively.

Donald Savoie's article "The Search for the Holy Grail: Maritime Cooperation" surveys the recent revival of interest in the Maritime provinces in greater regional integration. It is not the idea of political union that is gaining ground, but rather the notion of economic integration. Support for the latter idea is driven by the twin external threats of economic globalization and Canadian disunity. The reduced prospect for transfer payments from Ottawa is also forcing an emphasis on regional self-reliance. Savoie traces the long history of attempts to increase Maritime integration and concludes that the external threats alone have never been sufficient to get beyond entrenched interests of the individual provinces. This time the combination of factors may provide the ingredients of greater progress. These factors do not impinge on Newfoundland exactly the same way. Its interests will likely dictate a more selective degree of integration with its Maritime neighbours. A more vital player may be Ottawa. Its basic neutrality with respect to past Maritime integration efforts has not helped the cause, and, in the author's view, a more proactive federal role could secure the success of current efforts to achieve a common economic space in the Maritimes.

The distinct society on the other side of the country is the subject of Norman Ruff's chapter, "Pacific Perspectives on the Canadian Confederation: British

Columbia's Shadows and Symbols." The special brand of western alienation and isolation bred in British Columbia continues to shape its stance towards intergovernmental relations and the future of the federation. A much tougher economic climate and an increasingly Pacific-oriented population and trade flows have combined to heighten British Columbia's long-standing grievances with a federal system that is seen to extract more than it provides. The Vander Zalm government put an emphasis on "fair share federalism" and forced the federal government to respond with a more favourable procurement policy. A more difficult problem is the continuing deterioration of fiscal relations, as British Columbia led the western provinces in seeking greater decentralization of fiscal power. Other issues that dominate intergovernmental relations are the environment and, even more so, aboriginal land claims. British Columbia recently departed from its long-standing refusal to participate in land claims negotiations, but whether it can move fast enough to avoid destabilizing conflict, time and a provincial election will tell. Damaged by its association with the Meech Lake Accord and Vander Zalm's resignation, the Social Credit government has yet to take a prominent role in the constitutional debate and, at the time of writing, it is not yet evident how the issue will figure in the provincial election campaign. Norman Ruff contends, however, that both major parties share a common view of B.C.'s interests in these matters, and British Columbia could be the key western province to deal with in the coming year.

CONCLUSION: HOW TO SOLVE THE COMPOUND CRISIS

This overview began with the straightforward observation that the federation is in a state of crisis and has been for some time. Our contributors show how complex are the current issues. Indeed it is not too hyperbolic to conclude that we are facing a compound crisis in our political system.

An intense constitutional debate is beginning, against which the controversy over the Meech Lake Accord will pale in comparison. The debate will unfold against an economic backdrop of slow recovery from a recession that has left many unpleasant after-effects. The fiscal problems of governments at all levels are not expected to improve. The public at large remains fundamentally dissatisfied with governments and established political institutions. The ruling Conservative party in the federal parliament confronts these challenges with at most 15 percent of public support, and three provincial governments (New Brunswick, British Columbia and Saskatchewan) face electoral tests in the autumn of 1991.

The urgency of economic problems (and their dread twin of fiscal squeeze on governments) may well be the issue that sweeps all before it in the coming months. There is predicted to be only a very sluggish recovery of the Quebec economy, and in Ontario the recession leaves a litter of closed plants and unemployment lines. These realities will force the two most populous provinces to concentrate on competitiveness and productivity. At the same time they will prejudge the electorate to favour constitutional options that improve the chances for increased economic efficiency, but which do not increase the average citizen's vulnerability to economic shocks.

These contradictory objectives unfortunately leave a lot of room for debate about just which options can meet them. The Allaire Report and others have argued for reducing intergovernmental competition and duplication. The Group of 22 and others have advocated stronger guarantees of the economic union. The NDP government of Ontario and others have called for the protection of social programs and other national standards. The Parti Québécois on one side, and the Reform Party on the other, offer more radical changes which are often justified in terms of the goals of competitiveness and economic security.

If, as the Quebec government fondly wishes, there were a constitutional dialogue between Quebec and Ottawa, the compound nature of the constitutional crisis might be lessened. But this is impossible: there is too much sentiment in the west and the Atlantic provinces against formally asymmetrical powers for Quebec; and too much support in favour of Triple E Senate reform; the aboriginal leadership now rides a wave of public support for its broad-ranging demands; non-territorially based interest groups supported by Ontario are ready to do battle over national rights and standards; and the public at large favours direct participation in constitutional renewal. An Ottawa-Quebec deal is thus unsustainable and hence undesirable. It could be argued that each of the above issues would be better resolved separately from the high-stake politics of constitutional reform. However, the Canadian disease of pursuing policy objectives by constitutional means is endemic and probably incurable.

The very compound nature of the agenda does create opportunities for trade-offs and log-rolling in a comprehensive Canada Round. That said, there is also the risk that a broad set of proposals will satisfy no camp sufficiently well to create the broad coalition of support required to avoid a regime-fracturing deadlock. So Canadians would be well advised not only to hedge their bets, but also to consider carefully how much a failure of the federal system would cost. In the coming months, after intense debate and deliberation, renewed federalism may prove impossible. In that case Canadians both within and outside Quebec will have to put to the test their supposed qualities of tolerance, pragmatism and compromise to find arrangements that minimize the disruption and uncertainty of separation. And in this respect, a few more years of talk would be preferable to the incalculable consequences of a series of hasty unilateral declarations.

Simply put, current trends suggest that the coming drama may unfold in one of two scenarios. Arguably the worst scenario for Canadians is that the inter-weaving of economic, political and constitutional problems will prove so complex that proposed solutions will soon after sink out of sight and a series of worsening deadlocks will result. It may be that no one set of problems can be solved without simultaneous movement on the others, and that the compromises necessary to resolve the entire set of problems are beyond the capabilities of the system. Deadlock begets paralysis, which begets extremism, which begets breakdown.

In the second scenario, which is perhaps the most we can hope for, one envisages the steady and patient resolution (including postponement) of the individual items on the agenda. A consensus to settle one component of the agenda increases the chances of dealing successfully with those that remain. This scenario also relies upon a range of settlement devices, not all of which are constitutional. There would need to be an avoidance of take-it-or-leave-it options and package solutions too easily vetoed. It also assumes that both leaders and citizens recognize that tolerance is essential now to avoid breakdown later. Finally, it requires constitutional statesmanship, and humility and compassion in the face of the greater well-being of Canadian citizens.

On the face of it, the first of these scenarios may seem most plausible. Current trends appear likely to add conflicting elements to the constitutional stew and unpredictable events may heighten dissension. The second scenario requires more faith in the abilities of the current federal system to handle unprecedented strain. Allowing that these scenarios have been starkly painted, the chances for each occurring appear now to be about even. An assessment of the State of the Federation a year from now will produce a more certain judgement.

NOTES

1. The Institute has produced such a volume as the outcome of a project sponsored by the Business Council on National Issues. See R.L. Watts and D.M. Brown (eds.), *Options for a New Canada* (Toronto: University of Toronto Press, 1991). Other useful books include D. Smith, P. MacKinnon and J.C. Courtney (eds.), *After Meech Lake: Lessons for the Future* (Saskatoon: Fifth House Publishers, 1991); and R. Simeon and M. Janigan (eds.), *Toolkits and Building Blocks: Constructing a New Canada* (Toronto: C.D. Howe Institute, 1991).

2. Tom Courchene makes this argument in his paper "Canada 1992: Political Denouement or Economic Renaissance?" to appear in the forthcoming book by R. Boadway et al. (eds.), *Economic Dimensions of Constitutional Change* (Kingston: John Deutsch Institute, Queen's University, 1991).

3. Ibid.

4. See the Angus Reid polling results of the fall of 1990 referenced in David Hawkes and Marina Devine, "Meech Lake and Elijah Harper: Native-State Relations in the 1990s," in Frances Abele (ed.), *How Ottawa Spends: The Politics of Fragmentation* (Ottawa: Carleton University Press, 1991), p. 57.

5. For a good overview of aboriginal issues, current to early 1991, see Hawkes and Devine, cited above.
6. See *Le Devoir*, 2 July 1991.

II

Focus on the Constitutional Debate

2

Le Québec de l'après-Meech: entre le beau risque nouvelle manière et la souveraineté

Daniel Bonin

The demise of the Meech Lake constitutional accord has provoked a real sea-change in Quebec. Fruit of an exceptional consensus among the Quebec political community, the Bélanger-Campeau Commission has led both reborn sovereigntists and disappointed federalists to present their grievances towards Canadian federalism. The Allaire Report has thrown the constitutional ball back to the rest-of-Canada. The Allaire Report also pointed out the prospect of a referendum on sovereignty by the fall of 1992. Nonetheless, over the last few months, Premier Robert Bourassa has expressed his primary allegiance to federalism, to the great displeasure of the sovereigntist-leaning wing within his party, as well as the outright sovereigntists in the PQ.

This chapter first reviews the aftermath of the Meech Lake fiasco as Bourassa revealed to the rest-of-Canada (ROC) his reluctance to deal within a constitutional framework of 11 governments and announced the creation of the Commission to examine the political and constitutional future of Quebec. Second, the chapter highlights the most significant stances advocated by different groups or individuals before the Quebec Commission. Third, both the content of the Allaire Report and the Bélanger-Campeau Report are analyzed, as well as Bill 150, adopted by the Quebec National Assembly as the legislative expression of the so-called Bélanger-Campeau consensus. Whereas the Allaire Report fostered a radical across-the-board decentralization of the Canadian federalism, the Bélanger-Campeau Report in the end accepted the idea of assessing any constitutional offer that might come from the ROC, with however, — as with Allaire — the eventuality of a referendum on sovereignty in October 1992.

The author also reviews the federal strategy since the Meech Lake failure. The emphasis is on the stance of the Mulroney government for a "renewed Canada" leading to a set of constitutional proposals to be made by Ottawa in September 1991. Finally the author examines the political context in Quebec and Canada on the eve of the next Canada round.

FEU L'ACCORD

Le naufrage de l'Accord du lac Meech le 23 juin 1990 aura eu pour conséquence d'ouvrir la boîte de Pandore constitutionnelle que les partisans de l'entente de 1987 avaient cru voir définitivement scellée, deux semaines plus tôt, lors de la signature d'une version amendée de l'Accord, au terme de la longue et laborieuse conférence des onze premiers ministres dite de la "dernière chance", à Ottawa.

L'échec de Meech fut particulièrement éprouvant pour Brian Mulroney et Robert Bourassa: s'agissant du premier ministre canadien, que le Québec ne puisse réintégrer le giron constitutionnel dans l'"honneur et l'enthousiasme" compromettait à coup sûr son pari de la "réconciliation nationale" tout en fragilisant par le fait même ses chances de survie politique au Québec et dans le ROC (Rest of Canada); quant au premier ministre du Québec, le coup fut peut-être encore plus sévère à encaisser, lui qui voyait dans la ratification de l'Accord une occasion inespérée de se dédouaner rétrospectivement de son opposition circonstancielle à la Charte de Victoria en 1971, ainsi que d'effacer les stigmates du rapatriement unilatéral et de la proclamation de la Constitution opérés par Pierre Elliot Trudeau en 1981-1982, sans le consentement de l'Assemblée nationale du Québec.[1]

Au surplus, Robert Bourassa désirait à tout prix assurer au Québec une "paix constitutionnelle" pour au moins une décade, sur la base d'une reconnaissance des cinq demandes formulées par son gouvernement. L'enjeu était tel pour Robert Bourassa qu'il accepta le risque, sur le plan juridique, de souscrire à l'entente du 9 juin 1990 — qui s'inspirait directement des propositions constitutionnelles du premier ministre du Nouveau-Brunswick, Frank McKenna et du rapport Charest — en dépit notamment d'une possible prévalence de la clause Canada nouvellement introduite sur la notion de société distincte. Pour le premier ministre du Québec, il s'agissait avant tout de "démontrer la bonne foi du Québec envers ses partenaires".[2] Sourd aux objurgations des Lucien Bouchard et Jacques Parizeau hostiles à tout accord revu et corrigé, Robert Bourassa réaffirma plutôt de façon solennelle son attachement au Canada et au fédéralisme canadien. Mais c'était sans compter sur la volte-face du premier ministre terre-neuvien Clyde Wells ainsi que sur l'obstruction législative pratiquée à la onzième heure par le député autochtone manitobain, Elijah Harper.

L'échec de Meech, s'il provoqua des sentiments contradictoires au Canada anglais, aura été ressenti par une majorité de Québécois comme une nette rebuffade par celui-ci à l'endroit des aspirations légitimes du Québec.[3] A preuve, le défilé pro-souverainiste de plus de 300,000 Québécois le long de la rue Sherbrooke à Montréal, le jour de la Saint-Jean Baptiste, tout juste au lendemain du décès de Meech, symbolisa avec force et éloquence l'exaspération d'une majeure partie de la population québécoise face au cul-de-sac constitutionnel dont le Québec venait une fois encore de faire les frais. Au surplus, la victoire significative de Gilles Duceppe, porte-étendard du Bloc québécois pro-souverainiste, lors de l'élection partielle fédérale dans Laurier-Sainte-Marie en août 1990, avec plus de deux-tiers des voix obtenues, aura en quelque sorte cristallisé, en microcosme, la forte inclination des Québécois — confirmée depuis des mois par divers sondages — à l'égard de l'option souverainiste de même que leur désaffection croissante envers les libéraux de Jean Chrétien et les "bleus du Québec" de Brian Mulroney.

Mortifié à la suite du dénouement de la saga Meech, Robert Bourassa dut néanmoins tourner la page et tirer les conclusions du moment. Ravi d'accepter la main tendue offerte par le chef péquiste Jacques Parizeau — geste qui confortait d'autant sa légitimité du moment — le premier ministre du Québec n'en était pas encore toutefois à succomber aux sirènes de la vague souverainiste qui déferlait alors sur le Québec.

Comme les événements l'auront démontré par la suite, la débâcle de Meech se sera avérée au demeurant pour Robert Bourassa un malencontreux accident de parcours qui ne remettait toutefois pas en question, intrinsèquement, sa prime allégeance envers l'option fédéraliste — ou ses variantes — et partant aussi, envers la stratégie constitutionnelle lui étant afférente.

A cet égard, l'adresse télévisée du premier ministre du Québec à ses compatriotes le 23 juin 1990 constituait, de prime abord, un désaveu radical du traditionnel processus de révision constitutionnelle, fondé sur une négociation à onze gouvernements; selon Robert Bourassa, ce processus avait été discrédité en permettant les dérapages ultimes au Manitoba et à Terre-Neuve, lesquels furent encouragés en sous-main, de suggérer ce dernier, par le tandem Chrétien-Trudeau. Le gouvernement du Québec allait désormais se donner ce mot d'ordre: exit donc, dorénavant toute participation à des conférences fédérales-provinciales et/ou inter-provinciales où les intérêts directs du Québec ne seraient pas en jeu.[4]

Conscient de l'obsolescence de facto du programme constitutionnel du Parti libéral du Québec et de son gouvernement à la suite du rejet de Meech, Robert Bourassa n'avait d'autre alternative — sous peine de s'aliéner une majorité de la population québécoise — que de s'engager à tenir un vaste débat public sur l'avenir constitutionnel du Québec, au terme duquel celui-ci aurait pleine "liberté de ses choix" constitutionnels. Dans l'attente d'une définition de ce nouvel avenir constitutionnel, le gouvernement du Québec n'entendait désormais établir des relations avec le ROC que sur une base bilatérale, voire d'"égal à égal", selon la formule de Robert Bourassa, directement empruntée au vocabulaire péquiste référendaire. Au regard de cette nouvelle dynamique Québec-Canada, le gouvernement fédéral conservateur, fidèle allié du Québec durant l'épisode Meech, allait se voir confier, malgré lui, le rôle d'interlocuteur unique du Canada hors Québec en matière constitutionnelle.

L'initiative québécoise trouva peu d'écho auprès du gouvernement Mulroney, littéralement abasourdi par la tournure des événements. En fait, c'est du côté de Queen's Park qu'émanèrent, au cours des semaines suivantes, les réactions les plus vives à l'endroit du gouvernement Bourassa. Echaudé par son exclusion du pattern de négociations Québec-Ottawa établi par son "ami" Robert Bourassa, David Peterson aura précipité du coup la rupture de l'axe politique Québec-Ontario, lequel n'avait cessé pourtant de se consolider, depuis 1987, à la faveur de l'adhésion commune des deux provinces du Canada central à l'Accord du lac Meech.[5] Désireux, au surplus, de jouer les "Captain Canada" pour pallier au mutisme et au leadership affaibli du gouvernement Mulroney, David Peterson aura tenté, le temps d'un été, de prendre le contre-pied de la démarche québécoise: de fait, il se fit l'apôtre, a contrario, du renforcement du gouvernement central ainsi que du rejet de tout réaménagement constitutionnel bilatéral, de type Québec-Ottawa, qui remettrait en cause le principe d'égalité des dix provinces consacré par la *Loi constitutionnelle de 1982*.[6] Cependant, la croisade pro-Canada du premier ministre Peterson aura tourné court auprès des Ontariens : de fait, en le désavouant électoralement au début septembre 1990, ceux-ci entendaient protester contre un certain cynisme du personnage mais aussi, souhaitaient prendre congé d'un leader qui avait été associé de façon très étroite à un processus constitutionnel fortement décrié, et ultimement avorté.

Sur la scène québécoise, le premier ministre Bourassa n'aura pas tardé, après l'échec de Meech, à dévoiler la nature du forum appelé à réfléchir sur l'avenir du Québec. Une commission parlementaire élargie, dénoncée d'avance par d'aucuns comme une simple "collection d'intérêts", fut préférée à la formule des Etats généraux, chère au Parti québécois et à Lucien Bouchard, ainsi qu'au modèle de la commission d'enquête, jugé trop hors de contrôle du pouvoir politique.

Au reste, la commission parlementaire élargie, par sa durée, accordait un répit salutaire au parti gouvernemental pour compléter, en parallèle, un exercice comparable par l'entremise de son comité constitutionnel. Somme toute, c'est uniquement l'"intermède" estival de la crise autochtone à Oka et Kahnawake, conjugué au traitement tardif de la maladie du premier ministre Bourassa, qui auront retardé pour un temps la mise en chantier du processus participatif québécois.

LE FORUM DU QUEBEC

Instituée le 4 septembre 1990 sous l'autorité de l'Assemblée nationale à la suite du vote unanime des partis politiques québécois, la Commission sur l'avenir politique et constitutionnel du Québec s'inscrivait, du coup, dans la lignée historique des Commission Tremblay (1953), Commission Laurendeau-Dunton (1963) et Commission Pepin-Robarts (1978), lesquelles s'étaient déjà penchées auparavant sur les tenants et aboutissants de la problématique Québec-Canada. Forum multi-partisan et mixte (18 parlementaires et 18 non-élus), la nouvelle commission québécoise avait pour mandat spécifique "d'étudier et d'analyser le statut constitutionnel du Québec et de formuler à cet égard des recommandations". Dans l'esprit du consensus généré par l'après-Meech et compte tenu de l'impasse constitutionnelle à résoudre, le gouvernement du Québec et l'opposition péquiste firent aisément chorus pour endosser le préambule de la loi constitutive de la Commission proclamant entre autres que

> les Québécoises et les Québécois sont libres d'assumer leur propre destin, de déterminer leur statut politique et d'assumer leur développement économique, social et culturel (...) considérant la nécessité de redéfinir (ledit) statut politique et constitutionnel du Québec.[7]

Autrement dit, toutes les options étaient envisageables en principe sauf le statu quo, à la vérité. L'heure n'était pas encore venue pour que s'engage un bras de fer idéologique entre souverainistes et fédéralistes de toutes tendances, comme cela se produira au finish, lorsqu'il s'agira de favoriser l'une ou l'autre de ces orientations constitutionnelles.

Si du côté péquiste, la thèse à promouvoir — la souveraineté — ne faisait pas l'ombre d'un doute, en revanche le gouvernement du Québec se gardait bien de privilégier officiellement une option précise, préférant plutôt attendre le dépôt, cinq mois plus tard, des conclusions du comité constitutionnel de son parti. Cependant, le premier ministre Bourassa, en fidèle disciple de Jules Monnet, inspirateur de l'Europe communautaire, ne faisait pas mystère de sa prédilection pour sa fameuse "superstructure", modèle qui s'apparenterait à une future CEE, plus intégrée politiquement que celle d'aujourd'hui.

Soucieux d'offrir l'image rassurante de l'homme politique résolument pragmatique, Robert Bourassa se fit fort d'affirmer que

> ce qui va guider le gouvernement, ce n'est pas une formule politique plutôt qu'une autre, c'est l'intérêt supérieur des Québécois. Pour nous la valeur suprême, c'est l'intérêt, le progrès du Québec. Les formules politiques doivent être subordonnées, à notre point de vue, à cet intérêt, au progrès du Québec.[8]

En corollaire, la "priorité à accorder au renforcement de l'économie québécoise" constituait l'un des "paramètres" établis, d'entrée de jeu, par le premier ministre Bourassa. Il pouvait sans peine invoquer le soutien d'un Jacques Parizeau à ce chapitre. Les deux hommes s'entendaient au surplus sur le caractère incontournable de l'association économique avec le ROC, le chef péquiste posant toutefois, comme condition préalable, l'accession du Québec à la souveraineté.[9] Ainsi donc, en dépit des divergences déjà prévisibles entre les deux leaders par rapport à la finalité politique des changements à venir, Robert

Bourassa et Jacques Parizeau officiaient, à tout le moins, à la même "grande communion économique", pour reprendre l'expression piquante de Lise Bissonnette. Ce consensus initial, loin d'être un exploit en soi, traduisait plutôt l'adhésion de l'ensemble des élites québécoises — et dans une certaine mesure canadienne — aux valeurs issues des années quatre-vingts, fondées sur la prévalence du référent économique au regard du développement sociétal.[10]

En vertu du même parangon économiste, Robert Bourassa et Jacques Parizeau convinrent aussi, au prix de longues et laborieuses tractations, de nommer chacun *leur* "personnalité du monde des affaires" à la présidence de la commission parlementaire élargie; tous deux se disaient en effet impressionnés par l'"autorité morale de l'entreprise", selon les termes du leader péquiste. C'est ainsi que Michel Bélanger et Jean Campeau, désignés co-présidents du forum québécois, furent identifiés d'avance, à leur corps défendant et et de façon quasi caricaturale, qui au camp fédéraliste, qui au camp souverainiste; en définitive, ceux-ci auront été au centre de la première es-carmouche entre libéraux et péquistes, chaque parti n'entendant rien céder de ses prérogatives relativement au choix éminemment stratégique et symbolique de la présidence.[11]

La Commission Bélanger-Campeau [12], en raison de son caractère unique et des enjeux s'y rattachant, aura constitué en soi un événement historique, largement méditatisé (en particulier par la presse) au Québec et, dans une moindre mesure, dans le ROC.

Le fer de lance du forum québécois s'est avéré la participation publique aux travaux de la Commission. La contribution de la population, sous forme de mémoires, fut remarquable compte tenu des délais serrés fixés par la Commission; ainsi plus d'un demi-millier de groupes ou individus, provenant de milieux et de sphères d'activités représentatifs du "Québec profond", répondirent à l'invitation qui leur fut faite de présenter leurs vues sur le devenir politico-constitutionnel du Québec. A ceux-ci s'ajoutèrent une cinquantaine de spécialistes des sciences sociales, du droit ainsi que des personnalités du domaine culturel, des arts et des lettres. De début novembre 1990 à fin janvier 1991, la Commission aura entendu, dans le cadre des audiences publiques itinérantes à la grandeur du Québec, plus du tiers des groupes ou individus ci-hauts.[13] Le rapport de la Commission fut rendu public le 27 mars 1991. Nous y reviendrons plus avant.

Si une équité relative présida au choix des témoins à paraître devant la Commission, en contrepartie, la composition de celle-ci souffrit d'absences notables; de fait, rien ne pouvait raisonnablement justifier la mise à l'écart des autochtones et des groupes ethno-culturels comme membres à part entière de la Commission. Il est patent, en ce qui concerne les premiers, qu'il s'agissait d'une mesure revancharde appliquée en souvenir d'Oka, par le gouvernement du Québec, avec la complicité tacite de l'opposition péquiste; les deux partis craignaient en effet qu'en offrant aux autochtones l'accès à une telle tribune, ceux-ci ne fassent valoir ad nauseam leur propre vision du problème constitutionnel, ramenant sur le tapis, ce faisant, la question litigieuse des droits ancestraux revendiqués par les peuples aborigènes. Ce qui, à coup sûr, aurait influé sur la nature des débats à la Commission. Qui plus est, à l'heure où l'immigration constitue l'une des priorités du gouvernement du Québec, l'omission des communautés culturelles au sein de ce forum trahissait de la part du gouvernement Bourassa une rare incohérence.

Outre ces bavures, la légitimité de la Commission Bélanger-Campeau ne fut guère mise en cause si ce n'est par la Centrale des syndicats démocratiques (C.S.D.), frustrée surtout de ne pas en être, contrairement à ses trois autres grandes rivales québécoises, soit la F.T.Q., la C.S.N. et la C.E.Q. Autre critique, celle du député libéral de Papineau-St-Michel à Ottawa, André Ouellet, représentant de son parti à la Commission qui jeta un certain discrédit sur les audiences publiques en raison de l'omniprésence des témoins souverainistes à la barre.

Durant la première phase des travaux de la Commission, soit jusqu'au début de la réflexion à huis-clos des commissaires, fin janvier 1991, les témoignages — empreints de sérénité dans l'ensemble — des organismes, individus ou spécialistes sollicités se seront traduits par un éventail d'opinions qui, à l'exception des experts, n'avaient parfois aucun lien direct avec la question constitutionnelle. De fait, près du tiers des mémoires déposés par les organismes furent silencieux à propos des options constitutionnelles pouvant s'offrir au Québec; ces groupes virent plutôt la Commission comme un tremplin privilégié pour sensibiliser les commissaires et partant, l'opinion publique québécoise, aux réalités auxquelles ils sont étroitement confrontés telles par exemple, l'inégalité de développement de certaines régions, l'absence d'une politique de main-d'oeuvre, la dévalorisation de l'agriculture, l'avenir des francophones hors Québec,[14] etc.

Quant à la majeure partie des témoins, très vite il est apparu, au cours des audiences publiques, qu'une majorité d'entre eux favorisaient une révision en profondeur du système fédéral actuel. Un expert invité par la Commission, Charles Taylor, alla même pour sa part jusqu'à proposer une sorte de reprise de la Conférence de Charlottetown de 1864 — premier jalon de la future fédération canadienne — dont l'issue finale, en cas d'échec, signifierait ultimement "la fin du pays". [15]

Dès l'ouverture des travaux de la Commission, le ton aura été donné avec le mémoire-choc présenté par la Chambre de Commerce du Québec, lequel affirmait péremptoirement que "le fédéralisme pratiqué au Canada est un échec économique".[16] Précisant que le "malaise de ses membres vis-à-vis le fédéralisme n'est pas idéologique mais plutôt pragmatique", la Chambre en venait à prôner, parmi plusieurs recommandations, le transfert au Québec d'une vingtaine de compétences occupées pour l'heure par Ottawa, afin de mettre un terme aux chevauchements de juridictions, source de gaspillage de plusieurs milliards$ en fonds publics. Comme conséquence de cette redéfinition des compétences législatives, la Chambre proposait un nouveau partage fiscal entre le gouvernement du Québec et le gouvernement central sur la base du principe de responsabilité: une seule autorité dans chaque matière, responsable à la fois de dépenser et de taxer. Ce qui, d'après la Chambre, devait se traduire par l'élimination du régime actuel de transferts fédéraux-provinciaux et une remise en cause du système de péréquation. Au surplus, la Chambre préconisait, entre autres, une réforme de la Banque du Canada ainsi que le maintien du marché commun canadien.

Le refus de cet organisme de se réclamer d'une option précise sur le plan constitutionnel aura amené certains commissaires, selon leur inclination propre, à attribuer à ce mémoire tantôt une couleur souverainiste, tantôt un penchant en faveur du fédéralisme renouvelé. L'ampleur des transferts de pouvoirs proposés (près de 70% des programmes fédéraux), auquel fit écho — à un registre moindre — le Board of Trade (Bureau de commerce), eut pour effet par ailleurs de susciter le scepticisme chez bon nombre de commissaires (toutes tendances confondues) quant à la faisabilité d'une réforme aussi fondamentale du cadre fédéral canadien; la réserve soulevée avait trait tantôt à la formule d'amendement nécessaire à la réalisation de tels changements, tantôt à la volonté même du ROC d'y souscrire, compte tenu de son refus préalable des conditions minimales de l'Accord du lac Meech.

La Commission aura donné lieu mutatis mutandis avec le dépôt du mémoire du Conseil du Patronat du Québec, à une reprise du débat référendaire de 1980 du fait de sa conclusion touchant la rentabilité indiscutable du fédéralisme. S'appuyant sur une étude préalable préparée par l'économiste André Raynauld, le mémoire du C.P.Q. soutenait que le régime fédéral a permis au Québec, à l'instar des autres provinces canadiennes, d'enregistrer des gains remarquables, notamment depuis une vingtaine d'années. Les données soumises par le Conseil indiquaient un gain net se situant entre 800 millions $ et un milliard $ pour le Québec en 1988, tandis que pendant les trois dernières années, selon l'organisme patronal, la rentabilité du fédéralisme canadien aurait toutefois été moindre. Le bilan fiscal du fédéralisme canadien, tel qu'établi par le C.P.Q. pour 1988, ne tarda pas à être contesté par les souverainistes pour qui le Québec, la même année, a contrario, aurait essuyé une perte de 1,3 milliards $ en redevenant un contributeur net aux finances publiques fédérales.

Au-delà de cette guerre des chiffres et des divergences méthodologiques relativement à l'interprétation des *Comptes nationaux*, les deux co-présidents de la Commission québécoise estimaient dans leur bilan-synthèse de janvier 1991 que si se poursuivaient les restrictions budgétaires du gouvernement fédéral, en particulier celles qu'il impose aux transferts aux provinces, l'évolution du Québec vers une situation de contributeur net se maintiendrait également.[17]

Empruntant au besoin le verbe partisan, le C.P.Q. assortit son bilan globalement positif du fédéralisme canadien d'une sévère mise en garde contre l'"aventure" souverainiste, option jugée "suicidaire" au surplus, et dont les coûts de transition, selon le Conseil, compromettraient le niveau de vie et les "acquis socio-économiques" des Québécois.[18] De plus, le Conseil soutenait hardiment qu'un Québec souverain remettrait en question son appartenance au marché commun canadien, avec pour conséquence, l'isolement du nouvel Etat sur le plan continental; le C.P.Q. s'employait à présenter l'option souverainiste en porte-à-faux du courant actuel à l'échelle internationale poussant à l'interdépendance des Etats. Or, l'organisme patronal se trouvait à gommer du coup l'orientation résolument libre-échangiste à laquelle adhèrent l'ensemble des souverainistes, et le P.Q. au premier chef.[19]

Plaidant enfin pour une "constitution moderne", le Conseil du Patronat du Québec est apparu cependant, de tous les organismes patronaux ayant comparu devant la Commission, comme celui dont les propositions en matière de renouvellement du fédéralisme étaient les moins audacieuses. Disant réclamer une "plus grande autonomie des provinces", le C.P.Q. n'aura identifié paradoxalement que trois secteurs où "l'autonomie provinciale devrait être accrue", soit, en l'occurrence, l'immigration, la main-d'oeuvre et la politique familiale. Finalement, selon le Conseil, ce sont l'ensemble des provinces, et non seulement le Québec, qui devraient bénéficier de cette "décentralisation des pouvoirs". Du fait de la timidité des réformes proposées, le mémoire du C.P.Q., de même, entre autres, que de celui-ci de Jean Chrétien, soumis le mois suivant à la Commission, auront été définis par certains analystes politiques du Québec comme l'archétype même du "statu quo renouvelé".[20]

Environ la moitié des mémoires entendus à la Commission Bélanger-Campeau favorisèrent une gamme d'options un tant soit peu convergentes sur l'axe constitutionnel, allant de la "communauté nationale autonome" à l'indépendance, en passant par la souveraineté(-)association et une nouvelle Confédération Québec-Canada. Le cinquième des mémoires s'affichèrent fédéralistes et le reste de ceux-ci restaient neutres à l'égard des options en présence.[21] De toutes les prises de position prônant la thèse de l'autonomisme maximaliste (avec ses variantes), celle, très attendue, du Mouvement Desjardins est apparue de loin la plus spectaculaire, voire symbolique, en raison de la stature imposante de cette institution financière dont deux Québécois sur trois font partie (4,3 millions de sociétaires). En revanche, la cause souverainiste stricto sensu obtint déjà les faveurs, bien avant les audiences publiques de la Commission, d'un certain nombre d'organisations telles: les trois grandes centrales québécoises, les mouvements nationalistes et leurs filiales (Société Saint-Jean Baptiste, Ligue d'action nationale, Mouvement national des Québécois), le Parti québécois, l'Union des artistes et certains autres organismes, individus ou experts sollicités).

Les arguments avancés à l'appui de la souveraineté furent nombreux et de divers types. La plupart des motifs d'ordre économique invoqués à cet égard avaient, à toutes fins utiles, déjà été mis de l'avant par la Chambre de commerce du Québec dans son évaluation à l'emporte-pièce du fédéralisme canadien. L'économiste Pierre Fortin aura été l'expert qui, à la suite de la Chambre, articula le mieux l'éventuelle viabilité d'un Québec souverain, confortée sur le plan statistique par une étude postérieure réalisée par le Secrétariat de la Commission Bélanger-Campeau.[22] Répondant par ricochet au mémoire du C.P.Q., Fortin soutint que

> pour plusieurs raisons, la prospérité du Québec ne dépend pas de son statut politique: la corrélation entre le niveau de vie et la taille démographique des pays industriels est nulle, l'économie du Québec est intrinsèquement dynamique et performante, les frontières économiques transcendent les frontières politiques, la capacité financière de l'Etat québécois ne fait pas de doute et l'union monétaire avec le Canada n'est pas indispensable, bien que souhaitable et probable. Plus de souveraineté n'infligerait aucun tort sérieux à l'économie mais ne serait pas un gage de prospérité non plus; pour une Norvège et une Suisse, il y a une Nouvelle-Zélande et une Irlande.

Dépassionnalisant l'enjeu de la souveraineté, Fortin concluait son analyse comme suit:

> Si les Québécois en viennent à la souveraineté, ce ne sera (...) pas par pur enthousiasme puisqu'un tiers d'entre eux, tout au plus, ont régulièrement appuyé cette option depuis dix ans. Ce sera plutôt par constat pragmatique qu'ils n'ont guère d'autre choix.[23]

A un tout autre registre, certains tenants de la souveraineté auront affirmé, avec des accents déterministes, que l'indépendance s'avère "la voie tracée par l'histoire" et que le "sentiment nous y incline". D'autres renvoyèrent à la thèse classique des deux solitudes pour caractériser le "décalage politique" existant entre le Québec et le Canada, comme si les "deux sociétés n'évoluaient pas sur la même longueur d'onde, n'évoluaient pas au même rythme", chacune animée par sa propre "logique incompatible et contradictoire"; le tout s'exprimant, d'une part, par une aspiration légitime des Anglo-canadiens pour un Canada doté d'un gouvernement central fort et, d'autre part, par le désir d'une majorité de Québécois de pouvoir compter sur un gouvernement québécois tout aussi fort afin d'assurer leur survie comme collectivité distincte. D'aucuns allèrent même jusqu'à soutenir, avec une pointe d'ironie, que la souveraineté du Québec agirait en quelque sorte comme un catalyseur pour le Canada hors Québec;

suivant cette optique, les Anglo-canadiens pourraient finalement s'offrir leur "propre pays", affranchis qu'ils seraient dès lors d'un Québec éternellement rétif devant la dynamique de nation-building propre au ROC. Comme autre argument en faveur de la souveraineté, un témoin fit référence à l'"illégitimité" de la *Loi constitutionnelle de 1982* et de la Charte des droits et libertés proclamée "sans le consentement de l'Assemblée nationale du Québec", la Charte étant assimilée ici à un "instrument d'homogénéisation" judiciaire fondamentalement contraire aux intérêts du Québec.[24]

Il n'aura fallu qu'une quinzaine de jours environ pour que des clans distincts se forment au sein de la Commission Bélanger-Campeau et se maintiennent jusqu'à la fin de ses travaux, soit fin mars 1991. Les groupes en question consistaient en l'aile parlementaire libérale, en celle du Parti québécois, en le bloc fédéraliste né de l'alliance conjoncturelle entre le député libéral fédéral André Ouellet et de son homologue conservateur, Jean-Pierre Hogue et enfin, en un quatrième groupement dit des "non-alignés" réunissant des souverainistes déclarés dont notamment Lucien Bouchard, leader du Bloc québécois, Claude Béland, président du Mouvement Desjardins et les leaders syndicaux représentés à la Commission. Robert Libman et William Holden du Parti Egalité firent, quant à eux, bande à part durant une bonne partie des travaux de la Commission.

La supériorité numérique indiscutable des témoins souverainistes et autres autonomistes à la barre de la Commission n'aura laissé, tout compte fait, que la portion congrue aux adeptes inconditionnels du lien fédéral. Marginalisés au Québec par suite du consensus nationaliste qui aura régné dans la province depuis l'échec de Meech, les tenants du fédéralisme maximaliste n'en proposèrent pas moins selon Alain Dubuc, éditorialiste en chef à La Presse, "une vision défensive du Canada qui repose non pas sur les vertus de la fédération mais sur les risques inhérents à sa rupture".[25] En misant sur une analyse coûts-bénéfices qui n'était pas sans rappeler la stratégie du camp du "non" onze ans plus tôt, les témoins d'obédience fédéraliste faisaient le pari ambitieux de pouvoir opérer un retournement de l'opinion publique québécoise.

Dans la foulée de cette stratégie alarmiste, le commissaire André Ouellet et le témoin Jean Chrétien évoquèrent la possibilité qu'un Québec souverain puisse faire les frais, territorialement, d'une observance stricte de la loi fédérale de 1912 sur l'extension des frontières du Québec en vertu de laquelle cette province s'était vue octroyer le territoire actuel du Nouveau-Québec. Perspective similaire de la part du Parti Egalité du comté de Brôme-Missisquoi : celui-ci, inspiré par des déclarations antérieures de l'ex-premier ministre Trudeau selon qui le Québec, pas moins que le Canada, n'était à l'abri d'une éventuelle partition territoriale, suggéra la création d'un corridor reliant, à travers le territoire d'un Québec souverain, le Nouveau-Brunswick et l'Ontario, dans le but d'empêcher la pakistanisation du ROC. Au reste, le représentant de l'Assemblée des Premières Nations aura renchéri dans cette veine en soutenant que la souveraineté interne des autochtones était demeurée intacte au cours des siècles et que même l'indépendance du Québec ne saurait aliéner les droits des Premières Nations touchant leurs territoires traditionnels.[26]

Privés de leur leader — en convalescence — et désorientés devant la question constitutionnelle, les commissaires libéraux se sentirent difficilement en mesure alors de jouer les hérauts d'un fédéralisme, même renouvelé. Réagissant à l'expectative de ceux-ci, le tandem Ouellet-Hogue, vite rejoint par les commissaires du milieu des affaires, ne fut pas long à cueillir le leadership de l'option fédéraliste. Le ministre Claude Ryan, qui aura boudé faute d'intérêt la plupart des séances de la Commission, s'employa pour sa part à secouer ses collègues libéraux flirtant avec l'option fédéraliste en leur rappelant les mérites du fédéralisme; Ryan renvoyait notamment à l'exemple de la défense des libertés individuelles, lesquelles, en vérité, n'auront peut-être pas tant été garanties, durant l'histoire canadienne, par le jeu d'équilibre entre le gouvernement fédéral et les gouvernements provinciaux, que simplement par notre régime démocratique.[27]

Par ailleurs, le groupe des non-alignés, quoique souverainiste à l'instar de l'aile péquiste à la Commission, déploya davantage d'énergies que celle-ci à réaliser un consensus, en particulier sur la tenue d'un référendum, le plus tôt possible après le dépôt du rapport de la Commission en mars 1991. Avalisé par une majorité de témoins à la Commission (organismes et experts), le principe du référendum fut rapidement acquis, même auprès des fédéralistes "mitigés" au sein de la Commission, incluant nombre de députés libéraux. Le rapport du comité constitutionnel du P.L.Q., diffusé le mois suivant, allait consacrer de fait la nécessité de recourir au viatique référendaire afin de dénouer l'impasse constitutionnelle.

Restait désormais à déterminer la question à poser ainsi que les modalités entourant la tenue de ce référendum. Au moment même où, des rangs souverainistes, les pressions s'amplifiaient pour qu'ait lieu un référendum hâtif sur la souveraineté, l'intervention du professeur Léon Dion, à titre de premier expert invité, fut reçue comme une bouée de sauvetage par les libéraux québécois, mal à l'aise à l'idée de monter aveuglément à bord du bâtiment conduit par les souverainistes pressés. Conseiller officieux du gouvernement Bourassa et du P.L.Q., le "fédéraliste fatigué" qu'est Léon Dion se fit néanmoins une nouvelle fois l'apôtre de la circonspection en proposant d'accorder une "nouvelle chance" au Canada anglais, à la faveur d'ultimes négociations constitutionnelles. Or cette fois-ci, prévenait Dion, le gouvernement du Québec devrait tirer ses leçons de l'échec de Meech et partant, ne s'engager dans ce processus de négociations qu'à l'unique condition d'y contraindre formellement le Canada hors Québec "le couperet sous la gorge", c'est-à-dire par l'entremise d'un référendum sur la souveraineté advenant un refus de ce dernier d'adhérer aux nouvelles demandes du Québec.[28] Pareille stratégie de l'ouverture musclée n'allait pas tarder effectivement à porter ses fruits, dans les semaines ultérieures, au sein du Parti libéral du Québec et du gouvernement Bourassa...

D'UN RAPPORT A L'AUTRE

Le mutisme des libéraux québécois et de leur chef eu égard à la question constitutionnelle n'aura donc été que tactique, le temps en effet que le P.L.Q. dépose, le 28 janvier 1991, le rapport produit par son comité constitutionnel présidé par Me Jean Allaire. Du coup, le document libéral se trouvait à devancer de deux mois le rapport de la Commission Bélanger-Campeau, une manière en fait d'obliger celle-ci à composer avec les conclusions du rapport Allaire.

Fruit d'un ardu compromis au sein du parti entre fédéralistes et quasi-souverainistes, le rapport intitulé *Le Québec libre de ses choix* eut néanmoins l'effet d'une bombe, notamment dans le ROC, en proposant entre autres que le Québec possède dorénavant la compétence exclusive dans 22 secteurs, de l'environnement à l'assurance-chômage en passant par la main-d'oeuvre et la formation; selon le schéma proposé, le gouvernement fédéral n'en conservait que quatre (défense, douanes, monnaies et dette, et péréquation) tandis que neuf autres domaines deviendraient des champs de juridiction partagés. Cette décentralisation massive des pouvoirs, assortie d'une réduction concomitante du pouvoir de dépenser d'Ottawa, traduisait en fait la volonté des auteurs du rapport Allaire de proposer une "nouvelle structure Québec-Canada" afin de dénouer l'impasse politique, fiscale et constitutionnelle à laquelle le pays est actuellement confronté.

Le constat du rapport Allaire ne souffre aucune équivoque: "le Canada, dans sa forme actuelle, est devenu difficilement gouvernable" [29]; ainsi, le fédéralisme canadien, en proie déjà à d'"éternels conflits linguistiques et culturels", fait en outre les frais d'une crise économique et financière d'une nature sans précédent se traduisant notamment par de coûteux et improductifs chevauchements de compétences et un déficit national croissant. Hormis une brève mention de circonstance des avantages que le fédéralisme canadien aura conférés au Québec, le rapport Allaire se sera attardé plutôt à démontrer que, d'un point de vue historique, l'affirmation de l'autonomie et de la spécificité québécoises — dans le sens d'un nouveau partage des pouvoirs — aura été très souvent en porte-à-faux de la "tendance à la centralisation et à l'uniformisation du régime canadien". Or, selon le document libéral, ce sont ces "pratiques centralisatrices figées", dictées par des normes nationales "inflexibles", qui minent inexorablement le fédéralisme canadien et contribuent, partant, à la crise des finances publiques et à l'incapacité d'Ottawa de résorber les écarts de richesse entre les provinces. A cet égard, le rapport Allaire aura cherché à dissiper l'impression que le Québec entend faire bande à part; c'est pourquoi on tenait à affirmer que "le Québec n'est plus seul dans son camp (et que) (...) l'impératif de changement est aussi réel pour le Québec que pour les autres provinces".[30] Cependant, le document libéral aura été trop vite en besogne en établissant un parallèle boîteux entre la démarche hyperdécentralisatrice du P.L.Q. et les revendications régionalistes des provinces de l'Ouest et de Terre-Neuve notamment, d'abord et avant tout hostiles au traditionnel pattern opposant soi-disant le Canada central (le fameux "triangle d'or" Québec-Ottawa-Toronto) et les provinces périphériques.

Pour le rapport Allaire, le nouvel ordre politique et économique proposé par le Québec vise à tirer profit de l"espace économique canadien"; question de fonder leurs prétentions sur le plan de l'Histoire, les auteurs du rapport auront été jusqu'à se découvrir une filiation avec les Pères fondateurs de la Confédération par le fait de réclamer la création d'un "véritable marché commun", libre de toutes barrières tarifaires et obstacles au commerce. Clé de voûte de ce programme: une réforme obligée de la Banque du Canada "afin de mieux refléter les réalités régionales", des mécanismes de règlement des différends commerciaux, toutes conditions auxquelles adhèrent également les tenants officiels de la souveraineté(-)association. Or autant le marché commun canadien envisagé dans le rapport Allaire se fonde-t-il sur une dynamique décentralisatrice, autant hors Québec voit-on le "Canadian Common Market" comme allant de pair avec un gouvernement central fort.[31]

En contrepoint de son ambitieux projet de repartage des pouvoirs, le rapport Allaire n'aura consacré que quelques maigres paragraphes à la section touchant le "réaménagement de la structure politique canadienne" en vertu duquel toutefois nombre des institutions actuelles devraient, selon les auteurs du document, être revues et corrigées dans la perspective du nouveau pacte Québec-Canada: le Sénat, la Cour suprême, le Parlement et la Banque du Canada déjà mentionnée. S'agissant du Parlement en particulier, Lise Bissonnette observait finement qu'avec ses quatre champs de compétence à exercer de concert avec les provinces, celui-ci était appelé à n'être tout au plus

> (qu')un organisme d'exécution des desiderata provinciaux (...) (dont le) rôle ne semble pas devoir excéder de beaucoup celui du "Conseil communautaire" non-élu que proposait le Parti québécois en 1979. En somme, tout se passe comme si on maintenait un Parlement pour la forme, pour laisser à la proposition libérale une parenté avec le fédéralisme.[32]

En fait, la plupart des commentateurs politiques, qu'ils soient du Québec, du Canada anglais ou des Etats-Unis, eurent tôt fait de comprendre à la lecture du rapport que si celui proposait, pro forma, un nouveau pacte fédéral ou confédéral (rien n'est précis à cet égard), sa dynamique s'avérait en soi souverainiste ; suivant cette logique en effet, le Québec jouirait en théorie d'un statut particulier tel qu'il ferait figure ni plus ni moins d'Etat quasi-souverain au sein de l'Etat canadien, un scénario d'emblée inacceptable pour le Canada hors Québec.[33] Guy Laforest souligne à juste titre que le rapport Allaire — tout comme d'ailleurs le rapport Bélanger-Campeau, par la suite — se caractérise par "sa lecture dualiste de l'histoire du fédéralisme canadien"[34]; la relation politique entre le Québec et le ROC est bel et bien dépeinte ici sous l'angle de deux nations distinctes, en constant rapport de force. A ce chapitre précis du moins, le document libéral emprunte davantage au Livre blanc que le gouvernement du Parti québécois publiait avant le référendum de 1980 (*Une nouvelle entente Québec-Canada*) qu'au Livre beige (*Une nouvelle fédération canadienne*) produit à la même époque par les libéraux québécois dirigés alors par Claude Ryan. Le P.L.Q. aura accentué sur papier sa mouvance souverainiste dans la mesure où, à des fins stratégiques, le rapport Allaire brandissait l'éventualité qu'ait lieu, à l'automne 1992, un référendum sur la souveraineté assortie d'une offre d'association économique, en cas d'échec dans les négociations avec le ROC. L'on reconnaissait bien là dans cette "démarche à suivre" l'empreinte du professeur Léon Dion, tout comme l'idée d'un rapatriement massif de compétences exclusives pour le Québec avait été directement empruntée au mémoire présenté par la Chambre de Commerce du Québec à la Commission Bélanger-Campeau.

Le rapport Allaire aura été approuvé pour l'essentiel (mis à part quelques modifications ou ajouts mineurs) par les militants libéraux lors du congrès du Parti, les 8,9 et 10 mars 1991. L'événement révéla la division marquée existant entre les nationalistes et les fédéralistes au sein du P.L.Q. Déjà, au cours des semaines précédentes, chaque camp avait interprété le rapport qui, comme un "tout à prendre ou à laisser", qui comme une simple "base de discussion". Le premier ministre Bourassa, pour sa part, évoquait déjà alors, en termes sibyllins, un décalage possible entre le contenu d'Allaire et la position de son gouvernement.[35] Or, les libéraux nationalistes tenaient coûte que coûte à préserver la lettre et l'esprit du rapport Allaire; c'est pourquoi ceux-ci s'employèrent à faire mordre la poussière à l'aile fédéraliste du Parti, regroupée autour du ministre Claude Ryan, laquelle avait fait de la proposition d'amendement numéro 5 le symbole de son ouverture face au Canada hors Québec. La proposition des fédéralistes se voulait plus volontariste et plus engageante que la proposition initiale du rapport: ainsi, selon eux, le projet de réforme constitutionnelle ne devait plus uniquement faire l'objet d'une "présentation" mais aussi d'une "négociation" formelle avec le ROC.

Le désaveu encaissé sur cette question par le camp fédéraliste auprès de plus des deux tiers des 3000 militants présents fit craindre sur le coup un schisme au sein du P.L.Q.; Robert Bourassa parvint à l'éviter en réaffirmant à la clôture du congrès le choix préférentiel du parti et de son gouvernement en faveur du fédéralisme renouvelé, et ce, au grand dam cependant de certains éléments plus radicaux du P.L.Q., agacés par le "pragmatisme" idéologique de leur leader et inquiets à l'idée d'un détournement éventuel du rapport Allaire. Le gros des militants, qui avaient manifesté jusque là des velléités quasi-souverainistes, ne firent néanmoins pas de cas du parti-pris renouvelé du chef libéral, ce dernier exerçant à l'endroit de ses troupes un ascendant quasi-total. Au demeurant, c'était la deuxième fois que Robert Bourassa sauvait les meubles de son parti; de fait, le comité constitutionnel du P.L.Q. aurait vraisemblablement éclaté à la mi-janvier 1991 n'eût été l'autorité morale et l'intervention personnelle de Robert Bourassa qui permirent, à l'onzième heure, l'élaboration d'un compromis touchant le projet de résolution du rapport Allaire. Avec une habileté consommée, Robert Bourassa aura presque réalisé la quadrature du cercle au sein de sa formation politique; d'une part, il obtint du groupe fédéraliste qu'il souscrive au contenu intégral du rapport ainsi qu'à l'hypothèse du référendum sur la souveraineté alors que d'autre part, il forçait les souverainistes du comité à repousser l'échéancier référendaire d'une année (soit jusqu'à la fin de 1992) de manière à maximiser les chances de réussir le "test ultime" du renouvellement du fédéralisme canadien.[36]

Or, Robert Bourassa n'était pas devenu pour autant un prosélyte de l'indépendance. Si, a priori, il n'excluait pas le recours éventuel à cette option, celle-ci en revanche ne constituait pas une "fin en soi" à ses yeux. Ce qui importait davantage pour le chef libéral, c'était de protéger la sécurité culturelle des Québécois, objectif tout-à-fait réalisable selon lui au sein d'un nouveau cadre constitutionnel canadien.[37] Cependant, la stratégie bourassiste exigeait impérativement la tenue d'un "échéancier contraignant" afin d'obliger le ROC à remettre en question le statu quo. En administrant un véritable électro-choc au Canada anglais, Robert Bourassa cherchait à faire d'une pierre trois coups: d'abord, se doter d'un credo quasi-souverainiste, au goût du jour et à forte valeur symbolique. Modifiable au besoin, celui-ci permettait dans l'intervalle au gouvernement Bourassa de s'aligner à distance et de façon commode sur l'option souverainiste qui ralliait alors les intentions de vote de près de trois francophones sur quatre au Québec; deuxièmement, améliorer son "bargaining power" avec le ROC en faisant preuve de désinvolture calculée de façon à éviter, comme durant l'épisode Meech, de s'auto-piéger à l'avance avec des demandes minimales; et, enfin, conscientiser le Canada anglais au fait que, quoiqu'il advienne, le Québec possédera toujours la pleine liberté de ses choix constitutionnels et qu'à la vérité, il revient désormais au ROC de convaincre le Québec de ne pas opter irrémédiablement pour la souveraineté.

A quelques exceptions près, le rapport Allaire n'aura suscité que stupeur et intransigeance hors Québec. De fait, il choqua bon nombre d'observateurs et d'hommes politiques anglo-canadiens, tant par son ton amer envers le reste du Canada qu'en raison du caractère radical des réformes proposées. Il n'en fallait pas plus pour que le rapport Allaire soit qualifié tantôt de "ridicule" par un Gordon Robertson, tantôt de "plaisanterie" et d'"insulte" par un Jeffrey

Simpson; ce dernier, prophétisant au reste que le départ du Québec n'était qu'une "question de temps", allait même jusqu'à sonner la curée, en représailles, à l'encontre des leaders des partis nationaux et autres hauts-fonctionnaires provenant du Québec.[38] A Ottawa, le rapport Allaire fut proprement désavoué par les trois chefs fédéraux, le premier ministre Mulroney concoctant déjà, pour sa part, une réplique plus incisive qu'il livra dans la quinzaine subséquente (voir infra). Ailleurs, au Canada, de Vancouver à Terre-Neuve, la désapprobation fut tout aussi unanime, et particulièrement vive de la part de Clyde Wells. Néanmoins, il s'est trouvé des voix au Canada anglais, comme celle par exemple du chef du Reform Party, Preston Manning, pour louer la volonté du gouvernement du Québec d'aborder carrément la question du partage des pouvoirs entre Ottawa et les provinces.[39]

De leur côté, les souverainistes du Parti québécois et du Bloc québécois furent mutuellement d'avis que le "beau risque" nouvelle manière proposé par les libéraux[40] était, d'avance, voué à l'échec vu que nulle logique ne prédisposait le ROC à souscrire à l'"esprit" d'Allaire après que celui-ci n'eut même pas été capable d'avaliser auparavant le très modeste Accord du lac Meech.

Conscient du problème mais tenu à un optimisme de circonstance, Robert Bourassa aura vu dans le rapport de la Commission Bélanger-Campeau l'instrument tout indiqué pour "bonifier" le rapport Allaire, sous l'angle stratégique, de manière à y enchâsser d'abord la prime orientation fédéraliste privilégiée par le gouvernement du Québec et partant, y circonscrire le recours à l'option souverainiste. Il s'agissait aussi pour le chef libéral de tirer profit autant que possible de l'aura de légitimité dont était investie la Commission Bélanger-Campeau aux yeux de la population québécoise; ainsi afin d'accroître sinon maintenir intact son rapport de force avec ses éventuels interlocuteurs du reste du Canada, Robert Bourassa se devait de façon impérieuse, mais à un moindre coût, de quérir un consensus numériquement significatif parmi les commissaires, fut-il de façade au pis-aller.

Dans l'intervalle, le rapport Allaire — dont le dépôt fut perçu par quelques commissaires souverainistes comme "un missile Scud tombant sur la Commission" — apparaissait de plus en plus banalisé à la suite des commentaires de type dubitatif émis par certains ministres "seniors" du gouvernement Bourassa eu égard à la substance du rapport. A cet égard, le ministre des Affaires intergouvernementales canadiennes, Gil Rémillard, fit savoir à la mi-février qu'au demeurant, seul l'échéancier référendaire de 1992 n'était pas négociable dans le rapport Allaire.[41]

C'est armé de cet argument-choc que le gouvernement du Québec récusa peu après et de façon cavalière l'hypothèse de travail présentée aux membres de la Commission sur l'avenir politique et constitutionnel du Québec par les co-présidents Michel Bélanger et Jean Campeau; seconde bombe lancée après le rapport Allaire, la proposition de ces derniers, ébruitée de toute évidence par certains commissaires fédéralistes, prévoyait un référendum sur le principe de la souveraineté dès 1991 — avec possiblement la souveraineté à la clé en 1993 — dans le but précis d'augmenter la pression dans les négociations avec le Canada anglais. La contre-proposition libérale soumise par le ministre Rémillard procédait en revanche d'une tout autre philosophie; plaçant tous les commissaires devant le fait accompli, la position du gouvernement Bourassa apparaissait maintenant dépourvue de toute ambiguïté si tant est qu'elle visait clairement à "accorder une dernière chance au fédéralisme". La profession de foi fédéraliste à laquelle se livrèrent pour l'occasion le ministre et son chef se fondait sur la conviction que les Québécois, en dépit de leur forte inclination pour la souveraineté[42], souhaitaient néanmoins poursuivre le dialogue avec le reste du Canada. Cette assurance fut confortée par un sondage Multi-Réso-*Le Devoir*, réalisé début février 1991, révélant en effet que six Québécois sur dix abondaient dans ce sens quoique, en contre-partie, la même proportion de répondants s'affichaient incrédules face au succès final de l'opération.

A ce stade, les propositions déjà bien campées des commissaires péquistes et libéraux quant à l'option à privilégier dans le rapport auront eu pour effet peu à peu de transformer le conclave du Domaine de Maizerets (où se réunissait l'aréopage Bélanger-Campeau) en véritable "foire d'empoigne".[43] En fait, par ce bras de fer comme le souligne Gilles Lesage,

> tous (voulaient) un consensus (...) (mais) chacun souhait(ait) que l'autre fasse le compromis qui permette de l'atteindre (...) C'(était) une lutte de pouvoir pour savoir qui contrôlera(it) le calendrier, l'"agenda" politique au Québec: le gouvernement ou l'opposition. En même temps, l'un et l'autre craign(ai)ent comme la peste l'odieux d'avoir empêché le consensus, s'employant à semer les pelures de bananes sur le chemin du voisin et à le rendre (...) responsable de l'échec éventuel de la Commission. Neuf mois et (4,6) millions $ pour en arriver à cette catastrophe ? Bien des Québécois ne (l')auraient pas compris).[44]

Finalement, au terme de moult péripéties stratégiques de dernière heure, 33 des 36 commissaires donnèrent leur aval au rapport final d'une centaine de pages, additionné de 16 substantiels addenda signés par un ou plusieurs des 28 commissaires qui manifestèrent des réserves au sujet de la teneur du rapport.[45] Le rapport, intitulé sans façon *L'avenir politique et constitutionnel du Québec*, aura proposé uniquement deux voies de solution pour sortir le Québec de l'actuelle impasse politique et constitutionnelle: 1) "une nouvelle (et ultime) tentative de redéfinir le statut du Québec au sein du régime fédéral canadien" et 2) "l'accession du Québec au statut d'Etat indépendant". Au reste, le rapport recommandait, en vertu d'un projet de loi à être adopté par l'Assemblée nationale (projet de loi 150) la tenue d'une consultation référendaire sur la souveraineté en 1992 — soit entre le 8 juin et le 22 juin ou entre le 12 octobre et le 26 octobre de ladite année — et la création de deux commissions parlementaires: l'une mandatée pour "étudier et analyser toute question relative à l'accession du Québec à la souveraineté" et l'autre chargée d'"apprécier toute offre de nature constitutionnelle" qui pourrait émaner du ROC. En définitive, le rapport refusait de trancher en faveur de l'une ou l'autre des options ci-hauts.

Le "consensus à 90%" qui a émergé de la Commission Bélanger-Campeau n'aura constitué tout au plus qu'un consensus symbolique, voire bancal, et comparé par certains à un "buffet froid" dans la mesure où chaque camp interpréta son endossement du rapport comme bon lui semblait. Les souverainistes, d'abord frustrés par la défaite d'une série de leurs amendements pro-souveraineté, signèrent enfin le rapport après que ceux-ci eurent obtenu : 1) l'élimination de toute référence à un appel d'offres au reste du Canada, n'obligeant pas ainsi le Parti québécois à "cautionner un fédéralisme renouvelé"; 2) l'obligation que, pour être examinée, toute offre éventuelle en provenance du reste du Canada lie "formellement" le gouvernement du Canada et les provinces. Jacques Parizeau, comme bien d'autres, comprenait par là un engagement ferme et non-équivoque des législatures concernées pour que les offres puissent être prises en compte par l'Assemblée nationale du Québec. Or, plusieurs indices laisseraient croire maintenant que l'approbation des législatures n'est plus considérée à Québec comme un pré-requis incontournable: on justifierait ce revirement par le fait que des Parlements peuvent toujours tourner casaque, comme ce fut le cas à Terre-Neuve en juin 1990. Ainsi donc selon Lise Bissonnette,

> un simple accord personnel des premiers ministres, selon le modèle de 1987 au lac Meech, paraît donc suffire à M. Bourassa pour qu'il y voie un engagement "formel" d'Ottawa et des provinces.[46]

Dès la publication du rapport Bélanger-Campeau, plusieurs observateurs eurent tôt fait de déclarer Robert Bourassa grand gagnant de l'opération; ceux-ci donnaient comme preuve notamment le contrôle que le parti libéral était appelé à exercer sur les deux commissions parlementaires succédant à la précédente commission parlementaire élargie, ainsi que la marge de manoeuvre que le gouvernement s'autorisait en vertu des remarques subsidiaires insérées dans le 1er addendum du rapport par le premier ministre Bourassa et le ministre délégué aux Affaires intergouvernementales canadiennes, Gil Rémillard. La présentation, à la mi-mai dernier, du projet de loi pré-référendaire (projet de loi 150) par le ministre Rémillard aura confirmé, si besoin était, le désir non-équivoque du gouvernement Bourassa de garder la main haute sur tout le processus de détermination de l'avenir politique et constitutionnelle du Québec pour les mois à venir. Frustrés et amers après coup d'avoir cédé aux appels "consensuels" de leurs alliés non-alignés lors de la signature du rapport, les membres du Parti québécois étaient donc en mal de revanche; c'est pourquoi ils auront voté contre l'adoption du projet de loi 150 le 19 juin dernier en jetant l'anathème sur quelques-uns des *considérants* de son préambule, lesquels, pourtant, respectaient plutôt fidèlement l'esprit de l'ajout incorporé auparavant par le premier ministre Bourassa au rapport Bélanger-Campeau.

Un premier *considérant* précise en effet que le présent gouvernement du Québec "conserve en tout temps sa pleine faculté d'initiative et d'appréciation des mesures favorisant le meilleur intérêt du Québec", ce qui en clair signifie que ce gouvernement pourrait s'estimer justifié de ne pas tenir le référendum prévu pour 1992, en dépit par ailleurs de l'énorme risque politique que comporterait une pareille décision. Auquel cas s'impose naturellement l'hypothèse très plausible, et qu'alimentent des rumeurs persistantes, voulant qu'une élection provinciale puisse être déclenchée par le gouvernement Bourassa au printemps ou à l'automne de l'an prochain en remplacement du référendum. Un second *considérant* stipule que l'Assemblée nationale "demeure souveraine pour décider de toute question référendaire", une formulation qui traduit sans fard aucun la prédilection gouvernementale à tenir un référendum sur "toute offre d'un nouveau partenariat de nature constitutionnelle" plutôt que sur la souveraineté. Enfin, les deux *considérants* relatifs au rôle des deux commissions déjà mentionnées auront notamment donné lieu à de vives empoignades verbales entre le gouvernement et les députés péquistes; l'opposition officielle aura compris un peu tard en effet qu'elle faisait les frais, au profit des libéraux, de la composition des dites commissions, ces derniers bénéficiant de fait d'une majorité écrasante à ce chapitre en s'arrogeant onze des dix-huit sièges de chacune des deux commissions.[47] Mais, à la vérité, comme le souligne la directrice du *Devoir*

> on voit mal (...) comment il aurait pu en être autrement. Moyen extraordinaire
> d'exploration des options québécoises après l'échec canadien de juin 1990, la
> commission parlementaire élargie (aura) fait son oeuvre et l'Assemblée nationale
> reprend son droit. Le P.Q. ne peut réclamer de faire comme s'il n'avait pas perdu
> les dernières élections.[48]

L'on sait déjà que les deux commissions parlementaires nées de l'adoption de la loi 150 fourniront en fait une tribune idéale au gouvernement Bourassa pour exprimer sans détour qui son penchant fédéraliste, qui sa froideur envers la souveraineté. Le désir du premier ministre du Québec de vouloir présenter aux Québécois une "juste définition de la souveraineté et de ses implications politiques, économiques, sociales et culturelles"[49] aura conduit celui-ci, pendant l'étude du projet de loi à la mi-juin, à prononcer un vigoureux réquisitoire contre la souveraineté "pure et dure", sous l'angle de ses risques financiers. A la suite de cette intervention du premier ministre, les péquistes prêtèrent vite aux libéraux le dessein de se livrer à une "job de bras" aux dépens de l'option souverainiste, dans le cadre de la commission chargée d'examiner les tenants et aboutissants de la souveraineté. Si d'aventure le gouvernement Bourassa devait s'adonner à une telle stratégie, il s'exposerait en revanche à émousser lui-même l'épée de Damoclès qu'il brandit à distance pour négocier prestement les termes d'un "nouveau partenariat". Le cas échéant, l'on assisterait à une situation farfelue où le gouvernement libéral menacerait d'avoir recours à une option qu'il juge hasardeuse au demeurant. [50]

Dans l'hypothèse — réaliste — où des offres formelles de partenariat émaneraient du reste du Canada l'an prochain, l'on saura alors jusqu'à quel point le gouvernement Bourassa sabrera dans le rapport Allaire pour en arriver à une entente avec ses interlocuteurs hors Québec. La conclusion d'une telle entente revêt une telle importance pour le gouvernement libéral qu'il a déjà signifié, en juin dernier, son intention éventuelle d'étudier, par la commission parlementaire créée à cette fin, toutes offres du Canada anglais qui viendraient même après un référendum dont les résultats seraient favorables à la souveraineté du Québec. Quoiqu'il en soit, le gouvernement Bourassa devra composer avec la Commission-Jeunesse de son parti. Contraints en mars 1991, sous l'impulsion de leur chef, à rentrer dans le rang fédéraliste, les jeunes libéraux entendent bien cette fois, comme ils l'ont exprimé lors de leur dernier congrès annuel en août dernier, démontrer le poids réel qu'il occupe au sein du parti; c'est pourquoi ils comptent mettre le maximum de pression pour forcer le gouvernement, le moment venu, à ne pas brader l'essentiel de la position constitutionnelle adoptée par les militants au printemps dernier.

Il se pourrait par ailleurs que, incapables de pouvoir obtenir ultimement l'appui de dix, sinon de sept provinces à leur projet de révision constitutionnelle, les gouvernements québécois et fédéral s'entendent plutôt pour procéder à de nouveaux arrangements administratifs du type de ceux prônés récemment par le "Groupe des 22" ou évoqués, au préalable, par le ministre Gil Rémillard ainsi que par le gouvernement Mulroney lors du dernier Discours du trône à Ottawa[51]. Par ailleurs, le gouvernement du Québec avait déclaré, au moment de la présentation du projet de loi 150, qu'il se ferait un point d'honneur de réaffirmer les cinq demandes initiales de Meech — et, au premier chef, la reconnaissance de la clause de société distincte —, ainsi que le maintien de la clause *nonobstant*.

C'est à l'automne 1991, à la suite du peaufinage estival de la stratégie fédérale, qu'on assistera au véritable coup d'envoi de la décisive ronde Canada-Québec.

LA REPONSE DU ROC

Placés devant le fait accompli de l'aggiornamento constitutionnel réclamé par le gouvernement Bourassa aux lendemains de l'échec de Meech, le gouvernement fédéral et les autres provinces auront tenté, avec plus ou moins de synergie, de réagir aux initiatives québécoises au cours des mois subséquents.[52] En dépit d'une légitimité écorchée par les sondages répétés lui accordant à peine

15% des intentions de vote des Canadiens, le gouvernement Mulroney n'avait rien à perdre de plus et tout à gagner, au vrai, — tant du point de vue purement électoral que de celui de la postérité historique — en relevant le défi de débloquer l'actuelle impasse constitutionnelle.

La stratégie adoptée par le gouvernement fédéral conservateur se sera articulée et étoffée de façon progressive, au gré des événements québécois de même qu'au fil de discours ponctuels prononcés symboliquement hors de la Chambre des Communes soit en l'occurrence: à Gaspé (25 août 1990), Buckingham (16 décembre 1990), Toronto et Québec (12-13 février 1991). Le discours de Gaspé aura fourni l'occasion au gouvernement Mulroney de raffermir d'abord son autorité sur ses propres troupes, éprouvées par une série de défections au profit du Bloc québécois dans la tourmente du Lac Meech; dans ce discours et celui de Buckingham, l'accent fut mis tantôt sur la nécessité d'un étapisme constitutionnel — avec, à la clé, la redéfinition du processus de modification constitutionnelle —, tantôt sur l'opportunité de "réévaluer les rôles respectifs des gouvernements fédéral et provinciaux", condition sine qua non, selon ce gouvernement, pour réaliser un fédéralisme "moderne et flexible".

Entretemps, question de ne pas être en reste face à la Commission Bélanger-Campeau — dépeinte ironiquement par le *Ottawa Citizen* comme le "flying circus" du Québec — certaines provinces avaient déjà annoncé la création de leur propre organe de réflexion constitutionnelle (Alberta, Nouveau-Brunswick, Ontario, Manitoba, suivies peu après par la Colombie-Britannique et plus récemment encore par la Nouvelle-Ecosse); dans cette mouvance consultative, Ottawa emboîta aussi le pas en créant — ou annonçant la création — à l'automne 1990 de deux outils de consultation publique, soit le Forum des Citoyens, présidé par Keith Spicer, chargé de "sonder les coeurs et les reins des Canadiens ordinaires", ainsi que le Comité spécial mixte du Sénat et de la Chambre des Communes mandaté pour réviser le processus de modification de la Constitution.

Boudée au Québec et raillée par moult commentateurs à travers le Canada, la Commission Spicer aura souffert dès ses débuts d'un problème de crédibilité auprès de la population canadienne, alimenté en partie par l'idiosyncrasie de son président-poète. Les concepteurs du "plus grand exercice démocratique que le monde ait jamais connu", selon l'expression hyperbolique de son président, s'employèrent à faire de la Commission qui, un agora électronique diffusé "from coast to coast", qui le prétexte à d'innombrables "thérapies" de groupe politiques où chacun était sollicité à deviser sur une série de thèmes allant des langues officielles jusqu'au Québec et l'unité canadienne en passant par la question autochtone et la responsabilité des leaders.

Cependant, le groupe Spicer aura eu à subir les foudres mêmes de l'un des siens, soit le commissaire Robert Normand; ce dernier provoqua en effet un véritable esclandre en accusant, entre autres choses, ses collègues de la

Commission de "banaliser la question du Québec". Elliptique sur la question du partage des pouvoirs, le rapport Spicer aura plaidé en fait pour un fédéralisme peu ou prou asymétrique, lequel serait fondé sur une équité théorique entre toutes les provinces de même que sur les "besoins particuliers de chacune". En vertu de ce schéma le Québec se verrait reconnaître la préservation de sa langue et de sa culture françaises, bref son "identité propre" selon la nouvelle terminologie post-meechienne mise de l'avant par le groupe Spicer.[53] Affaibli par les quasi-dissidences des commissaires Robert Normand et Richard Cashin, le rapport Spicer aura essuyé au reste le cynisme d'une bonne partie de la presse francophone québécoise; *Le Devoir*, pour sa part, n'y alla pas avec le dos de la cuillère en qualifiant sans ambages le document de "roman à l'eau de rose" et de "recueil de lamentations" inspiré, au demeurant, par une "recherche obsessive du consensus".[54]

Le comité mixte co-présidé par le sénateur Gérald Beaudoin et le député Jim Edwards aura constitué le volet technique du processus participatif enclenché par le gouvernement Mulroney, en réponse à la Commission Bélanger-Campeau. Forum itinérant tout comme la Commission Spicer, le comité Beaudoin-Edwards fit aussi d'entrée de jeu l'objet de critiques, formulées à la fois par l'opposition et par certains observateurs, à propos de la nature même du mandat imparti au groupe de travail; en fait, on reprochait au comité de focaliser exclusivement sur la "plomberie" constitutionnelle en omettant d'examiner la question fondamentale du partage des pouvoirs. Le premier ministre Mulroney ne fut pas long à réagir puisqu'il confia peu après — sans tambour ni trompette — à une dizaine d'équipes de sous-ministres et de hauts-fonctionnaires fédéraux le soin d'examiner en profondeur, dans l'esprit du discours de Buckingham, l'ensemble des compétences partagées entre Ottawa et les provinces.[55]

Après avoir jonglé durant la durée de leurs travaux avec deux hypothèses de base susceptibles de modifier la Constitution, soit l'Assemblée constituante ou le référendum, le Comité Beaudoin-Edwards aura décidé, en dernier ressort mais de manière circonscrite, de retenir la seconde option; ce faisant, on s'ajustait prudemment au refus catégorique du gouvernement du Québec d'être partie prenante d'un exercice (l'Assemblée constituante) dans le cadre duquel les demandes du Québec pouvaient, une fois encore, faire les frais d'une éventuelle cabale orchestrée par un ou des participants — parlementaires ou extra-parlementaires — "en mal d'égalité" avec le Québec.

Afin de passer outre à la règle de l'unanimité, le Comité Beaudoin-Edwards aura finalement proposé le recours à un référendum pan-canadien de manière à attribuer une macro-légitimité populaire au processus. Pour la formule d'amendement proprement dite, le comité Beaudoin-Edwards n'aura pas innové; il aura fait sienne plutôt la proposition formulée par le premier ministre Trudeau à la conférence de Victoria en 1971. La formule de veto régional, morte-née à la suite de l'échec de la conférence, constituait néanmoins, à quelques détails près, une formule passablement opérationnelle et relativement équitable, dans la mesure où elle accordait un veto spécifique au Québec et à l'Ontario et pondérait sur une base régionale (l'Ouest et les Maritimes) le veto des autres provinces. L'endossement du veto régional par les libéraux, conservateurs et néo-démocrates confère une crédibilité certaine à la formule; le hic toutefois, c'est que le succès de l'opération repose désormais sur la "noblesse" constitutionnelle des huits provinces invitées à se départir d'un droit de veto spécifique au profit plutôt d'un quart de veto. Or la réaction de ces dernières ne s'est pas fait attendre. Dans les heures qui ont suivi le dépôt du rapport, quatre provinces, Terre-Neuve, l'Alberta, la Saskatchewan et la Colombie Britannique, signifiaient déjà leur opposition à la principale recommandation du comité Beaudoin-Edwards. Comme élément de compensation pour les provinces perdantes, Ottawa se proposait en revanche d'inclure dans son "agenda" constitutionnel une réforme véritable du Sénat.[56]

C'est peu avant Buckingham que le gouvernement Mulroney aura entrepris graduellement de lancer une offensive idéologique en faveur du fédéralisme. L'un des premiers gestes d'Ottawa fut de prendre dans son collimateur la Commission Bélanger-Campeau en y déléguant un groupe de fonctionnaires fédéraux du Conseil privé chargés d'assister les supporters du fédéralisme à la Commission ainsi que d'instruire le cabinet du premier ministre Mulroney.[57] Devant la vague souverainiste au Québec déferlant jusqu'à la Commission Bélanger-Campeau, le premier ministre fédéral prit le parti de simplement relativiser le phénomène en le qualifiant d'"éphémère", question surtout de sécuriser le Canada anglais. Ce n'est qu'au prix d'un intense "forcing" de Québec que le gouvernement Mulroney aura finalement consenti à régler le dossier de l'immigration entre Québec et Ottawa, ce dernier craignant comme la peste que son geste soit interprété dans le reste du pays comme une prime indirecte à un bilatéralisme par trop exclusif envers le Québec.

Outre la "menace" souverainiste au Québec, c'est aussi et surtout le dépôt du rapport Allaire qui, comme le soulignait Graham Fraser, aura forcé le gouvernement fédéral à intervenir plus vigoureusement — et également plus tôt que prévu — en faveur de l'unité nationale.[58] Les discours prononcés par le premier ministre Mulroney, à la mi-février 1991, à Toronto et à Québec s'adressaient à deux auditoires distincts mais ils comportaient essentiellement un seul message, soit l'engagement ferme d'Ottawa à réaliser un "nouveau Canada", mais en marge cependant de "toutes menaces ou ultimatums". Le discours de Toronto avait pour objectif de persuader les Anglo-Canadiens, réfractaires pour la plupart à son leadership, de sa foi fédéraliste ainsi que de son aptitude à gouverner le pays durant cette situation de crise. Il s'agissait aussi de les sensibiliser à la nécessité de procéder à d'inévitables changements politiques, administratifs et constitutionnels, lesquels devraient toutefois se conformer à quelques principes fondamentaux tels que, parmi d'autres, la Charte canadienne des droits et libertés de même que le "maintien de certaines normes nationales" dans le domaine de la santé et de l'environnement. Allusion on ne peut plus claire s'il en fut au rapport Allaire, présenté à mi-mots, dans le discours de Québec, comme un entreprise qui reviendrait à faire du Canada un "pays à temps partiel" dont la dynamique hyper-décentralisatrice mènerait tout droit à une "vente de feu des institutions canadiennes", et où le rôle d'Ottawa serait réduit à ne plus assurer que l'"intendance minimale". Dans son plaidoyer pour un "Canada reconstitué, fier de sa diversité et fort de son unité", le premier ministre Mulroney n'aura évidemment pas épargné les souverainistes bon teint. De fait, il n'hésita pas à les dépeindre sans ménagement comme des "démolisseurs du Canada" et sommés, pour ce, de présenter le fardeau de la preuve relativement aux coûts économiques d'une rupture par le Québec du lien fédéral.

Engagé résolument dans une croisade pro-Canada à l'instar de son prédécesseur libéral, Pierre Elliot Trudeau, une décennie plus tôt, le premier ministre conservateur s'inspira aussi de la stratégie trudeauiste en créant le "groupe de travail sur l'unité canadienne"; doté d'un budget de 8 millions$, le groupe est tributaire du Bureau des Relations fédérales-provinciales et chargé de mettre au point les stratégies constitutionnelles du gouvernement fédéral. Certains auront vu dans ce groupe ad hoc une réincarnation du Centre d'information de l'unité canadienne créé par le gouvernement Trudeau avant le référendum de 1980, lequel s'était consacré alors, avec force moyens, à la diffusion du credo fédéraliste au Québec. Il est vrai que nombre de hauts mandarins de l'époque Trudeau, Paul Tellier en tête, ont repris dernièrement du service dans le dossier constitutionnel selon les voeux du gouvernement Mulroney. Mais là s'arrête peut-être la comparaison. De fait, les protagonistes québécois et fédéral de 1991, en dépit de leurs divergences réelles sur le plan constitutionnel, entretiennent encore des contacts réguliers voire étroits entre eux, fruits de leur ex-collaboration durant l'épisode Meech.[59]

Sachant ses bases électorales du Québec, de l'Ouest et de l'Ontario sérieusement menacées par le Bloc québécois et le Reform Party, le gouvernement Mulroney aura décidé d'opter pour une stratégie de type attaque frontale contre ces deux formations politiques. A la faveur d'une sorte de trêve tacite provisoire avec les libéraux et les néo-démocrates conviés dès lors à un "front commun" pour l'unité canadienne, le gouvernement conservateur s'est trouvé du coup en mesure de mieux concentrer ses tirs sur les partis de Lucien Bouchard et de Preston Manning. En qualifiant ces deux partis d'"anti-fédéralistes" le gouvernement Mulroney faisait le pari audacieux de pouvoir rallier, ultima ratio, une majorité de Canadiens autour de l'image de son parti prêt à tout pour venir à bout de ces forces centrifuges, et voué sans relâche à la défense des valeurs-clés de la fédération canadienne. Défi de taille à la vérité

étant donné que ces deux partis, nullement en compétition sur les plans territorial et électoral, pourraient à eux deux décrocher, en toute vraisemblance, la
balance du pouvoir aux Communes à la prochaine élection fédérale en faisant
élire près des deux-cinquièmes des députés de la Chambre. Ce multi-partisme
à cinq, façon européenne, constituerait un scénario du pire dans l'optique
d'Ottawa, compte tenu que le Bloc voit son pendant de l'Ouest comme un "allié
objectif" — malgré leurs divergences idéologiques — et que toute stratégie
déstabilisatrice plus ou moins commune de la part de ces deux partis aurait pour
effet de fragiliser, à un niveau inégalé dans l'histoire canadienne, les institutions
politiques fédérales.[60]

A cet égard, le remaniement ministériel d'avril 1991 opéré par le gouvernement Mulroney se voulait d'abord et avant tout un moyen de se gagner les
faveurs de l'Ouest en nommant Don Mazankowski, Harvie Andre et Joe Clark,
tous trois de l'Alberta, à des ministères de premier plan soit, respectivement,
les Finances, la Réforme parlementaire et les Affaires constitutionnelles.
Rapatrié d'urgence des Affaires extérieures, Joe Clark aura été perçu par Brian
Mulroney comme l'"homme de la situation" dans le dossier constitutionnel; en
raison de la souplesse et de la crédibilité politique de son nouveau ministre, le
premier ministre conservateur nourrit l'espoir que celui-ci puisse réaliser
l'exploit de trouver un terrain d'entente entre le Québec, Ottawa et les autres
provinces. Clark aura effectivement tâté le terrain: au terme d'une tournée des
dix premiers ministres provinciaux, le ministre conservateur demanda au
gouvernement Bourassa qu'il reporte, voire annule son échéance référendaire.
En contre-partie, Joe Clark exhorta le Canada anglais à ne pas rejeter du revers
de la main les doléances du Québec. En présentant au surplus le nationalisme
québécois comme un modèle de fierté pour le ROC, le ministre fédéral préparait
mentalement, en douce, le Canada anglais à reconnaître dans les mois à venir
le caractère distinct — sinon "unique" — du Québec. Même si, au début juillet
1991 selon l'Institut Gallup, deux Canadiens sur trois auraient souhaité la
démission de Brian Mulroney de son poste de leader des Tories, le premier
ministre conservateur sera néanmoins parvenu, au cours des dernières
semaines, à recueillir hors Québec l'appui voilé d'au moins cinq
gouvernements provinciaux (l'Ontario, la Colombie-Britannique, le Nouveau-
Brunswick, la Nouvelle-Ecosse et l'Ile du Prince-Edouard) envers sa stratégie
constitutionnelle.

Dans l'intervalle, le gouvernement Mulroney aura fait en sorte aussi
d'obtenir que des chefs d'Etat ou de gouvernement étrangers légitiment son
combat intérieur pour l'unité nationale. Ainsi, les présidents des Etats-Unis et
du Mexique, Georges Bush et Carlos Salinas, le chancelier de l'Allemagne,
Helmut Kohl, et le premier ministre de la Lituanie, Gediminas Vagnorius,
auront tous quatre plaidé en faveur d'un "Canada uni", des prises de position
qui, pour certains souverainistes, apparaissaient sollicitées directement par le

premier ministre canadien.[61] Le chef du Parti québécois, Jacques Parizeau, se livra à un exercice similaire, mais à un registre plus modeste, en cherchant à s'assurer, le moment venu, d'une ouverture de la France face à la souveraineté éventuelle du Québec, en conformité avec la politique traditionnelle de "non-indifférence"de l'Etat français par rapport au Québec. Or, soucieux avant toute chose de ne pas compromettre leurs relations harmonieuses avec Ottawa, l'Elysée et Matignon s'emploieront de toute évidence, dans un esprit de "non-ingérence" cette fois, à repousser le plus tard possible toute manifestation de sympathie active à l'égard de l'option souverainiste québécoise. Par ailleurs, le leader péquiste avait déjà tenté plus tôt, fin février, de rassurer tant bien que mal les milieux d'affaires de New-York à l'idée d'un Québec indépendant.

Finalement, le Discours du trône dévoilé le 13 mai dernier, à Ottawa, fut l'occasion pour le gouvernement Mulroney de faire connaître les grandes lignes de la stratégie qu'il entend poursuivre dans la prochaine année, pour cristalliser son "projet de pays". En créant un autre comité mixte du Parlement — composé de quinze députés et de dix sénateurs — chargé de soumettre, de septembre 1991 à janvier 1992, les propositions constitutionnelles aux Canadiens, aux groupes autochtones et aux représentants des provinces, le gouvernement fédéral se trouvait du coup à gagner un certain temps puis aussi, à donner la réplique aux échéanciers constitutionnels des rapports Allaire et Bélanger-Campeau. De fait, après la consultation effectuée par le comité mixte, Ottawa proposera un plan d'action constitutionnel aux Canadiens le printemps prochain, six mois seulement avant l'échéance ultime établie par le gouvernement du Québec pour tenir un référendum sur la souveraineté. Mais auparavant, le premier ministre Mulroney aura mis sur pied un comité formé de 18 ministres auquel fut confiée la mission d'élaborer lesdites propositions constitutionnelles qu'Ottawa fera connaître à l'ensemble des Canadiens à la mi-septembre. Au fil de ses pérégrinations à travers le Canada, de Winnipeg à Charlottetown en passant par Niagara-on-the-Lake, le comité ministériel aura cherché à prendre en compte les demandes diverses des provinces.

Avec la mise en retrait du Québec à la suite de l'échec de Meech et vu les revendications pressantes manifestées hors Québec au chapitre constitutionnel, il était presque dans l'ordre des choses qu'Ottawa fasse de cette prochaine ronde de négociations une "ronde Canada". Mi-livre blanc, mi-livre vert, la série de propositions qu'Ottawa déposera à l'automne emprunteront vraisemblablement autant à l'énoncé de politique formel qu'au document de travail offrant des options propres à la discussion.[62] Les propositions fédérales devraient s'articuler autour des quatre questions suivantes: les principes ou les caractéristiques fondamentales du pays; le partage des pouvoirs entre les gouvernements fédéral et provinciaux; la question des revendications au-tochtones et la réforme des institutions canadiennes. Ces quatre grands thèmes visent à embrasser jusqu'à un certain point l'ensemble des requêtes provinciales. Le défi reste entier et de taille pour Ottawa, chaque province y allant de son cheval de bataille particulier: qui la société distincte pour le Québec; qui la réforme du Sénat pour l'Alberta; qui une "charte sociale des droits" pour l'Ontario; qui un gouvernement central fort pour le Manitoba, etc.

Le concept de société distincte aura suscité quelques échanges musclés entre certains ministres québécois et anglo-canadiens faisant partie du comité Clark. La pomme de discorde renvoyait pour l'essentiel : i) à la place même du concept dans le texte constitutionnel (soit dans la Charte des droits, dans le préambule ou enchâssé dans le corps même de la Constitution) et ii) à la substance intrinsèque de la notion (c'est-à-dire concrètement, devait-on reconnaître au Québec le droit de "protéger et promouvoir" son caractère distinct comme l'aurait garanti feu l'Accord du lac Meech?) . Or, à ce chapitre, la marge de manoeuvre s'avère étroite pour le gouvernement Mulroney: ce dernier est tenu en effet de satisfaire le gouvernement Bourassa — qui dit n'attendre rien de moins que l'Accord du lac Meech — et, d'autre part, il se doit de vaincre certains esprits récalcitrants dans le ROC pour qui le caractère distinct du Québec est synonyme de supériorité aux dépens des autres provinces.

Par ailleurs, il faudra voir jusqu'où Ottawa se rendra sur la voie de la décentralisation des pouvoirs aux provinces ainsi qu'en matière de fédéralisme asymétrique, un domaine qui concerne le Québec au premier chef. Déjà le 23 août dernier, le premier ministre Mulroney démentait de façon énergique les spéculations médiatiques voulant que le Québec exerce une pleine juridiction sur la culture et les communications notamment. Quoiqu'il en soit, il est déjà à prévoir qu'Ottawa ne procédera pas à un transfert massif de compétences vers le Québec ou les autres provinces tel que prôné dans le rapport Allaire et par plusieurs témoins entendus à la Commission Bélanger-Campeau.[63] En pareil cas, le gouvernement Bourassa aura fort à faire pour "acheter" puis "vendre" ensuite aux Québécois les offres fédérales; il faudrait alors qu'Ottawa propose en revanche au Québec — et/ou à d'autres provinces intéressées — la formule quelque peu ni chair ni poisson des ententes administratives de type bilatéral, laquelle offre cependant l'avantage de passer outre au recours de modifications constitutionnelles. Une telle éventualité serait de nature à peut-être rallier éventuellement le reste du Canada. Le gouvernement Bourassa, par pur souci pragmatique, pourrait aussi opter pour une telle solution, au risque toutefois d'être accusé par certains au Québec d'endosser alors une réforme tout au plus cosmétique du fédéralisme canadien.

Il semble acquis par ailleurs qu'Ottawa proposera la création d'un Sénat élu où l'Ouest et les Maritimes se verraient mieux représentés mais dont les pouvoirs resteraient encore à définir. De même en devrait-il être du futur Conseil de la fédération qui comprendrait des représentants de toutes les provinces et du gouvernement central. Le but de cette nouvelle instance consisterait notamment à institutionnaliser les centaines de rencontres fédérales-provinciales ayant lieu chaque année; le Conseil prendrait également en charge certaines questions-clés relatives à l'union économique telles les barrières commerciales interprovinciales ainsi que la mise au point des normes nationales touchant les futurs programmes co-financés. [64] S'agissant des constantes revendications formulées par les premières nations, il faudra voir si Ottawa proposera dans l'immédiat l'enchâssement du droit à l'autonomie gouvernementale des autochtones. Joe Clark convenait à la mi-août que l'Ontario se situait à l'"avant-garde" à ce chapitre, à la suite de l'entente signée avec les Amérindiens de cette province reconnaissant explicitement le droit à ces derniers de se gouverner eux-mêmes. C'est d'ailleurs à la lumière de ce contexte qu'il importe d'interpréter les offres répétées d'alliance stratégique de l'Assemblée des Premières nations auprès du gouvernement du Québec[65]; le but consistant ici pour le regroupement amérindien à enterrer la hache de guerre avec l'ex-ennemi juré d'hier, et partant de convaincre celui-ci de l'indissociabilité des causes québécoise et autochtone dans l'optique d'une réforme "radicale" du fédéralisme canadien.

Reste à savoir maintenant dans quelle mesure le gouvernement Mulroney parviendra à concilier les positions parfois incompatibles des acteurs en cause sans laisser le Québec sur la touche pour autant; du reste, l'erreur fondamentale à éviter serait de confectionner, selon le mot de Susan Delacourt, un "buffet constitutionnel" trop diversifié mais sans grande substance. [66]

Entretemps, la volonté ferme d'Ottawa, confirmée à la suite du Discours du Trône, d'intervenir au Québec dans les domaines de l'éducation et de la formation, de la santé, de l'environnement et du développement régional aura littéralement pris de court le gouvernement Bourassa. Perçues à Québec comme un geste provocateur autant par l'opposition péquiste que par le gouvernement, certaines de ces initiatives fédérales auront été interprétées par Graham Fraser comme faisant partie d'une suite de décisions incohérentes prises à la suite du Discours du Trône.[67] L'offensive centralisatrice entreprise par le gouvernement Mulroney aura par contre été reçue comme du pain bénit par les libéraux de Jean Chrétien; le P.L.C. aura vite compris tout le bénéfice qu'il y avait sur le plan électoral — fût-ce de façon circonstancielle — à exploiter au Québec le créneau autonomiste aux dépens des conservateurs, dût-il même faire chorus pour l'occasion avec le Bloc québécois. Pour intempestif qu'il puisse paraître à première vue, l'interventionnisme pratiqué par le gouvernement Mulroney traduirait peut-être une volonté de sa part de renforcer son profil "All-Canadian" auprès des deux tiers d'Anglo-Canadiens toujours réfractaires aux demandes du Québec.[68] Le but ultime consistant ici pour le premier ministre fédéral à se trouver en assez bonne posture pour "vendre" au ROC, l'occasion venue, une quelconque entente éventuelle avec le Québec.

Au reste, le gouvernement Mulroney continue de croire au succès de son entreprise constitutionnelle, voire à sa réélection lors du prochain appel aux urnes, prévu vraisemblablement pour 1993. Pour ce faire, il devra avant tout éviter toute(s) nouvelle(s) défection(s) au sein de son caucus québécois si, d'aventure, le livre blanc gouvernemental ne recueillait pas le consensus escompté. Le gouvernement conservateur mise beaucoup sur l'image d'unité qu'a voulu offrir le P.C. lors de son dernier congrès à Toronto, à la mi-août, lorsque les délégués du parti votèrent à 92% en faveur d'une résolution "confirmant" le droit à l'autodétermination du Québec. L'optimisme du gouvernement Mulroney tient aussi aux données d'un sondage Angus Reid publié au même moment et indiquant une possible victoire électorale du parti conservateur fédéral dans l'éventualité d'un redémarrage effectif de l'économie canadienne, conjugué au règlement de la question constitutionnelle. Un défi de taille pour le premier ministre fédéral qui, en fier émule de John A. Macdonald et George-Etienne Cartier, joue désormais son va-tout sur le sauvetage de la fédération canadienne.

VERS UNE NOUVELLE DONNE QUEBEC-CANADA

On se souviendra de l'échec de l'Accord du lac Meech comme probablement de l'événement-charnière à partir duquel le sort de la fédération canadienne se sera joué décisivement. Le fiasco de cet épisode constitutionnel aura provoqué une véritable onde de choc au Québec. Fédéralistes désabusés et souverainistes ragaillardis auront vu dans la Commission Bélanger-Campeau — fruit d'un consensus exceptionnel de la classe politique québécoise — l'occasion de présenter leur "cahiers de doléances" à l'égard du fédéralisme canadien. Le parti gouvernemental ne fut pas en reste: à l'instar du rapport Bélanger-Campeau, le rapport Allaire issu du comité constitutionnel du Parti libéral du Québec renvoyait aussi la balle des négociations constitutionnelles dans le camp fédéral en laissant planer toutefois, à la clé, la menace d'un référendum sur la souveraineté à l'automne 1992. Mais à la vérité, le premier ministre Bourassa aura, au cours des derniers mois, affirmé sa prime allégeance envers le fédéralisme canadien, au grand dam des éléments hyper-autonomistes de son parti ainsi que des souverainistes québécois. Pendant ce temps, hors Québec, le gouvernement fédéral s'employait par étapes à organiser une vaste consultation, à la faveur de divers comités ou commissions, et auprès de ses partenaires provinciaux, afin d'offrir des propositions de réforme du fédéralisme canadien qui soient acceptables à la fois au Québec et aux autres provinces.

Jusqu'à nouvel ordre, le gouvernement Bourassa se contente, de façon officielle, d'attendre patiemment les offres formelles du reste du Canada qui lui parviendront seulement au printemps 1992. Ayant exprimé, fin juin, sa "confiance raisonnable" dans les offres fédérales à venir[69], Robert Bourassa pourrait aussi se prévaloir éventuellement de l'invitation faite alors par Joe Clark de déléguer certains membres de l'Assemblée nationale (en l'occurrence ici, de son parti) pour participer aux travaux du comité mixte fédéral qui pilotera dès septembre l'étude des propositions constitutionnelles d'Ottawa. Le gouvernement Bourassa pourrait être tenté, durant cette période, de multiplier ses éloges du système fédéral, dans le but de montrer "patte blanche" au Canada hors Québec, tout en accentuant ses critiques face à l'option souverainiste. Par ailleurs, il n'est pas exclu non plus — quoique peu vraisemblable pour l'heure — que le gouvernement Bourassa, pressentant au fil des mois que l'impasse demeure infranchissable, décide de retraiter en douce et de s'aligner sur la souveraineté, ce qui provoquerait à coup sûr le départ d'un certain nombre de libéraux québécois fédéralistes, viscéralement hostiles à cette option.

Gratifié d'une avance confortable de plus de douze points sur les libéraux à la lumière de deux récents coups de sonde de l'opinion publique québécoise,[70] le Parti québécois est confiant pour sa part de voir le parti gouvernemental faire les frais à nouveau, comme pour Meech, de cette nouvelle tentative de renouvellement du fédéralisme canadien. L'optimisme des péquistes est conforté par un récent sondage Multi-Réso-*Le Devoir* réalisé fin-mai début-juin et indiquant une persistance de la ferveur souverainiste au Québec (57%)[71] Autre motif de réjouissance pour le Parti québécois: sa victoire décisive lors de l'élection partielle dans la circonscription de Montmorency, le 12 août dernier. Le P.Q. en fit un test symbolique en faveur de la souveraineté pendant que les libéraux relativisèrent la signification du vote en attribuant plutôt leur défaite à la morosité des électeurs devant la stagnation de l'économie québécoise. Par ailleurs, le Parti québécois entend bien pour sa part, au cours des prochains mois, jouer les trouble-fête du renouvellement fédéraliste, relayés en cela à Ottawa par ses frères d'armes souverainistes du Bloc québécois. A cet égard, les deux formations souverainistes ne se priveront pas le moment venu de rappeler au gouvernement Mulroney — pour fins de comparaison avec le Québec — son empressement à reconnaître l'indépendance des Etats baltes, et son engagement à faire de même éventuellement avec une Ukraine qui opterait pour sa souveraineté par référendum.

Lié par ricochet à la question constitutionnelle, le méga-projet hydro-électrique Grande-Baleine aura été reporté, en août dernier, d'au moins un an par son ardent promoteur, le gouvernement Bourassa, à la suite de l'opposition conjuguée d'Ottawa et des autochtones relativement au type d'évaluation de l'impact du projet sur le plan environnemental. Realpolitik oblige, la volte-face spectaculaire du gouvernement libéral eu égard à son projet fétiche répondit grosso modo à trois impératifs: d'abord composer avec l'opinion internationale; puis ne pas compromettre le lucratif contrat d'exportation d'électricité avec la New York Power Authority d'une valeur de 12,6 milliards $; et enfin, éviter à la veille du dépôt des propositions fédérales tout affrontement avec Ottawa et/ou avec les autochtones qui pourrait réduire à néant les chances du gouvernement Bourassa d'en arriver à une entente éventuelle avec ses partenaires fédératifs.

A l'heure où l'échec d'un certain fédéralisme multiethnique apparaît de plus en plus consommé en U.R.S.S. et en Yougoslavie, le sort de la fédération canadienne se révèle, pour sa part, on ne peut plus incertain. Solidaires d'Ottawa et résolues à lancer l'offensive en faveur du maintien d'un gouvernement central fort, les provinces anglophones auront ni plus ni moins relancé la balle constitutionnelle dans le camp québécois, au terme de la dernière rencontre annuelle des premiers ministres provinciaux — où le Québec fut absent — à Whistler, à la fin du mois d'août dernier. Or, la faiblesse relative de Robert Bourassa, politiquement parlant, face à un P.Q. auréolé de son dernier succès électoral, pourrait contraindre le gouvernement du Québec à radicaliser sa position constitutionnelle face au ROC. Le reste du Canada, pendant ce temps, espère encore — sans trop se faire d'illusions toutefois — voir émerger l'"Homme providentiel" qui parviendrait à préserver l'intégrité du pays; à la vérité cependant, nombre de Canadiens hors Québec sont de plus en plus convaincus que les Québécois ont déjà franchi — psycho-politiquement parlant — le Rubicon de l'indépendance.

Devant un Canada anglais qui entend rester ferme envers les demandes du Québec, Robert Bourassa constitue finalement l'ultime inconnue dans ce processus constitutionnel. Mais, tout compte fait, il importe peut-être moins de savoir qui du nostalgique de Meech ou de l'éventuel fédéraliste désabusé émergera au cours des prochains mois. Car, en dernier ressort, c'est le peuple québécois qui, quelque part en 1992, par voie référendaire ou électorale, sera vraisemblablement appelé à trancher entre le beau risque nouvelle manière et la souveraineté.

NOTES

1. Voir Michel VASTEL, *Bourassa*, Editions de l'Homme, Montréal, 1991, p.87.

2. Cité par Gilles LESAGE dans "Le gouvernement a-t-il renié son engagement du 5 avril?", *Le Devoir*, 12 juin 1990, p.8.

3. S'il est vrai que les huit législatures provinciales ayant ratifié l'Accord totalisaient près de 95% de la population du pays, il faut se rappeler aussi que des sondages successifs réalisés avant et après l'échec de Meech (cf. le sondage réalisé par CBC-*The Globe and Mail* en février 1990 et celui par la maison Gallup en juin 1991) ont révélé un refus majoritaire du Canada anglais de souscrire à l'idée d'accorder au Québec un statut de société distincte si cela devait se traduire ultérieurement par des pouvoirs accrus à cette province.

4. Malgré l'annonce du boycott de ces conférences faite par le premier ministre Robert Bourassa l'an dernier, le Québec a participé néanmoins à environ une rencontre fédérale-provinciale sur quatre (17 sur 70: compilation au début juillet 1991) et maintenu également des contacts réguliers au niveau des hauts fonctionnaires avec les autorités outaouaises. Voir Michel VENNE, "Le boycott

des conférences fédérales-provinciales par le Québec est officiel mais loin d'être complet", *Le Devoir*, 2 juillet 1991, pp. 1 et 4.

5. Pour une analyse plus approfondie de la question, voir Daniel BONIN, "Les vicissitudes de l'axe Québec-Ontario", *La Presse*, 12 octobre 1990, p. B3.

6. Voir le discours de David PETERSON, "L'Ontario dans un Canada en mutation", le 10 août 1990.

7. *Loi instituant la Commission sur l'avenir politique et constitutionnel du Québec*, L.Q. 1990, ch.34 et modifications subséquentes L.Q. 1990, ch.45.

8. Robert BOURASSA, Discours à l'Assemblée nationale à l'occasion de l'adoption du projet de loi instituant la Commission sur l'avenir politique et constitutionnel du Québec, le 5 septembre 1990.

9. Voir à ce sujet les déclarations de Jacques Parizeau et de Robert Bourassa lors de la séance d'ouverture de la Commission sur l'avenir politique et constitutionnel du Québec, le 6 novembre 1990. *Journal des Débats*, Assemblée nationale, Québec, première session, trente-quatrième législature, no 1, pp. 5-10.

10. Voir Lise BISSONNETTE, "Le minimum de courant commun", *Le Devoir*, 7 novembre 1990, p. A12.

11. Le choix des commissaires s'effectua presque sans anicroche, hormis la nomination par le premier ministre Bourassa — en l'absence de Jacques Parizeau — de deux hommes d'affaires apparentés au Parti libéral du Québec (MM. Marcel Beaudry et Charles-André Poissant), aux dépens du président de la Chambre de commerce du Québec (M. Jean Lambert), préféré par le Parti québécois. En revanche, le P.Q. força, in extremis, le chef du gouvernement à recruter un représentant du secteur de l'éducation et de la culture, soit en l'occurrence M. Serge Turgeon, de l'Union des Artistes, bien connu pour ses convictions souverainistes. De toute évidence, l'union sacrée entre libéraux et péquistes avait montré ses limites objectives.

12. La composition de la commission se présentait comme suit: le premier ministre du Québec; le chef de l'opposition officielle; un groupe de dix-huit membres qui n'étaient pas des représentants de l'Assemblée nationale du Québec dont les deux co-présidents; deux élus municipaux; quatre représentants du milieu syndical; quatre représentants du milieu des affaires; un représentant du milieu des coopératives; un représentant du milieu de l'enseignement; un représentant du milieu de la culture; trois députés de la Chambre des Communes élus au Québec; un groupe de seize députés de l'Assemblée nationale dont neuf représentants du parti gouvernemental; six représentants de l'opposition officielle et un représentant officiel du Parti Egalité (William Holden) auquel il faut ajouter un autre représentant sans droit de vote. Précisons enfin qu'à l'exception des deux derniers commissaires, chaque membre de la Commission avait un suppléant désigné.

13. De façon plus précise, les travaux de la Commission se sont échelonnés du 6 novembre 1990 au 23 janvier 1991. 492 groupes et individus ont soumis des mémoires dans les délais prévus et 115 autres mémoires ont été reçus après coup, pour un total de 607 mémoires. Au surplus, 267 groupes ou individus ont fait l'objet d'auditions devant la Commission à la faveur des audiences publiques et

du forum "Les jeunes et l'avenir du Québec". Voir *Rapport de la Commission sur l'avenir politique et constitutionnel du Québec*, Québec, mars 1991, pp. 4-5.

14. Refusant d'être assimilés à des "cadavres encore chauds" — pour reprendre le qualificatif brutal que leur avait servi l'écrivain Yves Beauchemin devant la Commission Bélanger-Campeau —, les francophones hors Québec attendaient beaucoup de la commission sur l'avenir politique et constitutionnel du Québec. Les vingt et une lignes qui leur sont consacrées dans le rapport n'auront pas suffi à combler leur attente; selon eux la contribution de la commission à leur endroit reflétait très clairement "le désintéressement du Québec à l'égard de la francophonie canadienne". C'est dans cet esprit qu'à l'occasion de leur Assemblée générale annuelle de juin 1991, les francophones hors Québec décidèrent de rebaptiser leur organisation pan-canadienne *Fédération des communautés francophones et acadienne du Canada*. Ce changement de cap traduisait par le fait même une nette distanciation avec le Québec; désormais le credo constitutionnel des francophones hors Québec allait se fonder sur un Canada central fort. Voir Chantal HEBERT, "Les minorités francophones ne comptent plus sur le Québec", *Le Devoir*, 17 juin 1991, p.1.

15. Voir Charles TAYLOR, "Les enjeux de la réforme constitutionnelle", dans Commission sur l'avenir politique et constitutionnelle du Québec, *Les avis des spécialistes invités à répondre aux huit questions posées par la Commission*, Bibliothèque nationale du Québec, 1991, Document de travail, numéro 4, p. 978.

16. CHAMBRE DE COMMERCE DU QUEBEC, *L'avenir politique et constitutionnel du Québec: sa dimension économique*, mémoire présenté à la Commission Bélanger-Campeau le 7 novembre 1990, p.2.

17. Op.cit., publié dans *La Presse*, 25 janvier 1991, p.B3.

18. CONSEIL DU PATRONAT DU QUEBEC, *Le Canada de demain: pour une constitution moderne*, mémoire soumis à la Commission sur l'avenir politique et constitutionnel du Québec, novembre 1990, pp. 14-15.

19. Au sujet de la compatibilité entre souveraineté et interdépendance, voir notamment les mémoires de Louis BERNARD, "Réponses aux questions posées par la Commission sur l'avenir politique et constitutionnel du Québec", dans *Les avis des spécialistes...*, op. cit., p. 66; Pierre FORTIN, "Le choix forcé du Québec: aspects économiques et stratégiques", dans *Les avis des spécialistes...*, op. cit., p. 343; et l'ASSOCIATION DES ECONOMISTES QUEBECOIS, *Mémoire à la Commission sur l'avenir politique et constitutionnel du Québec*, novembre 1990, p. 4.

20. Voir Michel DAVID, "Le CPQ trouve l'aventure souverainiste "suicidaire"", *Le Soleil*, 6 novembre 1990, p. A6 et Alain DUBUC, "Le statu quo renouvelé de M.Chrétien", *La Presse*, 18 décembre 1990, p. B2.

21. Voir *La Presse*, 24 décembre 1990, p. B1.

22. Selon cette étude, un Québec souverain serait prémuni contre une "explosion" de son déficit. Ainsi, avec le rapatriement des points d'impôts et des taxes prélevées par Ottawa et au Québec, même en embauchant immédiatement les fonctionnaires fédéraux du Québec, le déficit provincial ne subirait une augmentation que de 133 millions$ sur un budget total de 35 milliards $, d'après les calculs du secrétariat

de la Commission. Qui plus est, il y aurait approximativement 5 milliards$ d'économie potentielle en éliminant l'ensemble des dédoublements de services entre Ottawa et Québec. Cette estimation n'aura cependant pas intégré l'impact du partage de la dette nationale et du rapatriement des actifs fédéraux au Québec qui feraient l'objet d'une entente éventuelle avec le gouvernement central, une procédure dont les écueils ont déjà été entrevus par certains économistes du Canada anglais. Voir à ce sujet Paul BOOTHE et Richard HARRIS, "Alternative Division of Federal Assets and Liabilities" (ronéotypé) dans *Economic Dimension of Constitutional Change*, Conférence organisée par le John Deutsch Institute, Queen's University, Kingston, Ontario, du 4 au 6 juin 1991. Au demeurant, il importe de mentionner ici l'allégeance souverainiste de l'auteur de cette étude, Henri-Paul Rousseau, dont les données de base — non les conclusions — ne furent par ailleurs pas contestées par la plupart des sympathisants fédéralistes à la Commission. Voir Denis LESSARD, "La souveraineté économiquement viable selon la Commission B.-C.", *La Presse*, 21 février 1991, p. A1.

23. Pierre FORTIN, "Le choix forcé du Québec", dans *Les avis des spécialistes...*, op.cit., pp. 346 et 378. On se reportera au mémoire pour une démonstration complète des idées de Fortin.

24. Voir pour le paragraphe précédent les mémoires suivants: Gilles ROCHELEAU, *Pour l'Outaouais et le Québec, d'abord!* , mémoire préparé par le député du Bloc québécois de Hull-Aylmer et présenté à la Commission Bélanger-Campeau, décembre 1990, p.15; LIGUE D'ACTION NATIONALE, *L'indépendance normale et nécessaire*, mémoire à la Commission sur l'avenir politique et constitutionnel du Québec, novembre 1990, p. 30; SOCIETE SAINT-JEAN BAPTISTE (Mauricie), *Mémoire sur l'avenir politique et constitutionnel du Québec, novembre 1990*, p.11; Simon LANGLOIS, "Une société distincte à reconnaître et une identité collective à consolider", dans *Les avis des spécialistes...*, op.cit., pp. 577-578; PARTI QUEBECOIS, *La nécessaire souveraineté*, mémoire à la Commission sur l'avenir politique et constitutionnel du Québec, novembre 1991, p.20 et Guy LAFOREST, "Protéger et promouvoir une société distincte au Québec, dans *Les avis des spécialistes...*, op.cit., pp. 526-535.

25. Alain DUBUC, "Le fédéralisme mal aimé", *La Presse*, 15 novembre 1990, p. B2.

26. Voir EQUALITY PARTY (Brome Missisquoi Riding Association), *A constitutional brief to La Commission sur l'avenir politique et constitutionnel du Québec*, p.13 et ASSEMBLEE DES PREMIERES NATIONS, *Notes pour la présentation* par Konrad Sioui à la Commission parlementaire élargie sur l'avenir politique et constitutionnel du Québec, 20 décembre 1990, p. 9.

27. Voir Lise BISSONNETTE, "Le syndrome de l'orphelinat", *Le Devoir*, 10 décembre 1990, p. 12.

28. Voir Léon DION, "Pour sortir de l'impasse constitutionnelle", dans *Les avis des spécialistes...*, op. cit., pp. 278-280.

29. PARTI LIBERAL DU QUEBEC, *Un Québec libre de ses choix*, Rapport du comité constitutionnel du parti, 28 janvier 1991, p. 4.

30. *Ibid.*, pp. 4 et 26.

31. Voir à ce sujet Richard G. HARRIS et Douglas D. PURVIS, "Some Economic Aspects of Political Restructuring" (ronéotypé), dans *Economic Dimensions of Constitutional Change*, Conférence organisée par le John Deutsch Institute, Queen's University, Kingston, Ontario, du 4 au 6 juin 1991.

32. Lise BISSONNETTE, "Partir et rester I", *Le Devoir*, 1er février 1991, p. A8.

33. Voir notamment Marcel ADAM, "Un projet formellement fédéraliste dont la dynamique est en fait sécessionniste", *La Presse*, 31 janvier 1991, p. B2.

34. Voir Guy LAFOREST, *Des balises pour l'avenir. Le Québec et l'interprétation du fédéralisme canadien*, ronéotypé. Communication présentée dans le cadre du Forum sur l'avenir politique et constitutionnel du Québec, Acfas, 1991, mai 1991, pp. 9-15.

35. "L'essence de ce que *nous avons décidé* devra être accepté" déclarait Bourassa aux lendemains du dépôt du rapport Allaire. Cité par Denis LESSARD, "C'est la minute de vérité pour le Canada", *La Presse*, 2 février 1991, p. A2.

36. Voir Denis LESSARD, "Comment Bourassa a empêché l'éclatement du comité Allaire", *La Presse*, 9 février 1991, p. B1.

37. Voir VASTEL, *op.cit.*, p. 287.

38. Voir Jeffrey SIMPSON, "A l'insulte québécoise, la riposte canadienne", *Le Devoir*, 4 février 1991, p. 12 et le témoignage de Gordon ROBERTSON devant le Comité mixte spécial sur le Processus de modification de la Constitution du Canada, Deuxième session de la trente-quatrième législature, *fascicule no 6*, le 28 février 1991, p. 6:81.

39. Voir Michel VASTEL, "Les propositions du Québec pas si mal reçues", *Le Droit*, 9 février 1991, p.4.

40. Rappelons que c'est le premier ministre René Lévesque qui qualifia de "beau risque" la volonté du premier ministre nouvellement élu Brian Mulroney, en 1984, de s'attaquer à une réforme de la Constitution qui tiendrait compte des aspirations légitimes du Québec.

41. Dix jours plus tard toutefois, Robert Bourassa remit jusqu'à un certain point en question cet aspect-clé de la résolution du rapport Allaire, avec pour résultat que depuis lors un fort doute anime les "radicaux" du parti libéral quant à la volonté réelle du gouvernement Bourassa de tenir un référendum selon la date convenue plutôt qu'une élection de type référendaire.

42. L'appui à la souveraineté totalisait 41,0% (CROP-*La Presse*), en octobre 1989 et aurait grimpé jusqu'à 68,2% (Léger et Léger, *Le Journal de Montréal*) dans les intentions de vote en février 1991.

43. Voir Denis LESSARD, "La Commission B.-C., la foire d'empoigne", *La Presse*, 30 mars 1991, p. B1.

44. Gilles LESAGE, "Bélanger-Campeau: l'espoir d'un consensus repose sur les non-alignés", *Le Devoir*, 23 mars 1991, p. A1.

45. Les commissaires André Ouellet et Richard Holden auront exprimé leur dissidence face au rapport, outre l'abstention de Jean-Pierre Hogue.

46. Lise BISSONNETTE, "Considérant la dernière chance", *Le Devoir*, 16 mai 1991, p. A 10.

47. Le Parti québécois exigeait qu'on pratique une entorse aux règles habituelles de formation des commissions parlementaires afin d'accorder une représentation égale aux tendances en présence. Jacques Parizeau escomptait, à tout le moins, que son parti puisse se voir confier, comme c'est le cas pour les commissions permanentes de l'Assemblée nationale, la présidence de ces commissions. Le P.Q. n'aura obtenu que six membres pour chaque commission (dont deux sans droit de vote), et le Parti Egalité, un, comparativement aux onze représentants libéraux (incluant ici le premier ministre ou son remplaçant, ainsi que le ministre délégué aux Affaires intergouvernementales canadiennes, Gil Rémillard).

48. Lise BISSONNETTE, "Considérant...", *op.cit.*,

49. Voir ASSEMBLEE NATIONALE, *Projet de loi 150. Loi sur le processus de détermination de l'avenir politique et constitutionnel du Québec*, présentée par M. Gil Rémillard, Ministre de la Justice et ministre délégué aux Affaires inter-gouvernementales canadiennes, Editeur officiel du Québec, 1991. Voir le 14e considérant du Préambule, p. 4.

50. Lysiane GAGNON, "Une démarche incohérente", *La Presse*, 18 mai 1991, p. B3.

51. Voir Denis LESSARD, "Des ententes administratives règleraient une bonne part du problème constitutionnel selon Rémillard", *La Presse*, 25 avril 1991, p. B1 et Chantal HEBERT, "Mulroney offrirait aux provinces de nouveaux arrangements administratifs", *Le Devoir*, 25 mai 1991, p. A1.

52. Pour une analyse complémentaire de la dynamique politico-constitutionnelle dans le ROC, on lira ci-après le chapitre de Graham FRASER, "Slouching Towards Canada".

53. LE FORUM DES CITOYENS SUR L'AVENIR DU CANADA, *Rapport à la population et au gouvernement du Canada*, Ottawa, p. 140.

54. Voir Lise BISSONNETTE, "Les apôtres de l'amour fini", *Le Devoir*, 29 juin 1991, p. A18.

55. Voir Susan DELACOURT, "Teams of deputy ministers work on new plan for Canada", *The Globe and Mail*, January 31, 1991, p. A1 et Gilles PAQUIN, "Ottawa remet en question ses propres compétences", *La Presse*, 30 janvier 1991, p. B1.

56. Pour une analyse approfondie des commissions fédérales, voir dans le présent volume le chapitre de Kathy L. BROCK, "The Politics of Process".

57. Voir entre autres Gilles LESAGE, "L'"intelligence" fédérale s'organise, le vrai combat commence...", *Le Devoir*, 12 décembre 1990, p. B1.

58. Voir Graham FRASER, "Quebec dictating debate tempo", *The Globe and Mail*, February 18, 1991, p. A1.

59. Voir Denis LESSARD, "Québec-Ottawa, copain-copain comme jamais", *La Presse*, 18 mai 1991, p. B6.

60. Voir Lysiane GAGNON, "Bloc's wish list doesn't include winning election", *The Globe and Mail*, June 22, 1991, p.D3 et Daniel BONIN, "L'audacieux combat du Bloc québécois", *La Presse*, 4 avril 1991, p.B3.

61. Voir François BEAULNE, "Des interventions "quémandées" par Mulroney lui-même", *La Presse*, 8 mai 1991, p.B3.

62. Voir Graham FRASER, "Clark unlikely to claim panel has consensus", *The Globe and Mail*, July, 8, 1991, pp. A1, A5.

63. Voir Chantal HEBERT, "Ottawa offrira la société distincte et la culture au Québec", *Le Devoir*, 23 août 1991, pp.1 et 4. Voir aussi Edison STEWART, "Clark unity plan calls Quebec "distinct"", *The Toronto Star*, August, 22, 1991, pp. A1, A24.

64. Voir Graham FRASER, "Wrapping up a unity package", *The Globe and Mail*, August, 23, 1991, p. A4.

65. L'on réfère ici à la première offre faite au Québec par l'ex-chef de l'Assemblée des Premières nations, George Erasmus, le 27 avril 1991 et celle, plus récente, formulée par Ovide Mercredi, nouveau leader du regroupement autochtone, le 9 août dernier.

66. Voir Susan DELACOURT, "Clark performs delicate balancing act", *The Globe and Mail*, July, 23, 1991, p. A1.

67. Voir Graham FRASER, "Tories'good-news agenda falls prey to confusion", *The Globe and Mail*, June 3, 1991, pp. A1-A2.

68. Voir entre autres les résultats du sondage GALLUP publiés dans *La Presse* du 13 mai 1991, p. B1.

69. Cf. *Le Droit*, 20 juin 1991, p. 21.

70. Voir les sondages IQOP de la fin mai 1991 et Multi-Réso de mars 1991 qui accordent respectivement treize et quinze points d'avance au P.Q sur le P.L.Q.

71. Voir *Le Devoir*, 8 juin 1991, pp. A1, A4. Ce sondage contredit deux enquêtes précédentes réalisées par les maisons CROP (publiée le 1er mai 1991) et IQOP (publiée le 2 juin 1991) qui accordaient respectivement 48% et 49% des intentions de vote des répondants à l'égard de la souveraineté. Même si les résultats du sondage Multi-Réso renouent en quelque sorte avec la tendance exprimée dans les sondages antérieurs qui révélaient une forte inclination des Québécois en faveur de l'option souverainiste, il y a lieu de s'interroger par ailleurs sur la signification des deux sondages ci-hauts; ceux-ci tendraient peut-être à démontrer, mutatis mutandis, sinon la "volatilité" des répondants, du moins la confusion de plusieurs d'entre eux quant à la signification intrinsèque de l'option souverainiste. Mis à part une frange d'indépendantistes "purs et durs" comptant grosso modo pour près du cinquième des électeurs québécois, le reste des sympathisants actuels de la souveraineté (soit plus ou moins quarante pour cent des Québécois selon les tendances présentes) pourrait se partager entre : 1) une fraction de "flottants", sans véritable allégeance partisane et dont l'opinion, mimétique, s'ajuste au gré des événements marquants et du climat politique en général et 2) les "souverainistes-associationnistes" qui, politiquement parlant, adhèrent encore au credo péquiste de 1980, et dont l'appui à la souveraineté se fonde plus ou moins consciemment sur une volonté de maintenir des liens formels, politiques et économiques avec le ROC. A cet égard, Robert Bourassa traduirait dans une certaine mesure cette "ambivalence" sinon cette pulsion récurrente partagée à divers degrés par plusieurs Québécois au fait de vouloir "partir et rester" en même temps dans le Canada.

3

The Politics of Process

Kathy L. Brock

Au terme de la saga du Lac Meech, les premiers ministres du pays se jurèrent de ne plus jamais faire revivre aux Canadiens une telle expérience. Un nouveau processus constitutionnel aura pris forme entre-temps. Ce chapitre analyse ce processus et les enjeux politiques qui le sous-tendent.

L'article débute par une examen de la "crise de représentation" qui émergea durant les négociations autour de l'Accord du lac Meech. Les citoyens hostiles à l'Accord firent valoir que le processus de réforme constitutionnelle était non démocratique et non représentatif. Ceux-ci appelèrent donc à l'établissement d'un processus plus ouvert et partant, plus achevé. Même si cette requête n'épouse pas particulièrement les projets des gouvernements engagés en faveur de la réconciliation nationale, il importera néanmoins qu'on y réponde de façon positive d'ici peu.

La deuxième partie de ce chapitre passe en revue les initiatives de réforme constitutionnelle en cours actuellement; y est mesuré aussi le degré de participation publique. On se penche également sur les objectifs visés par la réforme constitutionnelle et les vues discordantes du Canada partagées par les acteurs en cause.

La troisième partie analyse les propositions de réforme constitutionnelle provenant du Québec et des commissions fédérales. L'auteure met ensuite en relief les divergences d'approche d'une commission fédérale à l'autre. Par ailleurs, les positions adoptées sur le plan constitutionnel par la Commission Bélanger-Campeau et le comité Allaire n'auront pas été sans heurter, à ce chapitre, le credo de nombre de groupes de citoyens à l'échelle nationale. L'auteure soutient du reste que les présentes initiatives fédérales en matière de processus constitutionnel comportent certains éléments pouvant donner lieu éventuellement à une entente entre les acteurs impliqués.

L'article examine également les options relatives au processus constitutionnel qui font appel au peuple tels que l'assemblée constituante, le référendum et les audiences publiques. En conclusion, Kathy Brock estime qu'on ne devrait pas nécessairement envisager le recours à des mesures extraordinaires pour mener à bien et rendre acceptable un processus de réforme constitutionnelle.

The failure of the Meech Lake Accord revealed fundamental tensions within the Canadian political system.[1] While many of the problems identified in the Accord were substantive, the process of constitutional reform came increasingly under attack. The 11 governments of Canada were accused by citizen groups of undermining their rights and changing the constitution to serve their own agendas while disregarding the will of the population. Solidarity among the 11 first ministers broke down as three governments threatened to prevent the Accord from being proclaimed as law. Visions of Confederation as a compact between the two founding nations clashed with the principle of provincial equality and the view of Canada as an evolving, diverse society. The exercise pitted citizens against their governments and governments against governments. By the end, the major players vowed to the public that a similar process of constitutional reform would never be allowed to happen in Canada again. In the wake of Meech Lake, the first ministers of Canada have been seeking a process of constitutional change that would reconcile the divergent interests that clashed in the Meech Lake process.

This chapter examines the politics of the constitutional process in the post-Meech era. It argues that the nature of constitution-making has fundamentally changed in Canada. If constitutional reform is to be successful, then it must reconcile citizen demands for greater participation with the governments' diverse agendas. This task is very difficult, but it is not impossible. Current initiatives and proposals provide insight into how it may be achieved.

The chapter is divided into three sections. The first section traces the demand for greater public participation in the constitutional process. It briefly examines the question of representation underlying this demand. The second section reviews some of the current initiatives on constitutional reform. Since the demise of the Meech Lake Accord, a number of constitutional committees and mechanisms have been created to find a means of resolving Canada's current constitutional dilemma. While most of the Canadian governments have undertaken significant action on the constitutional front, the chapter focuses on the initiatives of the federal and Quebec governments since they capture the conflict between citizen demands and the governments' attempts at national reconciliation in the wake of Meech Lake. In the third section, the main proposals for revising the constitutional process are evaluated. The chapter concludes that a new constitutional process must accommodate the demand for greater participation while drawing on the virtues of strong political leadership. Extraordinary measures are not necessary to achieve a satisfactory process.

THE NEED FOR CHANGE

The nature of constitution-making in Canada underwent a significant shift with the patriation of the constitution. Wider public consultation is increasingly expected and accepted as a result of the 1982 constitutional process. The federal government drew societal groups into the 1980-81 constitutional negotiations in an endeavour to legitimize its proposals after a stalemate with the provinces arose. This process as well as the substance of the Canadian Charter of Rights and Freedoms

> bypassed governments and spoke directly to Canadians by defining them as bearers of rights, as well as by according specific constitutional recognition to women, aboriginals, official language minority populations, ethnic groups through the vehicle of multiculturalism, and to those social categories explicitly listed in the equality rights section of the Charter.[2]

When these groups had special information or expertise or were needed to legitimize government initiatives, they were brought into the process. The perception that citizens had a right to participate in government decisions affecting the constitution was reinforced by the growing rights consciousness in society. Citizens had a vested interest in protecting their rights and a new sense of empowerment.[3]

Subsequently, the Meech Lake experience revealed that constitutional reform must be more open and more inclusive. Throughout the hearings, the Meech Lake process was criticized as hasty, undemocratic, elitist, unrepresentative, secretive, and a violation of Canadian political norms.[4] After a lengthy account of the Meech Lake process, Andrew Cohen concludes that the Meech Lake Accord was "constitution-making by stealth." The requirement of unanimity encouraged secrecy which was inconsistent with public expectations in "an open, pluralistic democracy." He concludes that by denying the popular preference for openness, the first ministers created problems for themselves. The public did not witness the concessions made by Quebec, and thus were suspicious of Premier Bourassa's claims made later in the process that he could make no further compromises. Quebec appeared unyielding.[5] The emphasis on secrecy and denial of the necessity of a more open process undermined support for the Accord and fuelled the opposition to it. The unravelling of Meech Lake clearly established that the process of amending the constitution was untenable.[6]

There was a related tension in the constitutional revision process that Meech Lake revealed. As Cohen hinted and as Alan Cairns has documented, the Accord brought government and citizen agendas into conflict and underscored a basic incoherence in the process. Cairns explains that:

> while federalism may still be largely about governments, federalism itself has lost relative status in the Constitution as an organizing principle. The Constitution is now also about women, aboriginals, multicultural groups, equality, affirmative action, the disabled, a variety of rights, and so on. Since it is not possible to separate clearly the concerns of the governments which dominate federalism from the concerns of these newly constitutionalized social categories, it logically

follows that the Constitution with its many non-federal concerns can no longer be entrusted exclusively to governments in the process of constitutional change. Government domination of the constitutional process structures outcomes in terms of one set of cleavages; the public hearings process responds in terms of different cleavages. The latter delegitimizes the former.[7]

Although the dichotomy does not always hold, the prevailing pattern is that the governments respond to the constitution along traditional linguistic and spatial lines, while the public responds in terms of special interests and sectoral divisions.

During the Meech Lake process, this division was highlighted when Quebec's interests were pitted against broader societal and special interests. Although the governments could reach agreement, the Accord became less attractive once it was viewed from the perspective of geographically dispersed citizens such as aboriginal people, women, multicultural and multiracial communities, the disabled, and the disadvantaged. For example, Quebec's desires for distinct society status, limits on the spending power, and control over appointments to national institutions, were incompatible with the aspirations of these groups. Whether these differences could have been reconciled had the representatives of the interest groups been consulted earlier in the process remains the subject of much speculation.[8]

What does the demand for greater participation mean in the aftermath of Meech Lake? First, the number of actors in the constitutional reform process has expanded. Among those leading the charge for a more inclusive process are aboriginal organizations, ethnic and racial minorities, and women's groups. They are asking that the process and product reflect social diversity.

Aboriginal peoples have given clear warnings that they must be included. During the election of the Grand Chief to the Assembly of First Nations (AFN) held at the annual meeting in Winnipeg in June 1991, all of the candidates stressed that this was a condition for the success of future reforms. The newly elected Grand Chief, Ovide Mercredi, announced that the AFN expected equal participation with the governments in constitutional negotiations. At the annual meeting the Chiefs voted to establish a First Nations Circle on the Constitution to help them formulate a position for future discussions. Given the role of Elijah Harper in blocking the Meech Lake Accord and the public sympathy his stand generated, political leaders realise that aboriginal peoples and other groups must be included. Indeed, in Quebec on 24 June 1991, after addressing a St. Jean Baptiste Day gathering, Prime Minister Mulroney stated that although Canada wants Quebec's signature on the 1982 constitutional changes, any federal proposals must extend beyond the 1987 package of reforms to garner acceptance in Canada.

Second, many citizens and groups are calling for the process of constitutional reform to be more open. Citizens criticizing the Meech Lake process desired more information on the negotiations as they were being conducted. Although most recognized the need to go behind closed doors at certain points to discuss sensitive issues and reach compromises, they also desired more information on the negotiating positions of governments and the reasons for changes in positions or decisions. Similarly, the absence of political debate and the "absence of serious justificatory position papers issued by the federal government...aggravate[d] the problem of assessing the relationship of the provisions of Meech Lake to any explicit constitutional philosophy."[9] The public requires a rationale for decisions undertaken by the governments which might have significant effects on the nation's development. A *fait accompli* cannot be presented to the public again without arousing more hostility and suspicion. Public debates and education programs are important in keeping the citizenry informed.

Underlying this demand for greater public participation in the constitutional reform process is a concern with the representative nature of Canadian political institutions. With some regret, Stefan Dupré observes that the nature of discourse during the Meech Lake debate signals a shift in the Canadian political system from the tradition of responsible government to one rooted in the principles of pluralist democracy.[10] Citizens demand that political institutions and the decision-making process reflect the diversity in society.

This demand for "mirror representation" has been challenged in the Meech Lake debates. Jennifer Smith observes that the concept of mirror representation is repugnant to any "independent-minded citizen" because it implies that leaders speak for their societal group on the grounds that they are "one of them." Their right to speak for people of the specific group can be questioned unless they have a mandate derived through a political or legal structure and those people have consented to be represented by them as in the case of many aboriginal peoples.[11] Further, she maintains that representatives of interest groups argue from the perspective of one set of issues and thus have a partial concept of justice. Other citizens "rely on governments to save them from interest groups, not expose them even further to their claims."[12] Similarly, Alan Cairns warns that if past public hearings are an indication, certain interests such as business or labour may be underrepresented in the process while others may dominate the forum.[13] In contrast to interest advocates, elected politicians and political parties allow for a fuller understanding of justice, the public good and how to balance competing demands.

Beverly Baines offers a different perspective. She argues that the most "invidious" lesson to be drawn from Meech Lake and previous constitutional exercises is that

> We have a constitutional past, present and, it would appear, future in which it is taken for granted that men can and should represent the interests of women, not just politically but also constitutionally. Certainly that has always obtained with our first ministers and, as well, it prevailed throughout the Meech Lake process;

every legislative entity, be it committee or assembly, that was charged with the
arduous responsibility of reviewing the Accord was undeniably male dominated.
...It seems, in short, that our gender is not supposed to matter in political spaces
and constitutional moments.[14]

Baines then cites numerous political and legal studies that have shown that men
do not necessarily represent women's interests very effectively.[15] She concludes that equality of representation of the sexes should be the goal of future
reform processes.

Is a more inclusive process a more representative one? It does not necessarily
follow that the exclusion or limited inclusion of certain interests results in
unrepresentative decisions. Indeed, given the voting power of many of the
unrepresented groups, elected politicians cannot afford to be seen as unsympa-
thetic to their needs. Conversely, "there is no *necessary* link between someone
who comes from a particular ethnic or class background and the behaviour he
or she will exhibit as a member of the elite."[16] Inclusion of all groups in society
would not necessarily result in more representative decisions or a consensus on
change.

Despite these conclusions, the call for a more representative process is too
strong to deny. Exclusion sends a very powerful message to the groups on the
outside and heightens hostility to the process. If a group perceives that a
conscious effort has been made to consider and incorporate its interests, then it
is less likely to castigate that process. In a recent study of the electoral system,
Paul Thomas explains that representation includes the issue of responsiveness
and asks to whom should legislators be responsive.[17] He suggests that symbolic
responsiveness is important, especially since the Charter has conferred recognition on certain social groups. Individuals' confidence in institutions dimin-
ishes if they are underrepresented in that institution. Usually, there must be a
material reward for the symbolic representation to be effective but the electorate
perceives that there are finite limits to the efforts of politicians to respond to
particular interests. The rationale underlying the call for more representative
institutions is not that individuals cannot speak outside of their own experience
or can speak only for their own experience, but rather that an unrepresentative
system appears dismissive of those groups. These concerns cannot be allayed
by simple assurances to the contrary. This was shown clearly in the Meech Lake
process with respect to women, aboriginal peoples, and ethnic and racial
groups.

Questions of representation strike at the heart of an institution. This was the
case in the last round of constitutional negotiations. The very legitimacy of the
constitution and the political system came under attack. Just as Quebec's special
place in the constitution cannot be denied if the constitution is to have future
validity, so too aboriginal peoples, women, ethnic and racial communities
cannot be denied their part in either the process or result of a redefinition of

Canada's constitution. As Cairns states, "Patient, honest explanation of the means and ends of constitutional change by leaders prepared to listen to citizens is the only viable alternative to the havoc-creating seamless web of future Meech Lake Accords."[18] To restore legitimacy and confidence in the constitutional actors and process, constitutional negotiations must be more representative of and responsive to the public.

To achieve this end, governments are resorting to greater use of consultative mechanisms in the constitutional arena. The use of task forces and legislative committees and public hearings during Meech Lake encouraged analysts and politicians to consider these as means of incorporating public input into constitutional reform in a more formal manner. In the wake of Meech Lake, governments have responded to the current constitutional impasse by creating new commissions and conducting public hearings. It is to these bodies that we now turn.

CURRENT INITIATIVES

According to Peter Russell, there are three basic stages in the constitutional process. These are (i) public discussion, (ii) negotiations, and (iii) ratification.[19] At the point of writing, Canada is in the first phase. Governments have been investigating the grounds for negotiations through constitutional bodies. The Quebec government announced the Bélanger-Campeau Commission in August of 1990 in reaction to the failure of the Accord. However, it was predated by the Quebec Liberal Party's committee which was announced while the Meech talks were drawing to a close in the spring of 1990. The federal government responded by announcing the Citizen's Forum on Canada's Future on 1 November 1990 and the Special Joint Committee of the Senate and the House of Commons on The Process for Amending the Constitution of Canada on 17 December 1990. To signal the importance he was attaching to constitutional issues, the prime minister moved Joe Clark from his successful role as External Affairs Minister to the positions of president of the Privy Council and Minister Responsible for Constitutional Affairs. He is overseeing the creation of a Joint Parliamentary Committee dealing with Constitutional Affairs. Alberta, British Columbia, Manitoba, New Brunswick, Nova Scotia, and Ontario have all established committees or commissions to consult the public on the direction of future constitutional negotiations. All of the initiatives will be important in determining the success of future negotiations. However, the mandates and scope of some of the committees deserve special attention because they reveal the difficulties in reconciling public demands with government proposals for national reconciliation. The recommendations are analyzed in the next section.

Quebec has assumed a leading role in setting the agenda for the next round of constitutional negotiations. In January 1991, the Constitutional Committee of the Quebec Liberal Party, chaired by Jean Allaire, released its report. The Allaire Committee was charged with the task of preparing alternative scenarios in preparation for either the passage or failure of the Meech Lake Accord. The tight scheduling of the Allaire Committee's work gave the constitutional discussions in Quebec a particular sense of urgency. The Allaire Committee consulted party members and submitted its report to the General Convention of the Quebec Liberal Party in March. At that convention, the Liberal Party agreed to adopt the Allaire recommendations but made some minor amendments in relation to the Senate and application of the Canadian Charter of Rights and Freedoms to Quebec. They decided to proceed with negotiations on a revised federalism but hold a referendum on sovereignty if the talks failed. However, there was a discernible tension between the views of the majority of the delegates and Premier Bourassa who attempted to adopt a more conciliatory tone towards a renegotiated federalism with the rest-of-Canada.

The Quebec Liberal position was soon followed by the report of the Commission on the Political and Constitutional Future of Quebec, jointly chaired by Michel Bélanger and Jean Campeau. The Quebec National Assembly unanimously authorized the creation of the Bélanger-Campeau Commission on 4 September 1990. Its mandate was "to examine and analyse the political and constitutional status of Quebec and to make recommendations in respect thereof."[20] The Commission was composed of the two chairs jointly appointed by Premier Bourassa and Opposition Leader Jacques Parizeau, 16 Members of the National Assembly, 13 people from the private and public sector (the original Act specified 12 but both the educational and cultural sectors were represented instead of just one as originally conceived), 3 Quebec members of the House of Commons, and the premier and leader of the Opposition. The Commission received 607 briefs and selected 235 groups and individuals to appear before it during the public hearings. The Commission requested information from many experts. The Bélanger-Campeau and Allaire Reports clarify Quebec's position on the future process and substance of constitutional negotiations.

The federal government reacted to the initiatives begun in Quebec and some of the other provinces by creating a series of constitutional committees. Keith Spicer was appointed to head the Citizen's Forum on Canada's Future. The Spicer Commission was intended to provide Canadians with the opportunity to express their views on constitutional matters, to engage in an open dialogue with their fellow citizens, and to lower their mistrust of the process of redefining Canada. This was to be accomplished through general discussions, more thematic discussions and finally a focus on key issues.[21] The exercise culminated in a report released 27 June 1991. The mandate illustrated that the federal government was aware of the problems with representation and legitimacy that a constitutional process faced.

The Spicer Forum was structured to be highly accessible to citizens. To achieve this objective:

- national and regional offices were established;
- a toll-free Idea line in both official languages allowed Canadians from all parts of the country to phone in their views on the constitution;
- group discussions were held throughout the nation and led by trained moderators who reported back to the Commissioners;
- citizens were invited to write to the Forum;
- a separate Forum was set up to canvas student opinions; and
- the Forum was publicized through public appearances by Commissioners and moderators, advertisements, television and radio shows.

In all, the Spicer Forum consulted approximately 400,000 people,[22] a significant number but short of its original projection of 1,000,000. The participation rate was uneven across the country, and especially low in Quebec. The Forum also had a limited impact in the Maritimes. This affects the credibility of the Forum in speaking for all Canadians.

The task of the Special Joint Committee on Amending Formula was more specialized. Jointly chaired by Senator Gérald Beaudoin and Member of Parliament Jim Edwards, the committee was intended to consult broadly with the public on the amending formula with special attention to the role of the public in negotiations, the effectiveness of the formula, and alternatives to the current formula.[23] The mandate was aimed at correcting some of the perceived problems with the amending process as experienced in the Meech Lake negotiations.

The Beaudoin-Edwards Committee listened to testimony from citizens and constitutional experts. It travelled throughout Canada, heard 209 witnesses, and received over 500 briefs. During the hearings, many innovative ideas were expressed despite the technical nature of the topic. In particular, proposals for a constituent assembly and referenda to resolve the current situation were widely discussed.

The Joint Parliamentary Committee dealing with Constitutional Affairs is intended to bridge the work of the federal and provincial committees and to provide a clear direction for the federal government. Specifically, it is intended to comment upon federal government proposals for a renewed Canada.[24] Scheduled to begin in the fall of 1991 and table its report in February of 1992, the Committee is mandated to travel across Canada, to hold public hearings, and to consult with the provincial and territorial legislatures or individual members of them. Although composed of Parliamentarians, the Committee will be complemented by citizen panels that will advise on special constitutional interests.

Constitutional Affairs Minister Joe Clark had designated one of the panels specifically for Aboriginal Peoples. However, this proposal has been superseded by a plan for a parallel constitutional process for aboriginal peoples. Under this plan, the Assembly of First Nations (AFN) will consult its members and then report to the Committee. This process allows the AFN more control over the consultations and final recommendations than under the panel approach. The AFN will argue for full status at the constitutional bargaining table once talks between the federal and provincial governments begin. Some Métis are also establishing their own process. On 31 July 1991, the Manitoba Métis Senate Commission on National Unity and Constitutional Reform, after consulting with 950 Métis, released its report outlining the issues and consultation process. It will continue to consult with the Métis community until October 1991 and then the Manitoba Métis Federation will decide the future process of constitutional consultation for its people.[25]

The mandate, composition, and direction of the Joint Committee is revealing. First, the appointments of Joe Clark as Constitutional Affairs minister and Paul Tellier as Secretary to the Cabinet for Federal Provincial Relations are controversial.[26] Joe Clark enjoys the public confidence at a time when the prime minister and his government as a whole do not. Clark would provide the degree of legitimacy needed to advance the Progressive Conservative government agenda on constitutional reform. Paul Tellier is Clerk of the Privy Council, and the prime minister's most trusted bureaucrat. When he was appointed, the Liberals accused the prime minister of exercising control over the constitutional initiative behind the scenes despite Mr. Clark's insistence upon a degree of independence from the prime minister when he assumed the Constitutional Affairs position. This has fuelled speculation that the conclusion of the federal Committee has been predetermined. The departure of Gordon Smith from this position, on grounds of a personality conflict with Joe Clark, has also raised questions about whether a team of senior bureaucrats could be composed that would work together effectively to support the federal initiatives. The government has replied that the appointment of Tellier underscores the importance that the government attaches to the resolution of the constitutional issue. These concerns raise doubts about whether the Committee is genuinely open to provincial initiatives and to public input.

Second, the composition of the Committee indicates that the government is vesting ultimate decision-making authority in the political representatives. Rather than turning to outside channels or alternative mechanisms, the government is placing the onus of responsibility on the national politicians to chart the direction of the country. There are two ways to interpret this move. It may be seen as a means of asserting the government agenda with minimum opposition and input allowed from the public. Conversely, it may be seen as an important step towards restoring public confidence in the legislators by indicating that they are competent to do the job. The work of the Committee will reveal which interpretation is more accurate.

Third, the mandate of the Committee appears well-conceived. Specific mention of the need to "ensure aboriginal peoples participate fully in the development of the Government of Canada's plan for a renewed Canada and, in particular, on issues of special interest to them,"[27] would indicate that the government and Joe Clark realize that the process must be more open and inclusive. It acknowledges that aboriginal peoples' concerns may not be postponed while other constitutional issues are managed. This is an important departure from the Meech Lake rhetoric and example. Also promising is the Committee's power to hold joint sittings with provincial and territorial legislators and/or legislatures which permits the Committee to serve a liaison function and act as a coordinating body for all of the various initiatives on the constitution. While this might be viewed as a means of limiting provincial involvement to that of another special interest group, it may also be seen as an important means of gaining consensus on future constitutional reforms. The provinces will have further input in the negotiating stage of discussions. The mandate provides a basis for reconciliation of diverse interests provided that the Committee is willing to listen.

The constitutional initiatives in the other provinces will be important in determining the success or failure of the next round of constitutional talks. These initiatives involve the public to varying degrees:

- in August of 1990, Alberta created the Constitutional Reform Task Force which was chaired by Jim Horsman and intended to be "the most comprehensive review of the Constitution ever undertaken in Alberta."[28] By June 1991, the Committee had heard over 300 submissions and was expected to enter a new round of public hearings before preparing its report. However, the government position favouring decentralization seems to be at odds with the majority of presenters who favour a strong central government.[29]

- in December 1990, the Manitoba government created a Constitutional Task Force to review constitutional reforms with special attention to Senate reform, the Charter, the amending formula, the division of powers, Manitoba's constitutional priorities, and reform proposals by other governments.[30] Having heard 227 oral presentations and received over 80 written submissions, the Task Force is expected to report in the early fall. Its interim report specified its mandate, process and goal.

- in December of 1990, Ontario established a 12 member Select Committee on Ontario in Confederation headed by Tony Silipo to report on the social and economic interests and aspirations of Ontarians and what form of Confederation would best serve those needs.[31] The Committee has heard over 600 witnesses and identified key issues that should be addressed in future constitutional talks. Its original reporting deadline of 27 June 1991 has been extended until late October to allow it to consult as broadly as possible with Ontarians on these issues. It is contemplating holding a mini-constituent assembly before it reports.

- British Columbia's six-member Cabinet committee on the constitution reported in May.
- New Brunswick's nine-member Commission on the Province's Role in the Canadian Federation is in operation.
- Nova Scotia's committee on the future of Canada, appointed on 7 June 1991, will hold public hearings in the fall.

The federal opposition parties have responded to the government initiatives. The Liberals seem divided over whether to accept the proposals offered by their leader Jean Chrétien, which call for recognition of Quebec's distinctiveness, a renegotiated federalism, and a more inclusive amending formula with a possible referendum to resolve impasses.[32] The NDP approved a resolution on the constitution on 8 June 1991 which called for a new round of discussions for all Canadians and responded to many of the criticisms of the Meech Lake Accord. Particular attention was paid to the concerns of aboriginal people.[33] The NDP supports the idea of a constituent assembly as a means of negotiating change. Both parties have challenged the composition and proposed method of operation of the Joe Clark constitutional committee.

Citizen groups are also mobilizing. While the demands on the substance of negotiations is wide ranging, these groups are insisting upon a more open process of constitutional reform.[34] The National Action Committee on the Status of Women has also called for a constituent assembly to formulate demands outside Quebec followed by negotiations between Quebec, the rest-of-Canada, and the First Nations.[35] The Canada West Foundation has put forward a detailed proposal for a constituent assembly to rework the constitution. Various other citizen groups have also put forward proposals for constitutional change.[36]

One recent initiative which captured attention is the Report of the Group of 22. This group of citizens, including two former premiers and some notable Canadians, suggests that extraordinary measures like referenda, constituent assemblies, and radical change are not necessary to resolve the current impasse. Instead, they propose reworking the division of powers to conform to current practices and decentralizing some powers to respond to changing social and economic conditions. They consider their proposals to be pragmatic and attainable because they could be accomplished by Parliament alone or under the general amending formula. These changes could be made quickly to respond effectively to the current crisis.[37] Although the proposal does not address the concerns of the smaller and have-less provinces regarding limits on federal spending, it does suggest reworking the equalization scheme to assist these provinces if they assume greater responsibilities. However, it must be remembered that equalization is unenforceable. Thus, the smaller provinces would have to accept a promise for redistribution in exchange for their legal commitment to decentralization. One interesting characteristic of the report is that it does not treat Quebec and its agenda separately from the other provinces. While this might weaken its appeal in Quebec, the Group's solutions allow for the realization of many of Quebec's demands. Whether these would be sufficient to satisfy Quebec is not clear.

The Group of 22 proposal is especially interesting for two reasons. First, the proposal is consistent with apparent federal initiatives being developed within the bureaucracy. The federal government efforts on the constitution are being assisted by ten teams of Canada's senior deputy ministers who are examining the federal government's powers. This could provide the basis for a renegotiation of the federal-provincial division of powers which would lead to a greater decentralization of powers.[38] Second, the composition of the Group of 22 is revealing. As mentioned, the members are distinguished Canadians. Although they participated in the group as private individuals and not as representatives, they are drawn from all three parties and business. However, the NDP is only represented by Allan Blakeney and the *Report* represents a departure from the past and present stand adopted by the NDP on the division of powers and role of the federal government. One signatory to the proposal, Hugh Segal, has since been appointed Senior Adviser to the Prime Minister, effective August 1991. The membership of the Group seems to ensure that its proposals will not be brushed aside lightly.

At this stage in the constitutional discussions, citizens are being widely consulted. While the Spicer Forum has offered the most opportunities for the average citizen to express a viewpoint, the other commissions have been mandated to consult broadly with the public. Certain interests, such as those of Aboriginal Peoples, are receiving special attention. Governments realize the need to attune reforms to public demands. This is the important first step in making the constitutional process more open and inclusive. Whether the endeavour will be successful depends on how effectively governments incorporate citizen views into the final package of amendments and build a consensus within the Canadian community.

Thus, during the public discussion phase of constitutional negotiations, a number of solutions and proposals are being put forward. In the next round of discussions, these initiatives must be coordinated. The body that offers the best prospects for accomplishing this task is the federal Joint Parliamentary Committee under Constitutional Affairs Minister Joe Clark. Its mandate, composition and status as a national committee provide the basis for reviewing proposals and conducting negotiations with the various governments and societal groups. This task will not be easy given the diversity of views being advanced. The next section analyzes some of the proposals and their prospects for success.

PROPOSALS FOR RENEWAL OF THE CONSTITUTIONAL PROCESS

The diversity of views being put forward before and by the constitutional review committees and commissions complicates the agenda of constitutional reform. There is a division between the proposals emanating from Quebec and those from other jurisdictions in Canada. Both the content of the recommendations and the suggestions for the process for achieving substantive changes in Confederation vary. The following section examines the Quebec proposals and the proposals from the two federal committees.

QUEBEC SPEAKS

Quebec has established a clear agenda for the other governments to keep in mind while debating constitutional reform. Quebec's priorities as determined through the Allaire Report, the Bélanger-Campeau Report and the government's announcements, are for a renegotiated federalism, and failing that, Quebec sovereignty. Quebec has set a deadline of fall, 1992, for the conclusion of negotiations.

The National Assembly has approved Bill 150 putting the recommendations of the Bélanger-Campeau Commission and Allaire Report into effect.[39] The Bill authorizes the creation of two parliamentary commissions. One commission would examine matters pertaining to Quebec's accession to sovereignty. Included in its purview would be the responsibility to examine proposals from the federal government of Canada for an economic partnership.[40] The second parliamentary commission would assess and advise the Quebec National Assembly on any offers of a renewed federalism from the Government of Canada which formally bound the other Canadian governments.[41] The Bill authorizes October 1992 for a referendum on sovereignty should the negotiations with Canada fail.

What would a renegotiated federalism look like? The Bélanger-Campeau Report specifies certain minimum conditions:

- the necessity of creating a new relationship between Quebec and the rest-of-Canada, based on the recognition of and respect for the identity of Quebecers and their right to be different;
- a division of powers and responsibilities that assures Quebec of exclusive authority over those matters and domains which already fall under its exclusive jurisdiction, which means among other things eliminating

in these domains federal spending power and overlapping interventions;

- the exclusive attribution to Quebec of powers and responsibilities related to its social, economic and cultural development as well as to language;
- the transfer of tax and financial resources related to the powers and responsibilities which Quebec exercises;
- the maintenance of a Quebec representation in common institutions which fully reflects its particular situation in Canada;
- the guarantee that Quebec's consent be required with respect to any constitutional modification. However, it has been proposed that where applicable, Quebec enjoy the right to opt out of a transfer of a jurisdiction to the federal government, with reasonable compensation. Such right to withdraw with compensation would replace the right to a veto in such instances. [42]

In contrast to the Bélanger-Campeau recommendations, the Allaire Report specifies which powers would have to be renegotiated. [43] Quebec is waiting for the other Canadian governments to respond.

The Quebec position presents some important considerations for the other governments. First, both reports reject the notion that the provinces are equal in favour of the distinctiveness of Quebec. [44] If the outcome of the negotiations is going to reflect Quebec's distinctiveness and need for special powers to preserve itself within Canada, then the process must be structured to reflect Quebec's unique position. A process which does not concede the dual nature of Confederation and treats Quebec as one of ten provinces, is unlikely to meet Quebec's substantive demands. Thus, in future negotiations, the other governments are going to have to accept the special status of Quebec. This demand is based upon the tradition of asymmetry built into the Canadian constitutional settlement and rejects the current trend stressing equality of the ten provinces and intolerance of differences among them. [45] Second, Quebec objects to the fact that under the current general amending formula, constitutional changes could be imposed upon it which affect its fundamental interests without its consent, as happened in 1982. Conversely, the amending formula may also be used to obstruct changes that it deems essential to its survival in Canada as happened with Meech Lake. [46] This concern underlies its demand that future proposals from the Canadian government be binding on the other governments. It will not go through the humiliation of another Meech Lake. Thus, any proposals must be in a highly developed stage. This places limits on the bargaining room of other governments.

The most important consideration, though, pertains to conflicting visions of Canada. The Bélanger-Campeau Commissioners ponder "whether the rest of

Canada is capable of making choices that fully satisfy Quebec's own needs, aspirations and visions. Until now, such choices have been perceived or treated as being irreconcilable with other needs, aspirations and visions in Canada."[47] The Allaire Report is even more direct: "Support for multiculturalism in Canada works against the francophone population, which is considered by a very large proportion of Canadians as one cultural community among others, meaning it should be treated in the same way as the others!"[48] The binational vision of Canada clashes with the image of Canada as a mosaic comprising many peoples. As in the case of Meech Lake, this is a sensitive point of division.

THE NATIONAL RESPONSE

The first official national response came with the release of the report of the Special Joint Committee of the Senate and the House of Commons on the Process for Amending the Constitution of Canada (Beaudoin-Edwards). The Beaudoin-Edwards Committee made two sets of recommendations. The first set requires constitutional amendment. The second set does not.

First, it recommended the adoption of a regional amending formula. This new formula would replace the general amending formula as outlined in sections 38 and 42 of the *Constitution Act, 1982*, and the unanimity formula in section 41. Under the new formula most constitutional amendments would have to be passed by Parliament, at least two of the Atlantic provinces, Quebec, Ontario, and at least two of the western provinces with 50 percent of that population. Unanimity would be retained for minority languages, proprietary rights of provinces, the monarchy, and changes to the unanimity section. The Committee also recommended that the ratification period be shortened to two years.[49] Aboriginal peoples should consent to any changes affecting them and a biennial series of constitutional conferences should be created to deal with their rights. The Committee also recommended that the territorial legislatures approve any boundary extensions into their lands and that the pre-1982 requirement of the approval of Parliament and the territorial legislature concerned be restored for the creation of new provinces. The Committee thought that two institutional changes should also be made. The Senate should be reformed and Quebec's representation on the Supreme Court should be entrenched.

The second set of recommendations does not require constitutional amendment and thus could be acted upon immediately. The Committee recommended that the territorial governments and aboriginal peoples' representatives be invited to participate in all future constitutional conferences. A new constitutional committee should study the creation of a power to allow for delegation between governments as well as a provincial right to opt out of amendments with compensation under the proposed regional amending formula. The Committee recommended passage of a law authorizing the federal government to hold a consultative referendum on a constitutional proposal at its discretion. As if anticipating the work of the new committee under Joe Clark's direction, the Beaudoin-Edwards Committee eschewed a directly elected constituent assembly in favour of a parliamentary committee composed of parliamentarians that was broadly representative of the Canadian population, would act in concert with special task forces on aboriginal issues and other important constitutional matters, and would coordinate with provincial and territorial Committees. Its final recommendation was that Parliament's rules should be amended to require public hearings on constitutional proposals early enough in the process of reform to allow for changes.[50]

The Beaudoin-Edwards proposals aim to address the concerns with representation and legitimacy that surfaced during the Meech Lake process. First, they attempt to balance Quebec's concerns with the views associated with the public outside Quebec. It calls for a more representative process of amendment with meaningful public hearings. This meets citizen demands to a limited extent. But it did not call for a directly elected constituent assembly or an appointed assembly with members drawn from the legislatures and the special interest groups. This speaks to Quebec's refusal to participate in such a forum. However, it is inconsistent with the desire for a constituent assembly expressed by Premiers Wells, Rae, and Devine, and by many citizen groups. This casts doubt on the acceptability of this recommendation.

Second, the Committee has emphasized the role of the legislator in the process. This was a major factor in its decisions on referenda and the constituent assembly. A referendum would not be binding and would be held at the government's discretion. While the Committee recommended that the process be more inclusive and open, it accepted that a constituent assembly comprising people of various backgrounds would not necessarily make more representative decisions or be able to achieve consensus more easily.[51] This type of body would not solve the problems of representation. Instead, the Committee argued that:

> the mechanism which Canada needs now must consist of individuals chosen by the people as their political representatives. This conclusion stems, first of all, from our conviction that appointed assemblies would lack legitimacy in the eyes of the public. People want a sense of participation, and perhaps a sense of effective influence, in constitutional decision-making. Only a directly-elected body, we believe, can give Canadians this sense. As we argue above, however, there is no convincing case to be made for having separate elections for the purpose of composing a constituent assembly.[52]

The recommended parliamentary committee would maintain strong lines of accountability. The Commissioners conclude that this mechanism "must strike a balance between responsiveness to particular interests, and responsiveness to the general interest of the majority."[53] In dissent, the two NDP members of the

Committee argued that the recommended committee operates on the basis of elite accommodation and does not meet the demand for a democratic process, whereas a constituent assembly composed of politicians and representatives of the public would.[54] The recommendation coincides with current federal initiatives.

Third, the recommendations are intended to restore confidence both inside and outside Quebec. The report recognizes Quebec's demands for recognition and protection of its rights by stating that "Canada is a complex country, and the amending formula must take this complexity into account. The distinct or unique character of Quebec must be reflected in the amending procedure of the Constitution of Canada."[55] However, it is attentive to the needs of other provinces when it declares that "Just as the equality of individuals should not be seen as requiring identical treatment, so the equality of the provinces should not be seen as precluding the tailoring of roles and powers to the particular needs of people in any individual province."[56] It balances provincial equality with tolerance for differences among them, and reinforces this point by noting that strict provincial equality would conflict with the more fundamental principle of individual equality.

The recommended amending formula and the recommendation on delegation of powers would permit the degree of flexibility required to accommodate Quebec's demands for protection and more powers within Confederation. However, its acceptability to the other provinces is questionable. The formula is based upon regional, not provincial, equality. Smaller provinces would lose powers over amendments that they now possess. Provinces other than Quebec and Ontario might have reservations about accepting this arrangement. This concern was expressed by Lynn Hunter, the British Columbia NDP member, who dissented on the grounds that B.C. should also have a veto in a regional amending formula.[57] This casts doubts on the acceptability of this compromise to all of the provinces.

Finally, the Committee attempted to mediate between the interests of Quebec and aboriginal peoples. Significantly, the Committee sidestepped the issue of whether aboriginal peoples should be deemed distinct, as called for during the Meech Lake process. Instead, it noted that: the view of Canada as a duality was put forward years ago; aboriginal peoples were not included in constitutional negotiation in 1867 but their rights were recognized in 1982; and Canada has become increasingly diverse. On these grounds, they recommended aboriginal consent to amendments, invitations to future constitutional conferences, and biennial conferences.[58] The Committee has traded the symbolic issue of recognition as distinct societies for substantive gains including a process whereby recognition could be gained in the future along with such things as recognition of the right to self-government. In so doing, it has tried to defuse one of the tensions that undermined the Meech Lake Accord. Given that the rhetoric of distinctiveness has been raised, this recommendation may fail.

In contrast to the Beaudoin-Edwards Committee, the Citizens' Forum on Canada's Future (Spicer Forum) recommendations were broader according to its mandate. These should be briefly highlighted before analyzing the recommendations pertaining to process.[59] With respect to federalism and the national government, the Spicer Forum recommended that:

- the government should revisit its position on national institutions and symbols, especially those dealing with communications and transportation, and that a new constitutional preamble try to capture the essence of Canada;
- it should be recognized that special arrangements for provinces constitute a fundamental principle of Confederation. Thus, in the interest of equity, Quebec's special needs, especially linguistic and cultural protection, should be accommodated. In turn, this may reduce linguistic tensions. However, if Quebec is to separate, the break should be clean and final, and the costs made known to Canadians;[60]
- federalism and the division of powers should be reviewed with an eye to making the system more efficient; and
- the government should act to assume control of Canada's economic destiny.

The Forum also addressed the diversity of Canadian society. It recommended:

- reviewing the official languages policy and educating people as to the policy's benefits;
- cutting funding to multicultural programs while educating Canadians on the importance of cultural diversity;
- offering education in both official languages, limiting heritage courses, and encouraging exchange programs to foster a sense of unity and Canadianness;
- recognizing the contribution of aboriginal peoples to Canada, settling aboriginal claims, defining and implementing aboriginal self-government arrangements with the joint cooperation of governments and aboriginal peoples, and phasing out the Indian Act.

Finally, the Forum addressed the problems of representation and legitimacy, or leadership and democracy as it termed them. It observed that Canadians are angry with their leadership. In his foreword, Spicer suggested that the anger was general but also specifically directed at the prime minister.[61] The Commissioners identified as particular problems the lack of public participation in constitutional reform, and the tendency to resolve conflicts in private rather than in public bodies like the House of Commons. However, they deferred judgement on a constituent assembly followed by a referendum to another study group, and argued for reform of the operation of the House of Commons and especially the principle of party discipline, reform or abolition of the Senate, and the future use of public hearings. In the foreword, Spicer recommended that the government reconsider its decision against calling a constituent assembly.[62]

Although the Spicer recommendations are founded upon public opinion, they are unlikely to address the problems of legitimacy and representation satisfactorily. First, the recommendations are vague on the means of making the process more responsive despite the call for consideration of referenda, constituent assembly, and recall. This call is undercut by Constitutional Affairs Minister Joe Clark's refusal to consider a constituent assembly.[63] It was also weakened by Commissioner Richard Cashin of Newfoundland who argued that using devices of direct democracy to hold politicians to account is inconsistent with our parliamentary tradition of government.[64]

Second, the recommendation on multiculturalism does not resolve the problems of exclusion and representation identified by racial and ethnic communities. Cutting funding to multicultural programs and targetting it towards helping those groups integrate into Canadian society represents a form of assimilation which has proven unsatisfactory in the past. This is inconsistent with the demand expressed during Meech Lake by these communities for recognition of their cultures and contributions to Canadian society.[65] The Commissioners observed that these communities call for equality. This recommendation relegates multiculturalism to a secondary status while other recommendations assign primacy to the traditional French-English cleavage and to aboriginal peoples.

Third, the Forum reflected the division between Quebec and the rest-of-Canada in the unexpectedly low representation of Quebecers among respondents[66] and its recommendation to review bilingualism. The low participation rate of Quebecers indicates a suspicion of national commissions that address Quebec's concerns along with other Canadian problems. The recommendation to review bilingualism might send a powerful, alienating message to Quebecers and weaken the position of francophones outside Quebec at a time when conciliatory gestures are needed to bond the country. It was significant that Commissioner Robert Normand of Quebec protested the trivialization of the relationship between Quebec and the rest-of-Canada as well as the costs and operation of the Forum.[67]

Despite these weaknesses, the Spicer Report captured an important element of the current debate. If legitimacy and confidence in the Canadian system is to be restored, then the public's demand for openness and inclusion must be accommodated. The recommendations on national institutions and symbols, education, and information exchange between Canadian regions help accomplish this goal. As the Report notes:

> In the view of a great many participants, unity will not come from government programs to promote it; it will stem from our people themselves as we discover our commonalities, our shared history, what we've built together, and how much our ambitions and aspirations, for our families or for the country we live in, are shared by others who inhabit this land. The Forum's participants are asking their governments to make this sharing among citizens possible.[68]

Public participation must be guided by responsible leadership.

Taken together, these two national committees have attempted to find consensus on constitutional reform. The difficulty lay in reconciling citizen demands with governments' objectives. Both acknowledge that a more open and inclusive constitutional process is a mandatory first step, although they differ over means. Both reports attempt to accommodate Quebec's concerns with process while not disregarding the demands of the other provinces and citizens. The Beaudoin-Edwards recommendations are a solid basis for a workable compromise on process which coincides with the current federal initiatives.

THE FUTURE OF CONSTITUTIONAL REFORM

Are these arenas sufficient to meet the public demands for a more inclusive process? Do their solutions offer the answers for Canada as it proceeds into the negotiating and ratification stages of constitutional bargaining? As noted above, there is significant opposition to the current process and much disagreement over the recommendations offered by both the Beaudoin-Edwards Committee and the Spicer Forum. There are loud calls for the adoption of an extraordinary process of constitutional reform which would encompass governments and citizen groups. The merits and drawbacks of public hearings, referenda and constituent assemblies are being openly debated.

Public hearings are an important means of providing public input into the constitutional process without unduly restricting the politicians in the intergovernmental negotiations. The wide-spread use of hearings in the post-Meech era suggests that they are becoming an integral element of constitutional reform. As Beaudoin-Edwards explains, public hearings perform two functions:

> By holding hearings, Parliament would be responding to a major concern of Canadians, that of being heard on matters that concern them. Furthermore, the hearings would provide the opportunity for broader public understanding of constitutional issues.[69]

Hearings provide a basis for the exchange of information and views which stimulates political dialogue and helps build consensus. However, for this to occur, hearings must be held early enough in the process that proposals may be altered; they should be widely televised and accessible to the public; and politicians should be willing to justify and explain positions in public.

An effective constitutional reform process that incorporates public hearings will blend responsive political leadership with solid statecraft. The reports issued by the constitutional committees struck to listen to the public must reflect the opinions expressed at those hearings. This requires balancing majority and minority opinions. The governments must then use the committee reports to inform their positions. Once the process advances to the stage of intergovernmental negotiations, then the governments must remain receptive to the ideas emanating from other jurisdictions, especially if the ideas are intensely or broadly supported by the public. In this stage, discussions are likely to be conducted both in private and in the public eye. If a compromise is necessary to accommodate differences between two or more jurisdictions, then the politicians must be prepared to explain and defend it publicly. Citizens are more likely to accept intergovernmental bargains if they are based upon sound reasons which are clearly articulated, and if a benefit to them, their province or the nation accompanies the concession. If political leadership is combined with public debate and the process is properly managed, then the process "can build on itself: as society defines and evaluates its collective goals, it examines its norms and beliefs; in defining its purposes, it becomes better able to mobilize its resources and achieve its goals."[70] An effectively managed constitutional process with public hearings could help build consensus within Canadian society.

Public hearings are most easily incorporated into the public discussion phase of constitutional reform. To provide a greater opportunity for achieving national consensus in the negotiations stage of reform, the activities of the committees should be coordinated. If public hearings are used in later stages of reform, then they must be carefully managed. For example, Manitoba requires public hearings at the ratification stage of discussions. For hearings at this stage to be meaningful and not degenerate into rubber stamping a deal hammered out between the governments or obstructing necessary reforms, then jurisdictions requiring hearings should be first to ratify. Where serious problems are identified in the deal, then the first ministers should reconvene and address the matter. Where concerns lying outside the deal are raised, the governments should agree upon a separate process to handle those problems. Incorporating public input at this stage should not be unduly difficult if the process has previously been open and met the conditions outlined above.

Is a constituent assembly necessary in the next phase of constitutional reform to achieve the package of reforms necessary to maintain the unity of Canada? A variety of forms of constituent assembly have been suggested as a brief perusal of the submissions to the Beaudoin-Edwards Committee reveals. However, the model offered by Professor Peter Russell is most compelling. He proposes a constituent assembly composed of delegations from the ten provincial legislatures and the federal government which could be quickly convened and would operate within the current rules of the constitution. Each government would use its own selection and composition rules to choose delegates with a high degree of public legitimacy. The assembly, whose proceedings would be televised, would operate for a specified period of several weeks. A high degree of consensus would be established between delegates before they voted in blocks and the proposal advanced to the ratification stage. While one assembly with all governments as participants would be preferable, a two stage assembly may be necessary to overcome Quebec's objections to participating in such a forum. Ratification should easily follow a successful process.[71]

This form of constituent assembly is attractive but two difficulties require resolution. First, if the pattern of underrepresentation of aboriginal peoples, women, and ethnic and racial minorities in the legislatures is repeated in the assembly then these groups may not perceive a constituent assembly of legislative delegates as representative of their views. Second, the conditions do not obtain for a successful constituent assembly exercise. A recent study of constituent assemblies held in a number of countries indicates that they are most successful where a high degree of consensus exists; usually after a civil war, a revolution or major political disruption, or a group of colonies have decided to join together.[72] They have been less successful when used to revise constitutions.[73]

At this stage, it is not clear that an extraordinary measure like a constituent assembly is necessary for Canada. It would not necessarily incorporate the public to a greater extent. Being new, its legitimacy would be hard to establish. In contrast, the parliamentary committee recommended by Beaudoin-Edwards and in progress under Constitutional Affairs Minister Joe Clark has the potential to incorporate many of the benefits of a constituent assembly while operating within Canadian traditions. Parliamentarians must accept the responsibility if it fails or if its proposals do not work out. It can coordinate with legislators in other jurisdictions. The public may be brought into the process through the use of both advisory panels and hearings. If managed properly, this process combined with a series of first ministers' conferences has the potential to reinforce the lines of accountability and encourage responsible decision-making.

Finally, referenda have been suggested primarily for the ratification stage of negotiations. Unless authorized by the constitution, a referendum would only be consultative, not binding.[74] In strict terms, it would be a plebiscite, not a referendum. "The main difference between the two voting devices is therefore that a plebiscite is essentially a public opinion poll but a referendum automatically binds a government to enact a law (or to refrain from doing so) according to the voters' wishes."[75] Consultative referendum is the term in current usage for a non-binding referendum. Although referenda have been used infrequently in Canada, they have been often suggested as a possible means of settling differences in constitutional discussions.[76] Many presenters to both the Spicer and Beaudoin-Edwards Committees argued for a binding referendum on constitutional questions to be included in the constitutional process.

The Beaudoin-Edwards Committee explains one of the most persuasive cases for a referendum:

> A great number of witnesses took the position that the Constitution belongs to the people and the people must be enabled to pronounce on it. From their perspective, a referendum is one of the best means of giving citizens the feeling that the Constitution does indeed belong to them and of allowing them the last word on amending it.[77]

Referenda allow for a direct, democratic check on the decisions of legislators. This responds to the people's desires to be included by allowing them the final say on constitutional matters.

Referenda do not address the current problems in Canada with representation, despite impressions that they would. First, in Canada, votes would have to be subject to regional criteria or the interests of the national minority (Quebecers) or other regional interests in the federation would be jeopardized. The interests of geographically dispersed minorities, like aboriginal peoples, and ethnic and racial communities would be harder to safeguard. A referendum procedure that attempted to protect all of these interests would become complex and possibly unworkable. Second, results on referendum questions are open to interpretation as the 1980 Quebec referendum on sovereignty-association and the 1991 Soviet referenda on unity illustrate. Third, while a clear-cut solution to the question posed in a referendum might resolve an impasse, it also precludes a compromise solution characteristic of a bargaining process. Decisions in representative assemblies and first ministers' conferences may be scrutinized, delayed, revised, and negotiated. Thus, the final result may reflect a broader selection of public opinion than one arrived at through a referendum procedure.[78] This is important in Canada at a time when public opinion is so divided and citizens are questioning the viability of the political system. Finally, if a binding referendum were to be adopted, "it is most unlikely that the negotiations needed to effect this constitutional change could be confined to the amending process. To go ahead with a referendum before negotiating either the rules governing such a referendum or any matters of substance is indeed to put the cart before the horse."[79] Political leaders might end up embroiled in arguments over technical matters of process rather than the substance of change if a national referendum were to be used in this round of negotiations. This would decrease public confidence in the elected representatives and render the system ineffective in dealing with current constitutional problems.

In contrast to a binding referendum, a consultative referendum might be useful in the current process. Russell suggests a consultative referendum as a reasonable option if a deadlock in negotiations were to occur.[80] Similarly, the Beaudoin-Edwards Committee suggested that the federal government should be able at its discretion to hold a consultative referendum on constitutional matters either to build consensus or to aid in the adoption of a package.[81] However, the first two problems identified above would still hold.

CONCLUSION

Canadians expect an open, inclusive process of constitutional reform. Their expectations are justified by the Meech Lake process. However, the necessary changes to the process may be made within the existing formula. If the process is properly applied, then extraordinary measures, like constituent assemblies and referenda, will not be necessary. There is room for accommodating the concerns of the federal government, the Quebec and other provincial governments, and Canadian citizens generally without radical restructuring, which would be difficult to achieve at a time when consensus does not exist or is very fragile.

The ingredients of a constitutional process of reform which would help allay public concerns with legitimacy and representation may be identified. First, the current committees and commissions provide Canadians with an opportunity to air their views. The committee reports must reflect these views to build public confidence in the process. Government positions must be informed by the reports.

Second, in the negotiations stage of discussions, the findings and work of the various governments and committees must be coordinated. Open, visible dialogue must take place. Representatives of key citizen communities, such as the aboriginal peoples, must be included. If discussions go behind closed doors, then the governments must offer clear and convincing justifications for the decisions. Public education and exchange of information are important elements in building a national understanding and planting the seeds of tolerance and respect. Public justifications of decisions might also cause the first ministers to be more conscientious and attentive to public concerns behind closed doors and less likely to engage in the pressure tactics employed in the Meech Lake negotiations. They would not just be attempting to strike a deal, they would be sculpting a defendable pact. The Special Joint Committee dealing with Constitutional Affairs offers an opportunity to achieve these objectives in a more practical way than a constituent assembly at this point. However, it must act in good faith avoiding the appearance of partisanship or having a predetermined agenda.

Finally, the ratification process must be monitored. If possible, governments should conform to a time schedule agreed upon during the negotiations. If a realistic time frame which outlines approximately when certain actions will be taken is adhered to and departures are explained to the other governments, then much of the bitterness and the recriminations of the Meech Lake process might be avoided. Actions would conform to expectations. These measures should help to make the process more workable and acceptable to all Canadians.

One particularly important feature of future constitutional reform must be underscored. Aboriginal issues cannot be deferred or excluded from the constitutional agenda. After Meech Lake, this is a fact. The Spicer Forum noted that there was a high degree of consensus within the Canadian community on the need to satisfy aboriginal demands for self-determination.[82] This demand is no less pressing or legitimate than Quebec's demand for more autonomy. The Beaudoin-Edwards recommendations for aboriginal participation in the constitutional negotiations and a new aboriginal process are practical, equitable, and fair. The current initiative on the aboriginal process is promising. However, aboriginal involvement must include partnership in the next two phases of reform, if the process is to attain a high degree of legitimacy.

The current initiatives provide some basis for concluding that the issues of process may be resolved and a legitimate process of reform may be achieved. The deadline of 1992 provides a limit to the debates and procrastination by governments. However, if negotiations are proceeding and there are tangible results, then there might be room for extending the process. If the decline in support for sovereignty in Quebec and the recent signs of economic recovery in Canada continue, then they may provide encouragement that the present difficulties may be settled and are worth the effort. Whether the citizen demands for representation can be reconciled with the governments' agendas depends largely on the will and actions of the politicians. Public participation with strong, responsible political leadership may invest the constitutional process with the degree of legitimacy required for changes to the Canadian political system to be accepted.

NOTES

1.   I am indebted to the insightful comments offered by Orest Zajcew, Douglas Brown, and the reviewers of this publication on an earlier draft of this paper.

2.   Alan Cairns, "Citizens (Outsiders) and Governments (Insiders) in Constitution-Making: The Case of Meech Lake," in *Canadian Public Policy*, XIV, Special Supplement, 1988, p. 122. See also Cairns, "The Embedded State: State-Society Relations in Canada," in Keith Banting (ed.), *State and Society: Canada in a Comparative Perspective* (Toronto: University of Toronto Press, 1986), p. 66-7 and Cairns, "Ritual Taboo and Bias in Constitution Controversies in Canada or Constitutional Talk Canadian Style," in Alan Cairns and Douglas E. Williams (eds.), *Disruptions: Constitutional Struggles, from the Charter to Meech Lake*, (Toronto: McClelland and Stewart Ltd., 1991), pp. 216-17.

3. For an account of the impact of this process on governments' bargaining positions and styles, see Michael B. Stein, *Canadian Constitutional Renewal, 1968-1981: A Case Study in Integrative Bargaining,* Research Paper 27, (Kingston, Ont.: Institute of Intergovernmental Relations, Queen's University, 1989).

4. For summaries of these criticisms, see Canada, Special Joint Committee, *Minutes of Proceedings and Evidence of the Special Joint Committee of the Senate and of the House of Commons on The 1987 Constitutional Accord,* no. 17, 9 September 1987, pp. 129-31; Canada, Senate, *Minutes of the Proceedings of the Senate,* no. 166, 12 July 1988, pp. 2971-73; Manitoba, Task Force on Meech Lake, *Report on the 1987 Constitutional Accord* (Winnipeg: Government Printer, 1989), pp. 69-71; New Brunswick, Select Committee on the 1987 Constitutional Accord, *Final Report on the Constitution Amendment 1987* (Fredericton: Legislative Assembly, 1989), pp. 25-6; Ontario, Select Committee on Constitutional Reform, *Report on the Constitution Amendment 1987* (Toronto: Queen's Park, 1988), pp. 42-45; Canada, House of Commons, *Minutes of Proceedings and Evidence of the Special Committee to Study The Proposed Companion Resolution to the Meech Lake Accord,* no. 21, 8-12, 14, 15 May 1990, p. 9.

5. Andrew Cohen, *A Deal Undone: The Making and Breaking of the Meech lake Accord* (Vancouver: Douglas and McIntyre, 1990), pp. 271-72.

6. This has been extensively analyzed. For different perspectives, see Richard Simeon, "Why Did the Meech Lake Accord Fail?" in Ronald L. Watts and Douglas M. Brown (eds.), *Canada: The State of the Federation 1990* (Kingston, Ont.: Institute of Intergovernmental Relations, Queen's University, 1990), pp. 26-31; and Edouard Cloutier, "We the People: Public Opinion, Sovereignty and the Constitution," in Robert Young (ed.), *Confederation in Crisis* (Toronto: James Lorimer and Company, 1991), pp. 9-18.

7. Alan C. Cairns, "The Limited Constitutional Vision of Meech Lake," in K.E. Swinton and C.J. Rogerson (eds.), *Competing Constitutional Visions: The Meech Lake Accord* (Toronto: Carswell, 1988), p. 261.

8. See, for example, the debate over participation in Richard Simeon and Mary Janigan (eds.), *Toolkits and Building Blocks: Constructing a New Canada* (Toronto: C.D. Howe Institute, 1991), pp. 71-80; cf. Alan Cairns, "The Charter, Interest Groups, Executive Federalism, and Constitutional Reform," in David E. Smith, Peter MacKinnon and John C. Courtney (eds.), *After Meech Lake: Lessons for the Future* (Saskatoon: Fifth House Publishers, 1991), pp. 13-31; cf. Ian Scott, "After Meech Lake," in Smith et al., *After Meech Lake,* pp. 251-57.

9. Cairns, "The Limited Constitutional Vision of Meech Lake," p. 253.

10. J. Stefan Dupré, "Canadian Constitutionalism and the Sequel to the Meech Lake/Langevin Accord," in David P. Shugarman and Reg Whitaker (eds.), *Federalism and Political Community: Essays in Honour of Donald Smiley* (Peterborough, Ont.: Broadview Press, 1989), pp. 245-47.

11. Jennifer Smith, "Representation and Constitutional Reform in Canada," in Smith et al., *After Meech Lake,* pp. 75-7; cf. Alan Cairns, "Citizens (Outsiders) and Governments (Insiders) in Constitution-Making."

12. Ibid., p. 77.

13. Alan Cairns, "The Charter, Interest Groups, Executive Federalism, and Constitutional Reform," p. 27.

14. Beverly Baines, "After Meech Lake: The Ms/Representation of Gender in Scholarly Spaces," in Smith et al., *After Meech Lake,* p. 208.

15. Ibid., pp. 208-13.

16. Leo Panitch, "Elites, Power and Class in Canada," in M.S. Whittington and G. Williams (eds.), *Canadian Politics in the 1990s,* 3d ed. (Scarborough, Ont.: Nelson, 1990), p. 188.

17. Paul G. Thomas, "Regionalism, Parliament and Party Caucuses," in Herman Bakvis (ed.), *Representation, Integration and Political Parties in Canada,* Research Studies for the Royal Commission on Electoral Reform and Party Financing, vol. 14 (Toronto: Dundurn Press, 1991).

18. Alan Cairns, "Passing Judgement on Meech Lake," in Cairns and Williams, *Disruptions: Constitutional Struggles,* pp. 260-1.

19. Peter H. Russell, "Towards a New Constitutional Process," in Ronald L. Watts and Douglas M. Brown (eds.), *Options for a New Canada,* published in association with the Institute of Intergovernmental Relations, Queens University and the Business Council on National Issues, (Toronto: University of Toronto Press, 1991), pp. 143-145.

20. Quebec, National Assembly, First session, Thirty-fourth Legislature, Bill 90 (1990, chapter 34), "An Act to establish the Commission on the Political Future of Quebec."

21. Canada, Citizen's Forum on Canada's Future, *Fact Sheet,* 18 January 1991.

22. In addition, 300,000 elementary and secondary students participated through the separate Student's Forum. Canada, Citizen's Forum on Canada's Future, *Report to the People and Government of Canada* (Ottawa: Minister of Supply and Services, 1991), pp. 16, 29.

23. Canada, House of Commons, *Votes and Proceedings of the House of Commons,* 17 December 1990.

24. Canada, House of Commons, Third Session, 34th Parliament, Order Paper and Notice Paper, 17 June 1991, p. 17.

25. See The Manitoba Métis Senate Commission, *Report on National Unity and Constitutional Reform,* July 1991.

26. For public discussion of some of these concerns, see *Globe and Mail,* 29 June 1991, p. D3, 14 June 1991, p. A4, 13 June 1991, p. A3.

27. Ibid., p. 18.

28. Alberta, Constitutional Reform Task Force, "Alberta in a New Canada," 1990, p. 2.

29. Miro Cernetig, "Albertans may not share Getty's vision," *Globe and Mail,* 7 June 1991, p. A3.

30. Manitoba Premier Gary Filmon, Letter to Professor W. N. Fox-Decent, 5 December 1990.

31. Ontario, Select Committee on Ontario in Confederation, *Interim Report,* 21 March 1991, p. 1.

32. The Honourable Jean Chrétien, *Submission to The Commission on the Political and Constitutional Future of Quebec*, 17 December 1990, pp. 37, 39, 40-43, 47-48; cf. Hugh Winsor, "Liberals fall short of goals in repair work at Ontario talks," *Globe and Mail*, 17 June 1991, p. A4.

33. New Democratic Party of Canada, Resolution on the Constitution of Canada, Approved by Convention, 8 June 1991; cf. New Democratic Party, Canadian Constitution Discussion Paper, March 1991.

34. For a sampling of the different perspectives on the need for greater public participation in the process, see the submissions by Robinson Koilpillai of the Edmonton Multicultural Society, Richard Chartier of the Société franco-manitobaine, and Yvon Dumont of the Métis National Council to the Special Joint Committee of the Senate and the House of Commons on Process for Amending the Constitution of Canada, *Minutes of Proceedings and Evidence*, 18 March 1991, 10:67-78, 27 March 1991, and 18 April 1991, 17:6-18, 23:67-86.

35. Graham Fraser, "Difficult task tests minister's constitution," *Globe and Mail*, 17 June 1991, p. A4.

36. See, for example, Canadian Society of Muslims, *Oh! Canada! Whose Land, Whose Dream?* (Toronto, 1990).

37. Group of 22, "Some Practical Suggestions for Canada," June 1991, pp. 11, 13-25, 26, 27.

38. Susan Delacourt, "Teams of deputy ministers work on new plan for Canada," *Globe and Mail*, 31 January 1991, A1.

39. The National Assembly approved Bill 150 in principle on 14 June 1991.

40. For the initial proposal see, Quebec, Commission on the Political and Constitutional Future of Quebec (Bélanger-Campeau), *Report* (Quebec: National Assembly, 27 March 1991), pp. 80-1.

41. Ibid., pp. 81-2.

42. Ibid., pp. 48-9.

43. Constitutional Committee of the Quebec Liberal Party, *A Quebec Free to Choose*, (Allaire Report), 28 January 1991, pp. 60-2.

44. Allaire Report, p. 12; Bélanger-Campeau Report, p. 35.

45. For a discussion of the conflict between symmetry and asymmetry in Canadian federalism in a broader context, see David Milne, "Equality or Asymmetry: Why Choose?" in Watts and Brown, *Options for A New Canada*, pp. 285-307; cf. Thomas Courchene, "Forever Amber," in Smith et al., *After Meech Lake*, pp. 33-60.

46. Bélanger-Campeau Report, pp. 37-8.

47. Ibid., p. 39.

48. Allaire Report, p. 23.

49. Canada, Special Joint Committee of the Senate and the House of Commons on the Process for Amending the Constitution of Canada (Beaudoin-Edwards), *Minutes of Proceedings and Evidence* (Ottawa: Minister of Supply and Services, 1991), pp. 26-7, 67, 68.

50. Ibid., pp. 69-70.

51. Ibid., pp. 47-8.

52. Ibid., p. 50.

53. Ibid., p. 50.

54. Ibid., pp. 74-5.

55. Ibid., p. 22.

56. Ibid., p. 25.

57. Ibid., p. 77.

58. Ibid., p. 17.

59. The recommendations are drawn from Canada, Citizens' Forum on Canada's Future, *Report to the People and Government of Canada,* (Ottawa: Minister of Supply and Services Canada, 1991), pp. 121-38.

60. Ibid., pp. 57-62, 114, 124.

61. Ibid., p. 6.

62. Ibid., p. 5.

63. Susan Delacourt, "Constituent assembly plea rejected," *Globe and Mail,* 28 June 1991, A4.

64. Spicer Report, pp. 141-3.

65. See, for example, Manitoba, Task Force on Meech Lake, *Report on the 1987 Constitutional Accord,* pp. 12-15.

66. Spicer Report, p. 24.

67. Ibid., pp. 144-46.

68. Ibid., p. 46.

69. Beaudoin-Edwards Report, p. 54.

70. Robert Reich, *The Power of Public Ideas* (Cambridge, MA: Harvard University Press, 1990), p. 6; for a discussion of his ideas in the context of Canadian constitutional reform, see K. L. Brock, "The Demand for Greater Participation," in Simeon and Janigan, *Toolkits and Building Blocks,* pp. 71-4.

71. Peter H. Russell, "Towards a New Constitutional Process," pp. 150-54; cf. the submission by Russell to the Special Joint Committee of the Senate and House of Commons on the process for Amending the Constitution of Canada, *Minutes of Proceedings and Evidence,* 7 March 1991, 9:4-32.

72. Institute of Intergovernmental Relations, "Constituent Assemblies: A Comparative Survey," prepared for the Federal-Provincial Relations Office, Government of Canada, 15 March 1991, pp. 37-8.

73. Ibid., p. 45.

74. Canada, Federal-Provincial Relations Office (FPRO), *Amending the Constitution of Canada,* A Discussion Paper, December 1990, p. 15.

75. J. Patrick Boyer, *Lawmaking by the People: Referendums and Plebiscites in Canada,* (Toronto: Butterworths, 1982), p. 13.

76. FPRO, *Amending the Constitution of Canada,* pp. 16-17.

77. Beaudoin-Edwards Report, p. 36.

78. For a discussion of the weaknesses of referenda in a representative system see, David Butler and Austin Ranney, *Referendums: A Comparative Study of Practice and Theory* (Washington: American Enterprise Institute for Public Policy Research, 1978), pp. 34-37.

79. Peter H. Russell, "Towards A New Constitutional Process," pp. 149-50.

80. Ibid., p. 150.

81. Beaudoin-Edwards Report, pp. 41-2.

82. Spicer Report, pp. 126-27.

4

Slouching Towards Canada

Graham Fraser

Depuis l'échec de l'Accord du lac Meech, tout démontre que le Québec et le reste du Canada sont engagés dans des directions différentes sur le plan constitutionnel. Pour l'heure, en parallèle du gouvernement fédéral, le Canada hors Québec compte trois figures marquantes: Bob Rae, Preston Manning et Clyde Wells. La dernière conférence interprovinciale à Whistler aura révélé un certain leadership du premier ministre ontarien en matière constitutionnelle. Déjà auparavant, Bob Rae s'était distingué dans le dossier autochtone en reconnaissant le principe d'un gouvernement amérindien autonome dans sa province. Pour sa part, le leader du Reform Party, Preston Manning, aura forcé ni plus ni moins le gouvernement Mulroney à s'attaquer à une réforme des institutions parlementaires ainsi qu'à se pencher sur l'aliénation ressentie par les provinces de l'Ouest. Les pressions exercées par le parti de Manning sur les con-servateurs de l'Ouest expliquent pour une bonne part les difficultés du gouvernement Mulroney à obtenir un consensus sur la question constitutionnelle. Moins omniprésent qu'à l'époque de Meech, le premier ministre de Terre-Neuve, quant à lui, continue cependant de hanter les stratèges fédéraux, lesquels n'ont d'autre alternative que de concocter des propositions pouvant ultimement se passer de l'endossement de Clyde Wells.

Au cours de la dernière année, le gouvernement Mulroney n'aura connu aucun repos; de fait, outre l'impasse constitutionnelle proprement dite, le gouvernement conservateur eut à subir les affres d'autres crises: l'épisode d'Oka, la guérilla libérale au Sénat contre la T.P.S. et l'affaire El-Mashat.

En réponse à la Commission Bélanger-Campeau et au comité Allaire, le gouverne-ment Mulroney créa le Forum des Citoyens. La Commission Spicer, à l'instar des commissions Laurendeau-Dunton et Pepin-Robarts auparavant, se sera employée à diagnostiquer les maux profonds du pays, dont notamment la "désynchronisation" entre les citoyens et les élus.

L'auteur de l'article estime que les Québécois renvoient un peu trop systématiquement à Meech lorsqu'il s'agit d'évaluer les prochaines offres fédérales. A cet égard, le gouvernement Mulroney devra presque réaliser la quadrature du cercle: satisfaire d'un côté les Québécois tout en convainquant le reste du Canada que le Québec n'a pas reçu de traitement de faveur. L'auteur conclut en exprimant son pessimisme eu égard à l'issue de la présente ronde Canada, et quant aux chances d'un possible consensus national à la clé, compte tenu du désenchantement général des Canadiens à l'endroit du gouvernement Mulroney.

The year from June 1990 to June 1991 may turn out, in retrospect, to be when Canada decided it did not want Quebec. For, as the shock of the death of Meech Lake has gradually worn off, there have been increasing signs that, far from being guilt- or remorse-stricken at the effects of the death of Meech Lake, many English-speaking Canadians are gradually becoming accustomed to the idea of a political society that does not accommodate — or include — Quebec.

There have been a number of indications that the Canadian political society outside Quebec — the identity problem is evident in the fact that nobody knows what to call it, and so has called it everything from English Canada to Canada Outside Quebec (COQ) to the rest-of-Canada (ROC) to The Rest of Canada (TROC) — is heading in a very different direction from Quebec.

Quebec, as the constitutional policy of the Quebec Liberal Party makes clear, has already gone, psychologically if not legally. The gap between the minimum conditions for the Quebec government to sign a constitutional agreement and a recognizable national government for the rest of the country, once narrow enough to be bridged by the Meech Lake Accord, has now gaped open like a glacial crevasse. Rather than worrying about that chasm, the political class outside Quebec has been concerned with a series of other concerns: the aboriginal agenda, the environment, the state of the economy, the Goods and Services Tax and its by-product, cross-border shopping, Senate reform, and the future of Canada's social programs.

In fact, there are now three dominant political figures in Canada whose authority and influence are wholly independent of any support in Quebec: from left to right, Ontario Premier Bob Rae, Newfoundland Premier Clyde Wells and the leader of the Reform Party of Canada, Preston Manning.

Bob Rae is in the paradoxical position of being arguably the most bilingual Canadian politician in the country from outside Quebec — and in a political situation in which this is almost — not quite, and not yet — a liability. As New Democratic Party leader in Ontario and Leader of the Opposition, he almost certainly would have been defeated had he run for the federal leadership of the NDP, because he had so clearly, forcefully and eloquently supported the Meech Lake Accord.

David Peterson called the Ontario election primarily because of his concern about Quebec:

"The reason I called the election was I did not want an election in the province of Ontario in the future that would be a referendum on what's happening in Quebec," he told Georgette Gagnon and Dan Rath, referring to the Bélanger-Campeau Commission on Quebec's political and constitutional future. "I feared the consequences. I thought the situation would become absolutely ripe for oversimplified politics with a racist overtone that would be so destructive as everything reverberated across the country. I thought the voices of moderation and conciliation would be drowned in an impossible situation that would do irreperable harm to the country. That's why I did it — and I thought we could win. I thought we could have a strong hand to deal with things in a sensitive way to try to keep the country together in some semblance where you could recognize it."[1]

For a whole series of reasons, most of which had nothing to do with Quebec or the Meech Lake Accord, he was wrong, and Bob Rae became premier of Ontario.

Rae is the first provincial premier since Ed Schreyer who was a federal MP before moving to provincial politics; he was drawn to national issues first and foremost. It was, however, a reflex that set him apart from his cabinet, his caucus and his party. His colleagues were drawn into politics because of their concerns about battered women, child care, food banks, pollution and pay equity. After he was elected, he would almost apologize for raising what he jokingly called "the C word" at party meetings — aware that the constitution was widely identified in the NDP with an unholy alliance between Brian Mulroney and Robert Bourassa. The federal New Democratic Party had torn itself apart over the 1982 constitution; memories of that bitter experience were so deeply rooted that New Democrats instinctively recoiled from engaging in a gut-wrenching debate over constitutional principles.

Quebec unease about Rae, even before his desire to chart an independent course on the national unity question became clear, was summed up by a front-page headline in *La Presse* on 8 September, two days after he became premier: "Bob Rae connaît à peine Bourassa — Le Québec sera une province comme les autres." (Bob Rae barely knows Bourassa — Quebec will be a province like the others.)

Gradually, Rae began to make it clear that his approach to the constitution would be very different from Peterson's.

"The terms of the current Canadian federalism — its financial sharing, its cultural, social, economic and political institutions — can always be discussed and reformed. But Canada itself is not negotiable. We have come too far for that," he told the Ontario legislature on 19 December 1990. "The second point is that Ontario does not for one moment accept the proposition that the federal government speaks for 'English Canada' while the government of Quebec speaks for itself. Each government speaks for itself and for the people in its jurisdiction."[2]

Gradually, over the months that followed, he began to send out clearer signals about the directions he proposed to take on the federal-provincial and constitutional front. Conscious of the importance of Ontario's relationship to Quebec, he appointed a new delegate-general to Quebec City: the first time Ontario's representative would reside in the capital. But he sent other signals as well to the effect that Ontario would no longer act as Quebec's surrogate, acting on its behalf with the other provinces. The agenda would be wider and broader.

"I am saying that if we really want to have a Canada that will work, a federation that will work well, we have to recognize the social and economic elements of social and economic rights in this new federation," he said, speaking in French in the Ontario legislature — a clear a way of speaking to Quebec. "If we recognize rights in the constitution, if we recognize the possibility of having rights more broadly defined in the constitution, then that gives us the chance to say 'Well, now we can talk about how we divide powers in a different way.'"[3]

He indicated that he would not be entering discussions with what he called "a particular agenda in a kind of regional way," but was stressing certain principles:

> an affirmation of rights; an extension of those rights to include some broader social and economic principles as well; a determination on our part to use this round to make the country work better, more efficiently and more fairly and explicitly to deal with the division of powers question; to ensure that in fact Canada is capable of meeting the challenge of the 21st century. ...a willingness on our part to say categorically that we are prepared in this round on behalf of the people of the province, as we were in the last round, to recognize the unique character of Quebec, as well as some other basic principles: the rights of aboriginal people, the fundamental equality between men and women, [and] equality rights generally as part of a new Constitution.[4]

In that same speech, he indicated that he was unenthusiastic about a referendum, and favoured what he called "a constitutional convention, a gathering, certainly made up of legislators from provinces, territories, the House of Commons and native people, and I think that is the least number of people that need to be involved as we attempt then to find a genuine national consensus which will then have to go through the legislative process which is set out in our own Constitution."[5]

In the months ahead, Rae also stressed that he was determined to make the aboriginal agenda part of the process — recognizing aboriginal self-government in Ontario, and urging the premiers to invite aboriginal leaders to the annual Premiers' Conference. At the same time, he continued to talk about the need for a social charter, and repeatedly spoke about the importance of guaranteeing social programs — a message he underlined by announcing that his new deputy-minister for intergovernmental affairs would be the outgoing president of the Canadian Union of Public Employees, Jeff Rose.

At the annual meeting of premiers in Whistler B.C. in August 1991, he emerged as the most articulate spokesman of a provincial position on the constitutional question. He was among those who welcomed a federal involvement in education — a position that highlighted Quebec's absence. And his message was clear. "Any talk of a wholesale devolution of powers or of any dramatic moving away by the federal government from its responsibilities ... I don't think that has any real resonance or support in much of Canada and I think that's something the federal government is going to have to reflect on,"[6] he told reporters.

With the prospect of provincial elections in British Columbia and Saskatchewan electing at least one, and possibly two New Democratic Party premiers, the federal government will clearly have to reflect on everything Bob Rae says. So far, there is little indication that they have been doing so; federal strategists privately talk about Rae "positioning himself" for the constitutional discussions by stressing the aboriginal agenda, and suggest that being premier of Ontario will drive him, necessarily, towards a more traditional position, requiring him to modify his ideas about a social charter or a constituent assembly the way he had to drop his party's promise to create a state-owned automobile insurance system.

However, one of the elements being evaluated quietly as part of the constitutional package has been, in fact, a social charter. At this writing, the final package has not been agreed upon; however, a considerable amount of work had gone into including a social charter as one of the options in the package: a proposal for consideration that would involve guaranteeing the right to shelter, health care and a minimum standard of living in the constitution through a social charter. It may prove to be a way of responding to pressure from Rae and the NDP; however, it may simply open up a whole new front for ideological debate over the constitution.

"The social charter could ... be the spark that ignites some of the hottest political feuds in the national-unity debate," pointed out Susan Delacourt in the *Globe and Mail.* "Already, it threatens to pit left against right, English Canada against French Canada, centralists against decentralists, individual rights versus collective rights."[7]

Moving from the NDP to the Liberals, the major Liberal figure has not been Jean Chrétien, but Newfoundland Premier Clyde Wells, the most vociferous opponent of the Meech Lake Accord. But Wells, a dominant figure on the constitution for two years, lost some of his importance in the months following the death of the Meech Lake Accord. He had exercised his veto, shaken his fist at Ottawa and Quebec, and become a national figure for his resistance to the Accord. But, having established his rectitude and his rigidity, he lost his leverage, and shot his bolt. An indication of how his significance has diminished can be seen in a comparison of Jean Chrétien's gratitude, expressed on 23 June 1990, for the role Wells had played — and Chrétien's admission to the *Financial Post*, on 6 July 1991, that his opposition to the Meech Lake Accord had been a mistake.

In fact, the Liberal Party position adopted by the Quebec wing of the party in Sherbrooke on 25-26 May, which endorsed many of the key principles of the Meech Lake Accord and was supported by Chrétien, showed how far Chrétien had moved in a year. No longer could Clyde Wells be said to speak for the dominant thinking in the leadership of the Liberal Party. Moreover, it is highly likely that the federal proposal will be designed in such a way that it will not require unanimity — therefore avoiding the necessity of winning Wells' agreement.

Most of the other premiers have remained relatively quiet about the national unity issue. In some cases, they are scarred survivors of the Meech marathon, who, like superstitious sailors, have seen their comrades lost at sea: David Peterson swept overboard, John Buchanan carried aloft to the Senate, and William Vander Zalm leaping from the ship. In other cases, like Rita Johnston and Donald Cameron, they are new to the issue, and see no advantage in uttering more than platitudes. There is little to be gained by speaking out strongly on the issue, they have apparently decided; better to leave the question to those who are more comfortable with it.

But there is another significant figure who has emerged, and who has gained in strength and support: Preston Manning, leader of the Reform Party.

Manning, more than any other national politician, takes an uncompromising position towards Quebec, seeing the pressure for change there as a catalyst that will force change in the rest of Canada.

"First of all, let the people and politicians of Quebec define the new Quebec," he told his supporters at the Reform Party Assembly in Saskatoon in April. "We welcome the current constitutional ferment in Quebec because one of its effects will be to crack the Canadian Constitution wide open and force the rest of Canada to address the task of developing a new constitution, rather than attempting to patch up the old one."[8]

But, in another of the paradoxes of Canadian politics, Manning's rejection of any whiff of special status for Quebec opens the door to special status — since he sees what he calls New Canada mobilizing to restructure and redefine itself without Quebec.

However, he said it was only fair to the people of Quebec to add that whoever was negotiating on behalf of Canada would not be likely to be attracted by the concept of sovereignty-association.

"I was down in Quebec a couple of months ago," he told reporters later. "I got the feeling from reading, and hearing a bit from the Quebec politicians, that they kind of assume they'll be sitting across a table from a Pearson, a Trudeau, a Mulroney — someone who is really prepared to make concessions. But my point is that if you can no longer promise to keep the country together, if that incentive isn't there, what's the incentive to agree to anything? What that negotiation comes down to is each pursuing their own self-interest."[9]

Absent and unelected, Preston Manning nevertheless remains a figure of significance — in part because he continually personifies and reflects a desire, previously unacceptable, to see English-speaking Canadian leaders who are English-speaking Canadian leaders, rather than bilingual Montreal lawyers.

"Mr. Manning is a surrogate for the right wing of the Progressive Conservative Party and, when it comes to Quebec, also a surrogate for the right wing of the Liberal Party," observed William Thorsell. "Given Tory unpopularity among their traditional constituencies, Mr. Manning's influence is much greater than his power."[10]

His influence has already helped shape the federal government's concern about Parliamentary reform, and western alienation. His program has affected the government's agenda in a number of ways; his popularity acts as a substantial constraint on the ability of the federal government to respond to Quebec.

In fact, the strength of the Reform Party, and its ideological pressures on the western Conservatives, has made it all the more difficult for the Mulroney government to reach an internal consensus. To that extent, the fracturing widely predicted for the next Parliament, on the assumption that five parties will be running candidates (Progressive Conservatives, Liberals, New Democrats, Reform and the Bloc Québécois) has already had its impact on the ability of the Mulroney Cabinet to govern.

TEN MONTHS IN SHOCK

After the death of the Meech Lake Accord, the federal government was in a state of shock. The prime minister responded by naming as his chief of staff the former Secretary to Cabinet for Federal-Provincial Relations who had been the primary strategist on the constitutional file, Norman Spector. He was replaced by Canada's Ambassador to NATO, Gordon Smith. The minister responsible for the negotiation of the Meech Lake Accord, Lowell Murray, remained the minister responsible for federal-provincial relations — and, as Government Leader in the Senate, had a number of other distractions such as the marathon battle in the Senate over the Goods and Services Tax (GST).

In fact, for about a year, the federal government was in a constant state of crisis. First, the Meech Lake paroxysm, which began to monopolize the time and attention of senior decision-makers in spring 1990, and before its collapse on 23 June, saw the resignation of one Cabinet minister, Lucien Bouchard — the prime minister's closest friend in Cabinet — and three other Quebec Tories.

Ten days later, on 11 July, the death of Corporal Marcel LeMay in the attack of the Sûreté du Québec on the Mohawk barricades at Oka, and the subsequent blockage of the Mercier Bridge, began a second crisis that lasted until 26 September, when the Mohawks surrendered.

This was followed by the fight over the GST in the Senate.

In January, there was the Gulf War, followed by its major domestic repercussion, the Al-Mashat Affair.

Each one of these largely unrelated events had a number of elements in common. They gobbled up enormous amounts of time, thought and sleep of Cabinet members and senior government officials who were hustled into the adrenaline rush of daily emergency meetings of special committees, early morning briefings, late-night de-briefings, 24-hour hotline numbers, hot glowing television sets tuned constantly to Newsworld or CNN, and a proliferation of cellular phones. In the course of this frenzy, sleep-deprived politicians and deputy-ministers have said silly things.

Despite the series of other crises, the government made a number of strategic decisions in the fall of 1991, which the prime minister alluded to in his speech after the death of the Accord. To begin with, it decided that it would do nothing quickly. It would wait until the various provincial commissions had reported before responding in substantive terms. The government would study the technical problem of the amending formula. At the same time, there would be something — some *instrument* was the phrase used most often — for Canadians to express their values, what they had in common.

What this strategy did not appear to take into account was the degree to which consensus seemed to be hardening in Quebec around the idea of sovereignty, and the degree to which that consensus would be driven by both the Bélanger-Campeau Commission and the Quebec Liberal Party's constitutional committee presided over by Jean Allaire.

As a result, there began to be growing pressure on the federal government to *do* something. Or at least be seen to do something. The nature of that pressure meant that even those things that had been planned, and were part of the strategy, looked improvised and spontaneous.

A good example of this was the Citizens' Forum on Canada's Future, presided over by Keith Spicer. Even though something of that kind had been discussed since early summer, it looked as if it had emerged from the back of an envelope — complete with commissioners confessing they had been phoned the night before.

While Spicer was being ridiculed, his commissioners variously resigning or attacking each other, Quebec's Commissions seemed to be marching resolutely off into a sovereignist sunset. The sense of unease was increased by the news that committees of federal deputy ministers had been struck in order, it seemed, to look at how to dismantle their departments and give them to the provinces.

By the spring of 1991, ten months after the death of the Meech Lake Accord, four months after Allaire and two months after Bélanger-Campeau, things appeared to be somewhat different. The pressure on the federal government to be seen to act meant that the timetable was accelerated.

In Buckingham in December, and in Toronto and Quebec City in February, Mr. Mulroney made it clear that he was not going to dismantle the federal government, that the division of powers issue would be, as he put it, "a two-way street," and that Quebec could not expect to be a part-time member of Canada.

He was genuinely annoyed by the tone and sweep of the Allaire Report. It was also clear — as Bob Rae would point out in August, and as dozens of polls would make clear before then — that English-Canadian public opinion had a limited interest in full-scale decentralization of power to the provinces.

A REFLECTIVE PAUSE

By the spring of 1991, a number of things seemed to be happening.

In Quebec, there was a kind of reflective pause that showed in the polls. People who had not spoken out in the past were expressing a quite different form of reticence about independence. The polls showing that large numbers in the English-speaking community in Quebec expect to leave the province in the next five years[11] have stimulated some people to consider the trend towards an ever-more homogenous Quebec, regardless of its constitutional status. Gradually, it seems to be becoming permissible to talk about the costs of sovereignty without being accused of economic terrorism.

While there was a certain doubt being expressed in Quebec, there was a faintly more optimistic sense in Ottawa. Keith Spicer was no longer the subject of derision; some federal officials and journalists began to argue that he played a useful role as a kind of lightning rod, absorbing public rage and disenchantment at a time when a more traditional forum would not have worked. Joe Clark took over as Minister of Constitutional Affairs — and discovered that he had acquired a reservoir of trust in the country that would have been barely believable a decade earlier.

But public trust did not appear to be enough. In June, Gordon Smith was dismissed as Secretary to Cabinet for Federal-Provincial Relations, a victim of "poor chemistry," — further demoralizing an already depressed Federal-Provincial Relations Office — and the Cabinet committee on the constitution quickly discovered that it reflected the country as a whole: it was bitterly divided.

A group of the Quebec ministers in the federal Cabinet, led by Marcel Masse and Benoît Bouchard, were frustrated at the unwillingness of their Cabinet colleagues to accept the classic Quebec nationalist view of the country. Mr. Masse found that the initial document trivialized Quebec, while Bernard Valcourt expressed his Acadian frustration at Quebec's preoccupations. Joe Clark expressed confidence that he can build the kind of consensus in the country that exists in the Tory caucus — but his Cabinet committee did not manage to reach a consensus over the summer. In early September, the committee — and Cabinet's Priorities and Planning Committee — still had to make some key decisions on the nature of the federal proposals.

SPICER'S CRY: THE THIRD IN THREE DECADES

Keith Spicer emerged with an eloquent, but ultimately hollow cry, reflecting the rage and frustration that so many Canadians had been feeling towards their government. In late June 1991 he presented a Citizens' Forum report of a country in a crisis: out of sync with itself, unsure of its identity, unhappy with its leadership, irritated by language policy, resentful of secrecy, and suspicious of any whiff of provincial privilege or special deals.

It was not unique. For the third time in as many decades, the scraping sour notes of national dissonance were recorded by a federal commission — notes that are harsher because they come from across the country, and underscored with a new factor: crisis fatigue.

When he stood in front of a single microphone in the dramatic hall of the Museum of Civilization, across the river from the Parliament buildings, Spicer used the French word *désynchronisation* — literally, out of synchronization, out of sync — to refer to the disconnected relationship between citizens and elected officials. He could also have used the phrase to apply to the country itself. For 26 years after André Laurendau and Davidson Dunton issued their preliminary report and 12 years after Jean-Luc Pepin and the late John Robarts published their diagnosis and recommendations, Keith Spicer and his colleagues produced their own snapshot of the evolving national tantrum.

The report pointed out that in 1965, the Royal Commission on Bilingualism and Biculturalism (Bi-and-Bi) warned that Canada was passing through the greatest crisis in its history, and then in 1979, the Task Force on Canadian Unity, known as the Pepin-Robarts Report recalled that warning and renewed it: the crisis was graver and more critical.

"The Pepin-Robarts group also acknowledged in 1979 that 'even crises can become tedious and difficult to believe in if they go on too long and if nothing seems to happen,' " the Forum observed. "Through the winter and spring of 1991, we found the truth of this statement: the continuous series of crises has become tedious for many Canadians, and there is a measure of disbelief that, even now, change is imminent and may be damaging and disruptive."[12]

All three reports had significant elements in common. All three commissions found a country in profound ignorance of its different parts, and a country with contradictory visions, difficult to reconcile and even harder to resolve. For the third time in 30 years, a group of distinguished Canadians has asked whether Canadians want to live together, and emerged perplexed, slightly awed at the conflicting views of the country.

"Who is right and who is wrong?" the Bi-and-Bi Commissioners asked in 1965. "We do not even ask ourselves that question; we simply record the existence of a crisis which we believe to be very serious. If it should persist and gather momentum it could destroy Canada. On the other hand, if it is over come, it will have contributed to the rebirth of a richer and more dynamic Canada."[13]

Ironically, the approaches taken and the solutions proposed by all three groups were remarkably similar. Each one, in some way, tried to seek a way to acknowledge Quebec's status as a society.

The Laurendeau-Dunton Commission first coined the phrase "a distinct society;" Pepin-Roberts called for the recognition in the constitution of Quebec's distinctiveness and the historic partnership between English- and French-speaking Canadians. But André Laurendeau's desire to address the question of Quebec society was deflected and translated into official language policy and the Pepin-Roberts proposal of granting language policy and social and cultural matters to the provinces in exchange for greater economic integration was rejected — in both cases by Prime Minister Pierre Trudeau.

Both Laudendeau-Dunton and the Citizen's Forum have found that Canadians are misinformed about their country — Spicer wrote vividly in his preface that "this country is dying of ignorance, and of our stubborn refusal to learn."

"Sometimes the country seemed to us a multiplicity of solitudes, islands of self-contained activity and discourse disconnected from their neighbors and tragically unaware of the problem of the whole which contained them all," the Pepin-Roberts Task Force reported — in a sentence that could have slipped into the Citizens' Forum without a word changed. " When one spoke, the others did not listen; indeed, they barely seemed to hear."[14]

However, Canadians are now, at least, ignorant about different things. English-speaking Canadians in 1965 told the Bi-and-Bi Commission that Quebec was a backward, rural society when it was, by then, the most urban province of Canada, and that it was dominated by the Church and held back by its inadequate education system when the Church was dying in influence and the school system was being transformed.

In 1991, the Citizens' Forum found a disagreement about language laws in Quebec, the significance of official language policy, the nature of provincial equality, and the reasons for the failure of the Meech Lake Accord.

"A country that cannot guarantee equal rights to a citizen, whether from Lac St-Jean or Windsor, Matane or Vancouver, is not worth having," said a participant in a group outside Quebec. "If English Canadians couldn't accept the miniscule provisions of Meech, how will they accept a substantial change in the current Constitution?" asked a Quebecer, and one discussion group in Quebec concluded: "It is clear that the rest of Canada doesn't want us: it is therefore the time for us to affirm outselves."

The last notes of the report, fittingly enough, went to men from the provinces that represented the ultimate disagreement over the Meech Lake Accord, Newfoundland and Quebec.

Richard Cashin warned about the Americanization of the parliamentary system, through "American-style concepts of direct democracy" like a referendum, which "do not fit well within our parliamentary system."[15] And Robert Normand deplored that the relationship between Quebec and the rest-of-Canada was trivialized.

"The positive suggestions ... are either too convoluted in form or too timid in content to be adequate for resolving the problems in hand," he said, reflecting the gap between public opinion in Quebec and the rest of the country.[16]

Observing the state of "bitter confusion" in the country and "the Forum's inability to put forward satisfactory solutions," Mr. Normand concluded with what were, quite appropriately, the last words of the report: "Good luck to you, Mr. Clark." Joe Clark needs it.

...WAITING TO BE BORN

By the time this chapter appears, the federal proposal will have been published; as a result, this speculation may be proven wrong immediately. However, the various leaks and rumours that have swirled around the Cabinet committee meetings during the summer indicate that the federal proposal will suggest an elected Senate, and the creation of a Council of the Federation — a new federal institution filled by delegates from the provinces, who would take over the nitty-gritty of federal-provincial relations and monitor federal norms and standards for joint federal-provincial programs. A certain amount of authority over culture and communications would be offered to Quebec — although when Radio-Canada reported that this might go as far as a transfer of the network to provincial control, Mulroney denounced this as a "total fabrication."

Much of the intense debate that took place over the Cabinet table, with Quebec ministers like Marcel Masse and Benoît Bouchard arguing for more powers for Quebec and a restriction of the federal spending power, Acadian Bernard Valcourt criticizing Quebec's insensitivity to francophone minorities outside Quebec, and Ontario ministers like Barbara McDougall and Perrin Beatty calling for a retention of the federal power to spend in areas of provincial jurisdiction, will presumably be replayed, in some form, in public.

However, there are other dangers. One of the legacies of the Meech Lake Accord has been a bench-mark mentality in Quebec. When the report is produced, it will be immediately compared with what was offered in the Meech Lake Accord — and with the 22 powers sought by the Allaire Report. If political and public opinion in Quebec dismiss the report out of hand in the days following its publication, it will be increasingly difficult for the Quebec Tory MPs to maintain their solidarity with the caucus. Thus, one shoal that will have to be steered past will be the preservation of the government's majority; a massive walk-out of Quebec MPs would precipitate an election.

The other rocks to be avoided, of course, will be the feeling outside Quebec that the recommendations call for too much for Quebec. That is the circle to be squared, in a public environment in which everyone views someone else's gain as their loss, and someone else's benefit as their deprivation.

So as the autumn begins, Prime Minister Brian Mulroney can look forward to a difficult year ahead. It was been a difficult summer, despite a successful Progressive Conservative convention in August which endorsed Quebec's right to self-determination. Decima, the polling firm the government prefers, delivered bad news from a national survey in June. It found almost two-thirds of Albertans saying they probably would vote for the Reform Party, and 43 percent of Quebecers agreeing that "it is at least somewhat likely" that they would vote for the Bloc Québécois. Almost 60 percent of the Canadians polled were opposed to a trilateral free-trade agreement with the United States and Mexico, and almost half felt that Canada should exercise its right to get out of the free-trade agreement with the United States. The disenchantment with government is such that those polled felt not only that government involvement in the economy has hindered economic growth and the quality of life but also that a decrease in government involvement has hurt. The public mood did not improve over the summer. A Gallup poll released in late August showed support for the Tories at a historic low of 12 percent.

The challenge now becomes all the more complicated for the government. Can it put together any national consensus, or has its own unpopularity irredeemably tarnished any national proposal that it puts forward? Can the government separate its own electoral unpopularity from the constitutional proposal, or is the suspicion and distrust so high that any so-called non-partisan approach will be seen simply as another way of co-opting — or dividing — the Opposition? The government intended the Spicer Forum to act as a kind of pressure valve for the country to vent some anger and frustration — but it is not at all clear that disenchantment has diminished as a result.

In addition, there is the continuing risk of an unplanned, unforeseeable symbolic event that will further increase resentments, and drive a wedge between different parts of the country. The *Gens de l'Air* controversy in 1976, the trampling of the Quebec flag in Brockville in 1989; the Sault Ste Marie votes on municipal unilingualism in 1990, followed by the burning of Canadian flags at the *Fête Nationale* and the stoning of Mohawk elders and children during the Oka Crisis; the anger over Eric Lindros' refusal to sign with the Quebec Nordiques; the shooting of black teenagers by police in Montreal and Toronto, each one of these incidents further widened the gap of public sympathy and comprehension. Almost inevitably, there will be others.

To add to the complexity of the situation, there is the problem of timing and process. When the government's constitutional proposal is published, it is to be referred to a joint committee of the Senate and the House of Commons, which will hold hearings across the country. But in Quebec City, hearings were already being held by two committees set up by the National Assembly, one to study the implications of Quebec sovereignty, the other to study federal constitutional offers.

By the end of February 1992, the joint committee studying the constitutional paper is obliged to produce a report and, not long afterward, Mr. Clark will have to produce a final federal proposal that will take into account the report of the committee. He will not have much time: Quebec Premier Robert Bourassa faces his own deadlines. Quebec legislation requires that the wording of the question for a provincial referendum on sovereignty be tabled by the end of May; otherwise, a special session of the National Assembly will be called in July. Federal strategy is based on the assumption that Mr. Bourassa does not want to hold a referendum. But if one is to be avoided, he will have to have a federal offer attractive enough for him to sell vigorously to the province.

In calculating the outcome of the constitutional debate, federal strategists have yet to fix on a formula on how to end it, and how to ratify the results. It is increasingly taken for granted that they cannot hope for unanimity, and must build a package that can be ratified by seven provinces representing more than 50 percent of the population.

Will there be a federal-provincial conference; a proposal that is taken to the legislatures separately for ratification; or a Canada-wide referendum? The Beaudoin-Edwards Committee recommended a change to the amending formula — which would, in itself, require unanimous agreement — calling for four regional vetoes — but rejected the idea of a constituent assembly. Federal strategists are still uncertain, and are still looking for a process for what one called the "end game."

The puzzle, in its largest sense, may well remain unresolved by the federal proposal, in the name of public consultation. The challenge to come up with a consensus that addresses Benoît Bouchard's sense of a minimum necessary for a distinct society that makes sense, and at the same time preserves the Canada that Barbara McDougall and Kim Campbell feel they are citizens of, may prove insoluble. The federal Cabinet may be reduced to merely throwing out a series of options for public debate. In that case, the make-or-break points will be even harder to predict, as a weary country wrestles with suspicion, resentment, and conflicting goals.

For the unfortunate reality seems to be that Canadians and Quebecers remain out of sync with each other. Canadians have persistently been a decade or so out of date in their appraisal of Quebec, seeing it as a priest-ridden province when the Quiet Revolution was in full bloom in the mid-sixties, and being convinced that the Parti Québécois government was led by hijackers and terrorists in the mid-seventies. Now there is a tendency to view the current mood in Quebec as if it were a replay of the referendum of 1980.

In fact, it is very different. The referendum *Yes* campaign was idealistic, progressive, social-democratic in reflex — with occasional flashes of xenophobia. The current mood in Quebec, it seems to me, is confident, pragmatic, entrepreneurial, calculating — and, in a strange way, resigned, in a singularly joyless fashion, to a final failure of federalism after a final attempt to make this odd marriage work.

In contrast, the mood in Canada seems uncertain, cynical, neo-protectionist, mercurial — and, in an equally strange way, unprepared to believe that this final attempt might fail, and, with its failure, the country might slide into bitter recrimination and permanent secession.

We have arrived at this state of play after 30 years and four rounds of constitutional negotiations. In Quebec, those four rounds are generally viewed as two ties (Fulton-Favreau and Victoria) a defeat (1981-82) and a humiliation (Meech). In Canada, all four rounds are viewed as a massive concession to Quebec — because they happened at all. In light of those fundamentally contradictory perceptions of our recent past, it is not surprising that it is difficult to be optimistic about a resolution of our constitutional future, as we enter the fourth decade of constitutional preoccupation in Canada — and the bell is ringing for round five.

NOTES

1. Georgette Gagnon and Dan Rath, *Not Without Cause: David Peterson's Fall from Grace* (Toronto: Harper Collins, 1991), p. 176.

2. Ontario, *Official Report of Debates* (Hansard), 19 December 1990, p. 2893.

3. Ontario, *Official Report of Debates* (Hansard), 27 March 1991, p. 276. Author's translation.

4. Ibid.

5. Ibid., p. 278.

6. Susan Delacourt, "Unity Gap Displayed," *Globe and Mail*, 28 August 1991, p. A1.

7. *Globe and Mail*, 10 September 1991

8. Graham Fraser, "Quebec Referendum Opposed," *Globe and Mail*, 8 April 1991, p. A6.

9. Ibid.

10. William Thorsell, "Rae and Manning the Key Players as the Dice Start to Roll Again," *Globe and Mail*, 31 August 1991, p. D6.

11. Mario Fontaine, "L'indépendance ferait fuir 1 anglophone sur 2, mais près du tiers des Anglo-Québécois prévoient déjà qu'ils seront partis d'ici cinq ans," *La Presse*, 27 avril 1991.

12. Canada, Citizens' Forum on Canada's Future (Spicer Forum), *Report to the People and Government of Canada* (Ottawa: Minister of Supply and Services Canada, 1991), p. 51.

13. Canada, *A Preliminary Report of the Royal Commission on Bilingualism and Biculturalism,* (Ottawa: Queen's Printer and Controller of Stationary, 1965) p. 13.

14. Task Force on Canadian Unity, "A Future Together: Observations and Recommendations" (Ottawa: Minister of Supply and Services Canada, 1979), p. 6.

15. Citizens' Forum on Canada's Future, p. 141.

16. Ibid., p. 144.

III

Focus on the Issues

5

Constitutional Change and National Social Programs

Terrance Hunsley

Les Canadiens se posent des questions au sujet des objectifs nationaux sur le plan social, en rapport avec les soins de santé, les retraites, l'éducation et les service sociaux. Ils s'inquiètent et se demandent jusqu'à quel point les modifications apportées à la Constitution ainsi que les clauses éventuelles relatives à la décentralisation, au gouvernement autonome et à la société distincte n'amoindriront pas les critères actuels, et n'affaibliront pas du même coup notre aptitude à répondre aux défis sociaux qui s'annoncent. Toutefois, les objectifs nationaux existants ne sont pas aisés à définir. Assez peu de textes ont explicité jusqu'à présent les droits sociaux des Canadiens. A quels types de problèmes pourrait-on être confronté si l'on procédait à une décentralisation des pouvoirs au pays ou si encore le gouvernement fédéral décidait éventuellement de réduire sa contribution aux programmes sociaux co-financés?

Rappelant d'abord que les programmes sociaux à la disposition des Canadiens sont fondés sur des objectifs nationaux, le présent article souligne que les citoyens canadiens jouissent d'avantages sociaux qui, pour la plupart, sont à la fois comparables et transférables d'un océan à l'autre. Or, un certain jargon administratif a souvent pour effet d'occulter l'existence de ces avantages sociaux. Les droits et les objectifs sociaux s'inscrivent à l'intérieur d'un système global de programmes fédéraux et provinciaux co-financés, ainsi qu'au sein d'une myriade de règlements et d'interprétations juridiques formant, au total, une véritable infrastructure sociale à l'échelle pan-canadienne. C'est précisément cette infrastructure qui est en jeu dans le débat cons-titutionnel, dans la mesure où celle-ci pourrait faire les frais de toute réduction du pouvoir fédéral de dépenser.

Cet article examine le développement de l'infrastructure sociale au pays. Y sont analysés les faits nouveaux — telle la politique actuelle d'Ottawa consistant à retirer unilatéralement ses engagements financiers relatifs aux programmes co-financés — de même que la controverse suscitée par l'éventualité d'une décentralisation à ce chapitre. L'auteur montre que la protection sociale est liée directement à la clause de la constitution touchant la péréquation, tant en ce qui a trait aux transferts fiscaux fédéraux-provinciaux que sur le plan des droits sociaux des individus. Enfin, l'article conclut sur des suggestions susceptibles de bonifier le cadre constitutionnel afin de mieux clarifier les compétences dans le domaine social; il est aussi proposé d'éclaircir et de renforcer les droits sociaux, et de faire en sorte d'assortir responsabilités et pouvoir fiscal en cette matière.

INTRODUCTION

The (Meech Lake) Constitutional Accord and its eventual failure, pushed Canada into a serious constitutional crisis. The national debate that followed has become a test of the country's social solidarity, and its ability to withstand political stress. Superimposed on existing concerns about Canadian competitiveness in the global economy, have been a resurgence of Quebec nationalism, regionalism, and provincial government demands for more power in the federal structure.

Occasionally emerging from the political melee, and indeed not far from the surface at any time, are worries about constitutional responsibilities in social policy, and the implications of change for the structure of social programs. In a sense, the social contract has been framed within the context of the federal structure. The present set of programs form a kind of national infrastructure, which defines in its totality, the social benefits available to Canadians.

This chapter reviews the significance of the national social infrastructure, identifies some of the concerns that need to be addressed, and suggests means to ensure that Canadian social standards are not placed at risk in the redefinition of jurisdictions.

THE CONTEXT

Quebec's "five conditions," which played a major role in the formulation of the Accord, were established originally to allow Quebec to sign, with "honour and enthusiasm," the *Constitution Act, 1982*. They provided for the preservation of a French-speaking society, and for the transfer of governing powers necessary to preserve and advance the cultural identity of that society. As well, they would have increased Quebec's power within the federation itself.[1]

The Accord attempted to provide more or less similar powers to all provinces. However, its failure was often attributed, especially within Quebec, to a rejection of Quebec's desires for a distinct status. This general conclusion is certainly arguable, given that many groups (such as northern Canadians and Natives) opposed the Accord on other grounds; that it was perceived as broad decentralization of the federation; and that the process of formulating and presenting the Accord to the public caused resentment.

Nevertheless, the collapse of the Accord led to the formation of the Bélanger-Campeau Commission.[2] Although mandated to consider the constitutional and political future of Quebec, much of its focus was on the economic implications of a sovereign Quebec.

The Commission did not ignore issues of social programs and human rights. In fact, they were clear in calling for limits on federal social spending, and for the transfer of powers over immigration and training. However, social policy concerns were not central to their report, perhaps because Quebec has already achieved a greater degree of independence in its social policies, than have the other provinces.

The Allaire Report, which was eventually endorsed as representing the position of the Liberal Party of Quebec, was also clear in demanding the transfer of powers and the limitation of the federal role in social programs. It did however, assume a continuing federal role in providing equalization payments to Quebec.[3]

The federally-appointed Spicer Forum concentrated on encouraging people to express their views on Canadianism, and to identify common values. It was an interesting cultural experiment, and appeared to be gaining some degree of interest and credibility as people gradually got over their skepticism about initiatives and appointments of the current government. It touched social policy mainly in relation to policies on multiculturalism, reflecting a basic conservatism and preference to achieve a common identity over the sustenance and support of differences. The Forum also identified strong support for national programs like medicare, as well as an insistence that the federal government should be active in areas of national interest, regardless of jurisdictions. On the other hand, there also appears to be a desire for more direct participation in decisions taken by governments, and this implies a greater degree of decentralization in the administration of programs.[4]

At the same time, many provincial governments have been active in seeking to ensure that whatever powers go to Quebec, will also be given equally to them. Thus the issue of "asymmetrical federalism," which could mean a special status for Quebec, appears unlikely to get much support from government leaders.

The western premiers have gone a step further, suggesting that the federal government vacate the tax room presently occupied to raise revenues for participating in national social programs, and turn these programs completely over to the provinces.

More recently, some of the debate has turned towards consideration of the social contract and implications for social programs if the federation is restructured.

The Ontario Select Committee on Confederation has identified a need to review the application and protection of social benefits and social rights. They raised in their interim report the concerns of many witnesses that "changes in federal-provincial relations should not endanger social programs," and that rights to an adequate standard of living should in some way be enshrined in the Charter of Rights and Freedoms.[5] Such rights would cover social and economic interests, including income, employment and working conditions, health, education and social security. The Committee undertook to explore these suggestions in their further deliberations.

The New Brunswick committee on the future structure of the federation, also investigated the implications of restructuring federal-provincial jurisdictions for national social programs and the concept of national standards. The Committee sponsored a seminar on the topic, reviewing the historical role of national programs, their importance in the maintainance of social standards, and the social, economic, and political implications of change.

The federal New Democratic Party leader has also suggested in a recent statement that social rights will have to be strengthened in a revitalized federation, perhaps by reinforcing the present Charter.

Given these developments, and the dependence of social standards on the federal-provincial structure, it seems appropriate to look at the national infrastructure of social programs and policies, and to consider the implications of various options for change.

DEVELOPMENT AND ROLE OF THE "NATIONAL SOCIAL INFRASTRUCTURE"

The constitutional division of responsibility for social programs has been an important factor in the development of the social infrastructure. The *Constitution Act, 1867*, gave the federal government certain powers to govern, including residual power in areas not clearly designated to the provinces, the power to ensure "peace, order and good government," and an implied general spending power, all of which have been used to justify federal involvement in social programs.

On the other hand, provinces were given responsibility for "local matters," hospitals, charities and charitable institutions, municipal institutions, and property and civil rights, among other matters.[6]

Although at the time, there could have been little anticipation of the social conditions and needs of an industrializing society, this division of responsibility has been interpreted to give the provinces jurisdiction for almost the complete range of social programs. In fact, it was not until well into the present century that the federal government played a significant financial role.

The depression in the 1930s, reinforced by the centralizing of taxing powers at the federal level during World War II, resulted in a subsequent major growth of federal fiscal involvement in social programs. In fact, the development of the Canadian welfare state might be interpreted in hindsight as an exercise in restructuring the federation. We still are, in comparative terms, a decentralized federation. However, the development of social programs both reflected and fuelled a strengthening of the national role.

The temporary taxing powers were consolidated at the federal level, and were complemented by a series of constitutional amendments to allow for an increased federal funding role. Constitutional amendments in 1940, 1951 and 1964 allowed the federal government legislative jurisdiction over unemployment insurance, old age security and concurrent power over pensions. The spending power and the "peace, order and good government" clause, have been used to justify spending on family allowances.[7]

Social programs expanded dramatically in the three decades following the war. The federal ascendancy of the period, especially in fiscal matters, was fuelled by rapid increases in wealth, and by Keynesian economic policies which favoured the construction of national social programs to redistribute income, smooth out the business cycle, and support continuous growth.

An expanded equalization program gave have-not provinces a comparable revenue base from which to develop programs on a reasonably similar basis. On top of this was constructed (federal and provincial) cost-sharing mechanisms, contributory schemes and tax revenue provisions for social programs needed to support a modern industrial state. The result was a combination of federal and cost-shared provincial programs that formed an integrated "web," or social safety net. They included the Old Age Security (OAS) and Guaranteed Income Supplement (GIS) programs, the Family Allowance, Unemployment Insurance, financing for medicare and post-secondary education, the Canada Pension Plan, the Vocational Rehabilitation for Disabled Persons agreements, the Canada Assistance Plan agreements for social assistance and social services, the Occupational Training for Adults Act, and legal aid and social housing programs. Closely related as well were the various regional development efforts. Provinces funded primary and secondary education directly. Social programs grew steadily to the point where, in the mid-eighties, they represented almost 25 percent of the Gross National Product.

Policies which favoured guaranteed access to benefits gradually took over from the previous ethic of the administration of charity. This was encouraged by developments at the United Nations, and eventually at national and provincial levels, of codified human rights. These codes attempted to ensure that disadvantaged individuals and groups within the population were not left powerless in the face of discriminatory actions by private individuals, or the state. They also sought to establish a system of meeting essential needs as a basic guarantee of citizenship, rather than relying entirely on market forces, which always favour the economically strong.

The concept of citizenship had been growing gradually over a long period, with the removal of property qualifications in the nineteenth century, and the extension in the present century of voting rights to women, natives, prisoners, and people with mental disabilities. The meaning of what citizenship entails has also expanded from voting rights to various other entitlements.

Over time, a process of "acquired rights" took place, whereby access to social benefits became more and more a matter of entitlement, and the extent of these entitlements grew. This accumulation of entitlements took place as social programs were more clearly described in legislation, and as governments defined in regulations the benefits available. This latter action was intended in part to limit the amount of discretion exercised by program administrators, and in part to ensure that processes of determining benefits were public, and demonstrably fair.

As social and economic change took place, and the variety of programs was extended, change in one program became ever more likely to have effects on other programs. The need to clearly define entitlements grew. Moreover, in some cases, access to benefits required the exercise of professional or program judgement, and decisions or interpretations of situations or conditions established important precedents which then added to the entitlements. A good example of this is the variety of conditions covered by workers' compensation programs. In recent years, information has accumulated linking certain health conditions to the workplace, and workers' rights to benefits have been extended. In a similar vein, equality provisions of human rights codes or the Charter, have had the effect of extending benefits initially limited to certain categories of persons, to others who shared similar situations. This process of gradually extending rights complemented the tendency of government to respond to new needs by the development of new programs. They were part of what was generally known among social planners as "the incremental process" of building social protection into industrial society.

In the 1980s, strenuous efforts were made by federal and provincial governments to restrain, stop, or reverse, the development of the welfare state. Funding reductions for existing programs, privatization initiatives, and policies of devolution of responsibility, all attempted to limit the financial liability of governments for the social needs that accumulated in response to demographic, social, and economic change. The over-riding political ethic turned from national action to decentralization of social responsibility. The Charter of Rights and Freedoms, which accompanied the repatriation of the constitution in 1982, was a national project that supported the development of national standards. It was, in a sense, counter to the current momentum to constrain the welfare state. Indeed, it has been seen by some as an obstacle in the thrust to decentralize.

During the first few years of its application, the Charter has most often been invoked in court for the protection of individual rights and freedoms, by corporations and persons accused of crime. Disadvantaged individuals and groups have had great difficulty in using the Charter, in part because of lack of resources, and in part because Canadians do not have a tradition of using such an instrument for the protection of either social or collective rights. We do not, for example have the experience of people in the United States in pursuing class-action suits.

Nevertheless, the Charter has in some cases supported groups seeking the extension of social rights. It has the potential to over-ride provincial legislation, and to establish precedents in one province which may then need to be accomodated in others. For this reason, it is usually considered to have a nationalizing influence. It has also, of course, had a direct influence on national programs such as unemployment insurance. Moreover, as the courts appear to be moving towards a fairly broad definition of equality, there may be potential for longer term developments in favour of measuring either opportunity, or outcome, rather than procedure or process, in determining cases of discrimination, especially systemic discrimination.

The *Constitution Act, 1982* also secured and clarified the purpose and status of equalization, both as a financial transfer, and as a national social objective. Section 36 commits both federal and provincial governments to work towards equality of opportunity, to reduce disparities between regions, and to maintain in all provinces, reasonably comparable levels of public services at reasonably comparable levels of taxation. This clause does not appear to be, *prima facia*, justiciable, and there is therefore a lack of consensus as to its long-term effect. However, it stands as a clear expression of national social policy, and a strong articulation of national objectives. To an extent not perhaps fully appreciated, it may also become a base for the extension and protection of social rights, especially if social support programs become subject to challenge under international trade agreements.

In total, the combination of programs, benefits, and legal protections form a social infrastructure which is a vital part of the Canadian way of life. Although it is heavily dependent on bureaucratic, complicated, and often obscure federal-provincial financial arrangements, it has also become part of the Canadian national "psyche," or national identity. While most Canadians would have difficulty defining what it is to be Canadian, many would draw a distinction between U.S. society and our own. We consider ourselves to have a gentler, more peaceful society than the United States, and we attribute much of this to our social programs. This is most evident in the case of medicare, since many Canadians have either experienced the U.S. private health system, or know someone who has. It also explains in part the widespread resistance to the Canada-U.S. Free Trade Agreement, which many critics feel inexorably moves Canadian public policy into lock-step with that of the United States.

STRENGTHS AND WEAKNESSES OF THE NATIONAL INFRASTRUCTURE

The federal-provincial system of policies and programs, with its negotiations, cost-sharing, block-funding, and program-specific agreements, clearly has its strong and weak points. Some of these specific points will be considered in the section to follow. However, it is important first to make a general point that will be reflected as both a positive and negative factor; and that is the tendency for the overall standards of quality of social programs to be established and coordinated in the context of federal-provincial negotiations, working committees, and in the development process of both provincial and federal programs. The standards may not be clearly articulated, but they are reflected in the levels of benefits and conditions attached to them.

For many years, one of the strong points of this system was its bureaucratic nature. Bureaucratic policy analysis is strong in considering broad issues dealing with collectivities. Systematic and incremental development is consistent with large-scale bureaucracies. Although organized labour and other social policy advocates have played strong roles in the evolution of specific policy issues, much of the system of national programs grew in the conjuncture of now-cooperating, now-competing, but always growing, federal and provincial public services.

Because of its great size and diversity, and its small population, Canada has needed a strong government role, especially in matters of national or cross-regional significance. Many social programs such as those that support labour mobility, fall into this category. Because social programs are in essence public services (although they may be delivered by private organizations), their growth was reinforced by the overall expansion of the role of government.

During the years of rapid growth of national social programs, much of the discussion, research, and negotiation was carried out by the line departments which would ultimately become responsible for the administration and delivery of the programs. Because of this, emphasis was often placed on ensuring that they were adequately funded, and that there were provisions for development and growth.

Programs have often had a strong developmental thrust in areas where national standards or objectives have not been clearly identified. For example, the Canada Assistance Plan (CAP)was instrumental in helping provincial governments consolidate and modernize their approach to social assistance and social services. Pre-existing categorical programs serving the blind and disabled, and the unemployed, had often been inexpertly administered, enforced conditions that could vary significantly from community to community, and tended to stigmatize and humiliate the beneficiaries. Under CAP, provinces were given a financial incentive to rationalize and consolidate their programs, to establish a basic condition of financial need as the criterion for access, and to develop high quality administration. In fact, the federal-provincial consultations undertaken to develop CAP are often credited as an important cooperative exercise in national policy development. Definitions of programs and services tended to converge, and a strong, if informal, consensus on future directions for policy emerged.

In the seventies, the business of federal-provincial negotiations began to be taken more seriously by the central agencies of government because of their growing political and fiscal importance. Special departments were established for intergovernmental relations. These organizations have had a mixed track record in their influence, perhaps because their mandate focused on process, rather than the substantive areas of program expertise, or financial planning. In more recent years, federal and provincial finance departments have become more and more dominant in both financial and program negotiations, and the competition for some kind of financial advantage has become fierce.

With the exception of medicare, one would be hard put to find clear national standards in any single piece of federal cost-sharing legislation. In fact, the Canada Assistance Plan (CAP) sets out only a few standards, such as an appeal process for applicants who are refused financial assistance and the prohibiting of provincial residency requirements for eligibility for social assistance. Even these requirements do not apply to social services cost-shared through the Plan. Administrative procedures, sometimes confused with standards, must be followed in order to gain federal cost-sharing. Again in the case of CAP, provinces are required to define in law a level of "need," and to provide programs that meet that need. They are required to submit applicants for assistance to a needs test. But there is no restriction on what the measure of need will be; provinces can set it as high or as low as they wish.

There has been a recent exception to this, in that the federal government has imposed a 5 percent limit for cost-sharing purposes on spending increases in Ontario, British Columbia, and Alberta. The action has been unsuccessfully challenged in the courts on technical grounds — the lack of advance notice — but not on the question of whether such a limit is contrary to CAP's own requirement of establishing and meeting a need.

Yet in total, in the combination of benefits and rights, of negotiations and coordination, of conditions and service definitions, there is clearly an overall national standard-setting process. It is complemented by the clarification and expansion of rights which takes place through judicial interpretations, administrative regulations, and case-specific decisions.

The national standards in place most often do not constitute a standard of a particular service, but rather a cumulative standard of opportunity, of access to public resources, and in total, an overall minimum standard of living. Canadians generally know that they have a right to health care, to education for their children, to protection from starvation and homelessness, to protection from unemployment and work-related injuries, and to protection from at least some forms of discrimination. Moreover, they know that for the most part they can travel throughout Canada and still maintain these rights, even if they vary a bit from province to province.

The national standards are present in the infrastructure, and in a very general way, they reflect the international standards in human rights instruments which Canada has officially ratified. The Universal Declaration of Human Rights, as well as subsequent specific conventions and covenants, spell out the kinds of protection and support that member countries have committed to ensure for their residents. These are not average or minimum standards that establish a lowest common denominator. The standards are relative to the wealth and resources of each country, thereby supporting the idea of equity, and the right to call on a fair share of the resources of the society.

Canada's national programs also form a base from which progress can be measured, and policies judged. For example, there has been slow but constant progress in improving the income position of the elderly. Although never expressed formally, a national objective has existed, and was attained, to have the combination of OAS and GIS for an elderly couple, to be equal to the Statistics Canada Low Income Cut-offs (poverty lines). In fact, this objective originated in earlier collaborative work of Canada and other nations through the International Labour Organization, and was first formulated as a percentage (45 percent) of average industrial wage. Although the poverty-line objective was not attained for singles, the overall level of poverty among the elderly has been significantly reduced.

This achievement is in some contrast to the situation for poor young families, and single parent families. Their minimum living standards are determined by provincial governments, in setting minimum wage and social assistance levels. These measures are set far below the poverty line. The extent and depth of poverty among this population has increased dramatically in recent years.

National programs appear to strengthen both national identity, and public support for social standards. Moreover, the maintenance of national standards helps to achieve other social objectives, such as social equity, and the reduction of regional disparities. The fact that elderly benefits are the same throughout the country, and do not vary by region, narrows the income differentials between areas, since the elderly tend to be over-represented in the poorer sections. Unemployment insurance automatically responds to subsidize the economies of regions and communities in economic difficulty, and the special benefits for areas with higher than average levels of unemployment add a supplementary subsidy to surviving businesses in those areas.

It is significant that documentation prepared for the 1987 conference of first ministers lamented the fact that income security programs had been almost totally responsible for the narrowing of income differentials between the Atlantic provinces and the national average over the past two decades, rather than regional development programs.[8] This finding is important, not only for regional development policy, but also for the design of income security programs. In fact, it suggests the possibility that improved income security programs could make a greater contribution to national objectives. If the federal-provincial financial competition were removed, for example, between unemployment insurance, income support, and training and education (discussed below), these programs could be rationalized to improve the productivity of the lower end of the labour force.

The national infrastructure socializes the costs of market inequities, and of economic development and disruption. The Unemployment Insurance Program and Canada Assistance Plan respond automatically to increased need caused by recession. If a downturn is concentrated in one province or region, these programs automatically make more money available, thus using national fiscal power to assist when that province might not have been able to respond on its own. Similarly, the education system and adult training systems help to finance economic development. In the past, when a high school education was enough to launch a person into a middle-class career, the public education system was also an important equalizing instrument. Now, almost every mid-level occupation requires post-secondary education. With the gradual withdrawal of the federal government from funding post-secondary education, and with high dropout rates of disadvantaged children from high schools, the elite bias of the existing system can be expected to increase.

The national system is important to the improvement and maintenance of living standards; for social investment; and for pursuing principles and objectives of equality and social justice. On the other hand, this kind of infrastructure also has its weaknesses.

National programs are not easily changed to respond to changing needs, and can be inappropriately used. The Unemployment Insurance program for example, has been roundly criticized for its vulnerability to becoming a poorly designed income maintenance program, rather than a temporary income replacement program.

In more recent years, the attachment of social programs to the bureaucratic dimension of government has become a disadvantage. Political opinion has turned against government bureaucracies. Reducing the role of government in the economy has become a rallying cry for several political parties. During the 1980s, the old incrementalist approach of Canadian social policy was swept away in devolutionist and privatizing political strategies.

The national infrastructure is also a source of harmful and inefficient political/financial competition, especially between federal and provincial governments. The interface between Unemployment Insurance and the cost-shared social assistance programs, as one example, is a financial battleground for scores of federal and provincial officials who try and push costs back and forth into each other's area of liability. These struggles take place at taxpayers' expense, but with no net benefit accruing. In fact, they often stand in the way of rationalizing important policy areas. Both the income support field, and the adult training and education field have been "policy victims" of these struggles.

In some cases, as with employment training and counselling, there are overlapping jurisdictions, and duplication of services. Despite the competition, efforts at coordination of programs have been helpful in reducing some of these problems. The federal-provincial agreements on enhancing the employability of welfare recipients, signed during the mid-eighties, appear to have achieved some success in at least managing the areas of overlap.

In a sense, the national infrastructure for social policy is parallel to the national fiscal structure. It delivers the bill where the money is. The superior taxing powers, and broader access to credit when deficits are necessary, as well as being the fiscal agent of equalization, suggest that the federal government spending power is appropriately used in pursuing national social objectives.

On the other hand, this may mean that the whole system can be manipulated by powerful central interests. Recent fiscal decisions made unilaterally by the federal government have substantially altered, and will continue to alter, the existing and emerging infrastructure. Federal withdrawal or limiting of funding for CAP, medicare, post-secondary education, social assistance, social services, social housing, Family Allowances, Old Age Security, and tax-related family benefits, have substantially altered the status quo, in ways which again change the nature of the federation.

The federal government in recent years has sought various ways to pass some of its deficit to provincial governments, and this has caused dramatic shifts in the nature of federal-provincial fiscal arrangements. One such change has already been commented on, being the imposition of a 5 percent limit on spending increases under the Canada Assistance Plan, affecting Ontario, Alberta, and British Columbia. Although these are relatively wealthy provinces, they do have close to half of the country's poor among their populations. Moreover, the freeze is being imposed just at the time that a recession will cause increases in need for assistance. In Ontario, which is feeling severe impacts of the recession and adjustment to free trade, and which had just announced plans to significantly improve benefits for low wage workers, the effect is dramatic.

At the same time, limits on the growth of equalization payments are now biting into provincial revenues in poorer provinces, thus undermining the capacity to deliver comparable levels of public services. Yet the existence of the equalization program has often been advanced by the federal government as a rationale for not providing more generous cost-sharing arrangements with poorer provinces.

Layered on top of these shifts of funding responsibility to provinces, has been an apparent policy to pull federal funds completely out of health care and post-secondary education. This represents perhaps the most substantial change in federal and provincial funding responsibilities in the last 15 years. When in 1977, the federal government shifted from cost-sharing to "block-funding" its contribution to health and post-secondary education, part of the rationale was that these programs had reached a certain maturity in their development. Essentially, they needed to be maintained with some appropriate investment for continuing refinement; thus, the label of "established programs financing."

The agreement reached at the time was for an overall funding level to be established, based on per capita contributions to the provinces. These contributions, in total, represented the block fund, and would be transferred to the provinces with few conditions — essentially the principles of medicare (universality, comprehensiveness, accessibility, portability, and non-profit administration). Provinces had no restrictions on how they spent the money for post-secondary education.

In order to provide for inflation, for increased population demand, and for some improvements, the understanding was for the block fund to grow at the overall level of the economy, as reflected in the GNP. However, instead of paying the money all out in cash, the federal government made part of its contribution by reducing its overall income tax on individuals and corporations, thereby providing an opportunity for the provinces to increase their taxes by an equal amount, and in effect, shifting tax power to the provinces. These "tax points" that were shifted, would then continue to grow each year in value, basically at the rate of the overall growth of the economy.

Although it no longer had control over the value of the tax transfer, the federal government did have control on the total value of the block funds. Therefore, whenever the total commitment was reduced below the growth in the economy the full reduction would come out of the cash transfers. The block fund growth rate was reduced starting in the fiscal year 1983-84, when the Liberal government imposed its "six and five" limits on the amount corresponding to the post-secondary education portion. After the Conservatives took power, the growth rate was again reduced, on the entire fund, to "GNP minus 2" (percent), then frozen for two years and after to be limited to "GNP minus 3."

The overall effect is for federal cash contributions to reach zero in a very short time, since the value of the tax points continues to grow. The exact date at which this happens is difficult to predict, since it will depend on the interaction of factors such as population growth, interprovincial migration affecting population, and changes in the value of tax points that might result from economic growth rates and tax policy changes. Nevertheless, as early as 1995 or 1996 in Quebec, and soon after the end of the present decade in other provinces, (sooner in Quebec because they receive a larger portion of their contribution in tax points) the federal government will be effectively out of the cash funding of these major programs. Thus, a large part of the national infrastructure is being provincialized through fiscal measures, even while people with constitutional responsibilities are talking about the need to consult and involve Canadians in any changes to the constitution.

It is difficult to predict what the national influence will be on social programs when federal money is no longer available. In all likelihood, it will be substantially reduced. Provincial governments no longer look to the federal government for expertise on program-related issues, but concentrate more on interprovincial consultations. Within provinces, arguments about federal requirements, or incentives of federal cost-sharing, already have much less influence on fiscal decision-making.

Unilateral federal withdrawal from social program funding also puts in jeopardy the process that is often referred to as "executive federalism." This is the overall process of federal-provincial negotiation and agreements which bind both orders of government to maintain the standards that exist. As each program is put in place, agreements are made with time frames which may not correspond with the legislative mandate of any particular governing party. Moreover, other programs will be designed, much like the pieces of a jigsaw puzzle, that presume the continuation of existing programs. (Provincial programs for seniors, for example, often use the qualification for the Guaranteed Income Supplement, as a needs test for subsidized services, or even income supplements.) In this way, the commitment to maintain standards, and the translation of these commitments into entitlements, engages federal and provincial governments collectively as well as individually. Federal action to undermine funding standards in specific programs will have the reverse effect of weakening commitments in a broad range of programs.

Nor is it evident that the provinces will maintain the national characteristics of social programs and benefits. Quebec, for example, is already considering the imposition of user fees for the use of hospital emergency wards in "non-emergency" situations. They are also intending to claw back part of the value of health and medical care, through the income tax system. In a similar vein, several provinces have decided to treat the receipt of the Goods and Services (GST) refundable tax credit as income in determining social assistance rates, thus undermining the redistribution objective of that national program. In other cases, provinces have also reduced social assistance to people who receive inflation adjustments in benefits from the Canada Pension Plan.

In summary, there are many strains and have been for some time, on the national social infrastructure. The fiscal economic and social trends underlying these strains have contributed to a malaise not only in how Canadians view their social infrastructure but also in the broader constitutional arrangements. The constitutional debate is partly to deal with these concerns, but is also raising new challenges to social policy.

PROS AND CONS OF CONSTITUTIONAL DECENTRALIZATION

All of the constitutional proposals made to date (Meech Lake, Allaire, Bélanger-Campeau, Western Premiers) have had a common characteristic; they move power away from the federal government. In one way or another, they are decentralizing proposals. So it may be useful to look in a general way at the implications of decentralization.

One of the potential benefits has already been suggested. This is the possibility of rationalizing the income security — labour market — adult education program and policy structure. Revolutionary changes could be possible, and are needed, in this area. The present combination of programs are inadequate from almost any measure: they provide insufficient income for the poor; they produce serious disincentives to be employed, with marginal tax rates running well over one hundred percent; and they are ineffective in increasing the productivity of the labour force. Decentralization could result in federal enabling legislation, national standards, and provincial delivery of an integrated set of programs.

Another potential development in the decentralization process, is for municipalities to gain a much more substantial role in the federation. Canada's economic future may well be built around a number of growing metropolitan regions, with large economic hinterlands. Municipalities have to date been considered simply as creatures of the provinces. However, they will exercise significant clout in the future, and it is appropriate to put some formal social responsibility where economic and political power may be located.

Moreover, it may be that municipalities will come to realize the benefits that could result if they were to take on a role of social advocacy on behalf of their residents. Provincial politicians have done this for years in the federal-provincial arena. The municipal role could be especially effective, since the totality of federal and provincial policies are best measured locally, in the observable quality of life. The involvement of municipal politicians in such current projects as "Healthy Communities" and "Safer Communities," reflects this recognition that local issues are a microcosm of the complete range of public policy. In the increasingly competitive policy environment, local politicians will be asked to represent a broader range of human concerns.

On the other hand, it is important to question whether decentralization of responsibility for social programs would be accompanied by decentralization of accountability for social conditions, and by decentralization of the fiscal capacity necessary to maintain national standards.

The answer to the first part of the question may seem obvious, in that provincial governments are just as accountable to their constituencies as is the federal government. However, the constituencies of social programs are not as organized at the provincial level, especially in smaller provinces, as they are nationally. Moreover, provinces have not in the past been as likely to commit themselves to assuring future resources, as has the federal government. They do not ordinarily index social benefits to inflation, for example. Nor, with the exception of Quebec, are they as likely to codify specific entitlements to social benefits.

The reason for this may be the answer to the second part of the question, in that many provinces do not have the fiscal capacity to ensure a continuing level of benefits, for example, in a recession. Economic development and downturns may hit different regions differentially, and it may be that drawing upon the fiscal strength of the nation is necessary to avoid having the unfortunate become even more the victims of economic change. A related concern is whether the federal government is prepared to vacate substantial areas of "tax room," in order to allow provinces to move in and establish a sufficient base for social programs. The scenario of decentralized expenses without substantially changed taxing powers would be a death sentence for social programs, and especially for national standards.

A similar question arises in relation to the current federal deficit. At present, the federal policy is to pass some of this deficit over to the provinces through funding reductions. This presents the option for provinces to either cut programs and absorb the political backlash, or increase their own deficits. The provinces are more vulnerable on both counts: it is difficult to close hospital beds without a public reaction. Yet they will incur the wrath of other governments, as well as risk having their cost of credit increased, if they incur high deficits. A third option, for both orders of government, is to increase taxes in order to pay down the deficit. A fourth option is to promote full employment through lower interest rates and a devalued dollar, and to allow inflation to ease the burden of debt. With the broadest taxing powers, as well as the fiscal policy levers controlled federally, it would seem that decentralization could undermine these latter possibilities.

Another question has to do with the future of equalization, either as an intergovernmental transfer system, or as a dominant objective of Canadian social policy. Equalization is one of the few objectives that the Constitution obligates both federal and provincial governments to pursue. Yet the financial commitment to this principle rests on a broad national consensus. While Canada was a distinct economic entity with trade flowing east-west, there was a strong economic self-interest underpinning the willingness of richer provinces to have some of their resources redistributed to poorer areas. When dominant trade flows have become north-south, and strong policy influences are emanating from the U.S., Canada as a national entity may depend more on its social solidarity than on shared economic interests. Whether social solidarity will be strong enough to maintain the consensus supporting equalization, is open to question.

There is another issue associated with equalization. The fiscal transfers are calculated to allow poorer provinces to provide comparable public services. But government is becoming a smaller factor in the overall economy, and more and more functions, including a variety of health and social services, are being privatized. Even if a core program of intergovernmental transfers for equalization of public services is maintained, it is questionable whether it will have the needed scope and flexibility to respond to regional differences or fluctuations in social demand (need), or to maintain services in areas where decreasing population results in fewer resources, but higher per capita costs of service and administration. Thus equalization may have a smaller overall impact on reducing regional disparities in a country with a shrinking role of government.

There may be a need to pursue the broad equality (including equalization) objectives through methods other than intergovernmental transfers. This could mean an increased role for transfers to individuals. National income guarantees for children and/or tax credits or vouchers for the purchase of education, child care or health care, could become the format for future federal contributions in a country with program responsibility more clearly established at the provincial level. Such approaches would constitute a significant change in direction for Canadian policy, and would dramatically change the social infrastructure.

Decentralization also raises an issue about the "effectiveness of jurisdiction," or perhaps the limits of sovereignty of a federated country in the context of a globalized economy. It is questionable whether the nation-state in the future will be able to respond to social and economic conditions through traditional social policy mechanisms. All countries are recognizing that the regulation of global trade can only be achieved by passing governing powers "upward," to international bodies.[9] The banking industry, for example, is substantially regulated at the international level. As regional trading blocks become more internally integrated, there will be efforts to harmonize policies over a broad range. Indeed it may be that countries that are unable to adjust their policies to function in the new, more competitive environment may find themselves at a disadvantage internationally, or even unable to maintain their own social policy agenda.

Future configurations of social policy may continue to vary as much as at present. However, all countries will have increasingly to be cognizant of both the impact of policy on international competitiveness, and the potential threats of the global economy to social standards. One option may be to have international social agreements that parallel the trade arrangements. In the meantime though, we could be pushing social responsibility downward, while economic responsibility is moving either outward or upward. The result could be increased vulnerability of social policy to erosion of standards.

An absolutely vital issue in the context of decentralization, is the accountability void that could arise if the nature of the existing social contract is radically changed. Canadians are generally considered to be more pragmatic than ideological in their orientation to policies and programs. The fact that rights and standards have not been clearly articulated has not been a source of great dissatisfaction, except for social advocacy groups. Nevertheless, disengagement and decentralization may well leave many Canadians uncertain as to their rights for benefits and services. Moreover, people who may be in favour of decentralization of administrative responsibility for programs, may nevertheless insist on some form of national guarantees for programs that they consider critical to the national interest.

Decentralization then, should perhaps be accompanied by a decentralization of social accountability, through the extension and strengthening of social rights. It is interesting that the Charter of Rights and Freedoms has been seen as a centralizing influence, in that it has the potential to override provincial administrative authority in determining whether equality rights are being respected by the state. But a strengthened Charter could be an essential element of decentralization if it clarified the right to protection and support in a manner consistent with the resources of the country, principles of social justice, and international standards. It could also be vital in gaining public confidence in a decentralized federation.

Social rights could be protected in an amended Charter, or through the development of a separate social charter which also spelled out the values and principles to be upheld by social policy. In either case, an important objective would be to entrench the rights that Canadians already have in principle. As mentioned earlier, Canadian governments, both federal and provincial, have ratified several United Nations covenants over the years. These lay out clear standards for social programs, and are relative to the overall resources of the society. They include minimum income guarantees, a right to education and training, to health and social services, to equality of treatment and status, and to policies devoted to full employment. Unfortunately these international commitments, while official public policy in Canada, have not had status in domestic law.

THE IMPLICATIONS OF CONSTITUTIONAL OPTIONS

The precise implications of constitutional change would depend on the specific powers that might be decentralized, and on the consequent modifications in federal responsibility. It might be possible, for example, to replace the federal financial influence with a new and clear constitutional role in standard-setting. Alternatively, "executive federalism" might be broadened to "cooperative federalism" by the creation of new national institutions which combine federal and provincial political representation with other social partners such as business, labour and the voluntary sector, in the monitoring of social conditions and the development of proposed standards.

Several options for constitutional change have been enumerated by Herperger and Watts.[10] Among these are some that do not necessarily decentralize per se, but rearrange existing powers. The training and labour market adjustment programs, for example, might be decentralized, while income security could be rationalized and integrated at the federal level. This might be an appropriate move, especially since most of income security costs are currently federal, and most of personal services (social, health, education, etc.) are provincial. Both areas suffer from inefficiencies and internal contradictions. Lars Osberg has suggested that federal responsibility might be extended to guarantee living standards and opportunity for children (as at present it does for seniors), while the provinces take over labour market programs (adult welfare, unemployment insurance, training, etc).[11]

The option of "asymmetrical federalism" (special powers to Quebec for preservation of their culture, or new arrangements with native peoples) does not necessarily raise social policy problems. In fact, Quebec has already undertaken arrangements that differ substantially from other provinces. The Quebec Pension Plan runs in parallel to the Canada Pension Plan. Harmonization has been achieved without tying provincial hands, in that Quebec was first to introduce flexible provisions for age of retirement. They also invest the pension funds in a radically different way than those of the CPP.

Quebec has a higher number of tax points than the other provinces in the Established Programs Financing (EPF) block fund, meaning that the federal withdrawal from funding will take place more quickly there. On the other hand, after the federal transfer reaches zero, Quebec could be in the anomalous situation of being required to make transfers back to the federal government. As well, since part of Quebec's extra tax points were taken as partial payment of federal contributions under the Canada Assistance Plan, it has also had a different arrangement in that area. To date, that difference may be only a surface element, but this could change in the future if the federal limitation of CAP contributions is extended beyond the "have" provinces. Moreover, Quebec has been running its own income tax system, and has a different family allowance system. Quebec has also, even under existing legislation, developed a health and social service delivery system that is unique in its integration. So to a certain extent, asymmetrical federalism already exists in the social policy field.

In the case of native peoples, the issue has centred around self-government, even though this has to date been rather vaguely defined. Courchene has suggested that native peoples be given provincial government status.[12] Again, from a social policy point of view, such an arrangement would not seem to raise special problems, perhaps because the federal Department of Indian and Northern Affairs has, in a sense, been exercising many of the roles of a provincial government already. Presumably, self-government would not preclude harmonization of social rights in line with internationally-respected standards.

If "asymmetry" were carried to the point of sovereignty-association or outright separation of Quebec, then Canada would have another exercise to go through to consider what policies are appropriate in the new rest-of-Canada situation. Half of the population would be in Ontario, and even more of the economic power. This could lead to different approaches in some areas. René Lévesque used to say that English Canada would be happy after Quebec separated since they could then have a more centralized education policy. Much of this, however, would depend on the new economic circumstances that the two new countries would find themselves in.

A confederation-of-regions option would open up the field of social policy to a whole new set of possibilities, probably few of them good if no overriding commitments existed. Presumably each region would seek consensus on what form of social policy it wished to pursue. However, it is likely that any equalization provisions that crossed regions would be minimal. Equalization within regions would be more likely, and this would expose the vulnerability of weaker regions to maintaining social standards in the increasingly competitive economic environment. If such a structure, or a structure of strengthened regional institutions within a federal system, were to evolve, some form of common market would likely be a part. In such case, there would be a need to deal with harmonization of policies, including social policies, in order to avoid a vicious cycle of ever-decreasing social standards.

This is the situation that Europe is trying to avoid in developing the European social charter as part of the overall agreement on the single market. The European Charter on the Fundamental Social Rights of Workers lays out the objectives and principles of social rights in the context of international competition, including protection for overall social standards. The European Commission has adopted a plan of action for implementing the various sections of the Charter, and is currently negotiating the legal framework for the social rights specified within it.

CONCLUSION

A country in the process of economic transformation, in the midst of a constitutional crisis, and busily dismantling the federal-provincial arrangements that have supported the national social infrastructure, needs a firm direction in social policy.

Neither a centralizing nor a decentralizing thrust in itself is appropriate for social policy in the future federation. There are several ways that a workable package of responsibilities could be configured; this chapter has touched on a combination that might warrant consideration. The suggested package of changes includes the following:

Clarifying and giving constitutional status to national social objectives. An expansion of the equalization clause could achieve this, and would engage the responsibility of both orders of government. It is appropriate to clarify these objectives in a manner independent of social programs and benefits themselves, since achieving them involves more than the traditional range of social programs. Achieving health, for example, requires more than just a good health-care system. Economic policies, environment policies, housing and urban development, and many other policy areas are implicated by the objective.

There could be a constitutional recognition of a federal role to promote the achievement of national objectives and national social standards. These are standards of living and social entitlements, rather than administrative or program delivery measures.

Existing rights and entitlements, currently represented by ratified international criteria and covenants (e.g., the Universal Declaration on Human Rights and the U.N. Convention on Economic, Social, and Cultural Rights) could be codified and given legal status in the form of a Canadian Social Charter. Future covenants and conventions could also be given status in domestic law.

A national institution could be established with political representation from federal and provincial governments, and from the social partners — labour, business and the voluntary sector — to monitor and report on social conditions and the implementation of the Social Charter.

With these over-arching instruments in place, it would then seem possible and desirable to *recognize the special status needs of Quebec, and of Native Canadians.* Quebec could develop its own system under a distinct society clause, and with the powers necessary to protect its culture. Native Canadians could be given rights to self-government, perhaps in the form of provincial status as suggested by Tom Courchene.[13] In both instances, the expectation would be that the constitutional social objectives, and the entitlements of the Social Charter, would be respected.

With the exception of income guarantees, *the direction of most social programs would be provincial,* with federal contributions to assist in achieving national objectives and standards. Because of superior taxing powers, and because Canadian families are spread throughout the country, there is a strong rationale for suggesting that the federal government remain responsible for guaranteeing basic incomes for seniors. Children could be added to this responsibility, since they make up the other portion of the traditionally dependent population. Extending the Guaranteed Income Supplement to cover children would provide a strong nationalizing instrument, and would help to offset the growing inequalities currently victimizing young and single-parent families.[14]

This measure could also open the way for a major consolidation and rationalization of adult education and training, temporary income support, and labour market adjustment programs at the provincial level. This is one of the areas of greatest sensitivity in current debates on jurisdictions, and is vital for the viability and competitiveness of the labour force. Removing income support for children from the current provincial social assistance programs would almost completely eliminate the traditional "welfare trap" that haunts Canadian social planners. Low-wage workers cannot support children, and therefore welfare is often the only viable option. Taking children out of the welfare calculation removes a disincentive to be employed, while also supporting incomes of low-wage working families. The possibility to more effectively integrate training and unemployment insurance and to improve labour productivity is significant.

While provinces would have primacy in social services — health, education, training, income support — *the federal government would have a concurrent power to make contributions in all areas for purposes of achieving national standards.* These need not represent cost-sharing of the infrastructure of programs and services, but would support consultation and standards development, service development support in areas of national importance, and measures to ensure interprovincial compatibility and portability of entitlements. Instead of cost-sharing, after reformulating responsibilities as suggested here, there would be a need to rebalance taxing powers in line with the new social responsibilities.

In total, these changes offer a means to improve the functioning of social programs, to transfer social rights from a bureaucratic to a constitutional context, and to enhance the ability of both federal and provincial governments to fulfill their responsibilities. They should provide both a decentralizing, and a nationalizing thrust. Hopefully, they also suggest an acceptable context for Canadians to clearly recognize Quebec as a distinct society, and to respond to the needs of aboriginal peoples.

In the long view, the success of Canadian federalism will probably be measured by our ability to "muddle through," to adjust and adapt our system, and to stretch our understanding of Canadianism. This need not be an insurmountable challenge; the process of constructing the national social infrastructure is itself an example of flexibility and the management of diversity. But the unifying concepts of the future cannot rely on shared cultural backgrounds, or even (as much) on the continuing process of negotiation between two dominant cultures. Nor will economic interdependence provide the glue of national unity. It would appear that social policy will need to be removed from the "residual" category of public policy, and challenged with the task of defining the essential features of a viable Canadian social community.

NOTES

1.   Georges Mathews, *L'Accord: Comment Robert Bourassa fera l'indépendance* (Montréal: Le Jour, 1990).

2.   Quebec, Commission sur l'avenir politique et constitutionnel du Québec, *Commission on the Political and Constitutional Future of Quebec* (Bélanger-Campeau), *Report* (Quebec: Assmeblée, Documents Parlementaires, 1991).

3.   Constitutional Committee of the parti libéral du Québec, *Un Québec libre de ses choix: Rapport du Comité constitutionnel* (Montreal: Quebec Liberal Party, 1991).

4.   Canada, Citizens' Forum on Canada's Future (Spicer Forum), *Report to the People and Government of Canada* (Ottawa: Minister of Supply and Services Canada, 1991).

5.   Ontario, Select Committee on Ontario in Confederation, *Interim Report*, March 1991.

6.   For a more complete discussion of existing constitutional jurisdiction over social policy see Keith Banting, *The Welfare State and Canadian Federalism* (Montreal: McGill-Queen's University Press, 1987).

7.   Ibid., p. 52.

8.   First Ministers' Conference, *Report of the Federal-Provincial Task Force on Regional Development Assessment*, (Ottawa: Minister of Supply and Services Canada, 1987).

9.   Thomas J. Courchene, *Global Competitiveness and the Canadian Federation*, paper prepared for University of Toronto Conference, "Global Competition and Canadian Federalism," 1991.

10. Dwight Herperger and Ronald L. Watts, *Looking Forward, Looking Back: Constitutional Proposals of the Past and their Relevance in the Post-Meech Era* (Montreal: Council for Canadian Unity, 1990).

11. Lars Osberg, "Rights and Responsibilities: Canadian Federalism for the Future," April 1991 (unpublished).

12. Thomas J. Courchene, "How About Giving Natives a Province of Their Own?" in *Globe and Mail*, 18 October 1990.

13. Ibid.

14. Osberg, "Rights and Responsibilities."

6

Conflict and Cooperation on the Environment

Donna Tingley

Le but de cet article est de fournir un survol des relations fédérales-provinciales dans le domaine environnemental. Il est question d'abord de deux cas types qui illustrent la tradition de coopération existant au chapitre de l'environnement entre les deux niveaux de gouvernements. Le premier cas renvoie à la gestion de la "pêche intérieure" pour laquelle les gouvernements ont conclu, de manière informelle, certains arrangements fonctionnels; d'autre part, des ententes formelles entre les gouvernements fédéral et provinciaux furent signées afin de tenir compte de la position des provinces dans la mise en application de la Loi sur les pêches. Le deuxième exemple, soit les "normes en matière d'eau potable", se traduit par un mécanisme de coopération en vertu duquel les normes fédérales entrent en vigueur par l'entremise des législations provinciales.

L'article examine ensuite l'évolution de la Loi canadienne sur la protection de l'environnement (LCPE) de juridiction fédérale, et en particulier la "doctrine de l'équivalence" qui est exposée dans la version finale de la loi. L'auteure soutient que l'inclusion de la notion d'"équivalence" a suscité chez les environnementalistes une nette désillusion envers le gouvernement fédéral, compte tenu de l'engagement officiel d'Ottawa eu égard à la protection de l'environnement.

En conclusion, l'article propose une analyse des décisions judiciaires ayant donné lieu à une interprétation du décret fédéral "sur les lignes directrices visant le processus d'évaluation et d'examen en matière d'environnement"; plus spécifiquement, l'auteure se penche sur le litige qui est apparu à la suite de la construction des barrages Rafferty et Alameda en Saskatchewan.

INTRODUCTION

We are told by constitutional lawyers that "the environment," as we now know it, was not of concern to the drafters of the *Constitution Act, 1867 (BNA Act)*, and consequently, the power to enact legislation in respect to it was not granted exclusively or explicitly to either the federal or provincial level of government.[1] Rather, both levels of government were given powers that have indirectly authorized them to pass environmental laws; for example, "seacoast and inland fisheries" — federal; "local works and undertakings" — provincial; "the criminal law" — federal; and "property and civil rights" — provincial.[2] Pursuant to these powers, all governments in Canada have enacted laws dealing with environmental concerns ranging from wildlife protection[3] to pollution prevention[4] to the allocation of water resources.[5]

One could easily imagine that this situation would have given rise to federal-provincial constitutional squabbles over who had the right to pass environmental laws. Generally speaking, this has not been the case. Until recently, federal-provincial relations in the area of environmental protection have been less than acrimonious. This has been due in part to the notable timidity with which the federal government has approached environmental regulation. The federal government has consistently failed to press the limits of its constitutional authority to pass environmental laws. In the area of environmental protection, the federal government (and indeed the provinces) have occasionally engaged in a form of "jurisdictional buck-passing" — in difficult situations, they have claimed that "it" is the other government's responsibility, thus justifying their own inaction. Even where federal environmental legislation has been enacted the government has demonstrated a lack of interest in enforcing its legislative requirements.[6] Reasons for this may include the high cost of administering national environmental laws; a reluctance on the part of the federal government to interfere with provincial decisions on the management of provincially owned resources; or simply that environmental protection has not been a serious priority for the federal government.

The provinces, in turn, have had close to a free rein to formulate environmental regulatory regimes to deal with local problems and priorities. In most jurisdictions this has included a scheme for assessing the environmental effects of proposed projects as well as limitations on the release of contaminants. Collateral to the legislative requirements, the provinces have developed administrative enforcement and compliance policies which support the overall regime. Thus, the provinces have been virtually unfettered in their ability to tailor their environmental laws to their own needs, and if necessary to shield developments from environmental requirements in the interest of competing social objectives such as local employment.

In short, in the past, the federal and provincial governments have been able to "work things out" constitutionally in the area of environmental protection. The theoretical question of which level of government is responsible for "the environment" has confused students and environmental practitioners; but for government officials who appear comfortable working in the grey area of what is in effect concurrent jurisdiction, any problems have been overcome through cooperative efforts.

Without question, the social milieu in which federal and provincial legislators operate changed at some point during the 1980s. The public became deeply and personally concerned about the environment, and in particular, about the effects of environmental contamination on human health. They conveyed their concerns and expectations to the politicians, and in particular, to the federal government.[7] The response, at both the federal and provincial levels was the introduction of new programs, policies and laws. However, it was the federal government that came under particular pressure to enact tough new enforceable standards in relation to the emission of contaminants which were perceived to have a negative impact on human health. The federal government was uniquely able to establish enforceable national environmental standards; as well, the federal government, whether rightly or wrongly, was seen to be less likely to sacrifice its environmental standards under pressure from resource developers, as had been the case with many provincial governments.

The focal point of the federal government's response to this public concern was the passage in 1988 of the *Canadian Environmental Protection Act* (CEPA). In my view, the evolution of CEPA and its eventual enactment was a milestone in the development of federal-provincial relations on the environmental question. This is not because it altered the relationship between the two levels of government in any significant way, but rather because it focused the attention of all parties on the vexing question "who should have the primary responsibility in Canada for environmental protection?"

Environmentalists, in particular, were extremely disappointed with the efforts of the federal government to pursue strong environmental legislation through CEPA. One consequence of their lack of confidence in the federal government was the many subsequent lawsuits, initiated by environmentalists, that have required the federal government to comply with its own environmental requirements, and in particular with the "Environmental Assessment Review Process Guidelines Order" (EARP). Lawyers in Canadian environmental law organizations had long suspected that a legal challenge to EARP would be successful. It was not until the successful court action initiated by the Canadian Wildlife Federation, however, that the door was opened to environmentalists across Canada to legally challenge local projects. Discouraged by their discussions and exhortations with the federal government, they willingly initiated litigation to force EARP on unwitting provinces and resource developers. This litigation[8] does in fact have the potential to redefine the boundaries of the federal and provincial governments' ability to legislate to protect the environment.

The purpose of this chapter is to provide an overview of federal-provincial relations in the environmental area starting with a description of cooperative mechanisms to protect the environment; the development and passage into law of CEPA; and concluding with the aftermath — the EARP litigation and legislative efforts to clarify federal environmental assessment requirements.

LESSONS IN FEDERAL-PROVINCIAL COOPERATION

It is instructive, at the outset, to illustrate federal-provincial cooperation on the environment with examples. The two examples presented, "fisheries" and "drinking water standards" demonstrate a pragmatic, practical response to two important environmental concerns, the management and protection of Canada's fisheries and the guarantee of a minimum standard of drinking water across the country. Both are achieved within a complex constitutional framework where neither jurisdiction has the exclusive power to legislate.

FISHERIES

The following passage describes the state of constitutional law in Canada with respect to the federal government's power over "seacoast and inland fisheries":

> Under this head of power the federal government is given the exclusive power to enact fishery regulations and restrictions. It may prescribe the manner of fishing and the times and places where one may fish, and it may provide penalties for violation of its enactments. However, the clause does not convey any proprietary rights in relation to the fisheries to the Dominion. These remain with the provinces. Consequently, it has been held that the federal government could not grant exclusive fishing licenses. Marketing aspects of fishing and labour relations have also been held to lie within provincial jurisdiction.[9]

Pursuant to this power, the federal government has enacted the *Fisheries Act* which contains provisions with respect to the protection of the fishery, and to a certain extent, fish habitat.

Although the Act does not regulate the matter of water quality in Canada, this has been an indirect result because of the need to ensure a minimum quality of water that is sufficient to support the fishery. This can lead to a conflict with provisions in provincial acts that *do* directly address the matter of water quality in the province. For example, section 36(3) of the *Fisheries Act* provides as follows:

> (3) Subject to subsection (4), no person shall deposit or permit the deposit of a deleterious substance of any type in water frequented by fish or in any place under any conditions where the deleterious substance or any other deleterious substance that results from the deposit of the deleterious substance may enter any such water.

Subsection (4) of the same section authorizes the federal Cabinet to enact regulations authorizing the deposit of a deleterious substance in specified circumstances and a limited number of authorizing regulations have been passed pursuant to this provision.

The difficulty is that federal authorizations can run head on into provincial legislation regulating water quality. For example, in Alberta, water quality is regulated under the *Clean Water Act*. That Act requires that various specified facilities obtain a permit to construct (s.3) and a license to operate (s.4). Conditions attached to these permits and licences usually limit emissions from the facility into the relevant watercourse. Compliance with the permit or licence operates as a bar to prosecution under the general water pollution provision section in the Act (s.17).[10] It is conceivable that a facility licensed under Alberta's water quality protection legislation could be in contravention of Canada's fisheries management legislative scheme. Not surprisingly, this causes extreme anxiety on the part of provincially licensed facilities who fear a "double jeopardy" scenario.

As a result, a number of mechanisms, both formal and informal, have evolved to coordinate the complex matter of administering the fishery within the federal context. The following is an example of an informal mechanism. For the past several years, the Fish and Wildlife Division in Alberta Forestry, Lands and Wildlife has drafted new inland fishery regulations that are then forwarded to the federal departments of Justice and Fisheries and Oceans for enactment. The draft is reviewed and then the regulations are formally adopted, more or less unchanged, by the federal Cabinet.[11]

A second example arises from the difficult matter of the enforcement of the *Fisheries Act*. The Act is administered and enforced by provincial officials who are appointed as fisheries officers under section 5 of the Act.[12] Enforcement of the federal statute by Alberta Forestry, Lands and Wildlife enables officials to coordinate their efforts with environment officials, such that the licensees under provincial legislation are not charged under the federal act.

This arrangement was formalized by the "Canada-Alberta Accord for the Protection and Enhancement of Environmental Quality" signed on 8 October 1991, for a term of five years.[13] The overall purpose of the Accord was to provide for better coordination between the two governments to solve pollution problems.[14] The Accord deals with such matters as ambient environmental quality criteria and objectives and national baseline pollution control requirements.

Of particular interest are sections 13-14 of the Accord which deal with enforcement.

13.   Canada and the Province agree to appoint officers designated by either government to facilitate inspection for compliance with national effluent and emission standards and guidelines. Appropriate arrangements for inspection of facilities would be determined by specific agreements.

14.   (1) Canada agrees to take enforcement action pursuant to this Accord:

   (a) at federal facilities unless otherwise agreed to under Clause 13, above;
   (b) at the request of the Province; or

 (c) where the Province cannot, or for some reason fails to fulfil its obligations pursuant to this Accord, with respect to matters of federal jurisdiction administered by the Province.

(2) In instances where Canada for some reason fails to take enforcement action under subsection 1, paragraph (a) or (b) with respect to federal requirements, Canada and Alberta may agree that Alberta take action as required on behalf of Canada.

These sections, and the similar sections in agreements with other provinces have come under considerable criticism.[15] Notably, the accords have no legal force in that there is nothing in the *Fisheries Act* that authorizes the minister to delegate enforcement authority through an agreement.[16]

This arrangement also seems to have led some officials within both the federal and provincial levels of government to believe, incorrectly, that responsibility for fisheries management has been *delegated* from the federal government to Alberta. For example, in a letter from a senior official in the federal Department of Fisheries and Oceans, to a noted environmentalist the following conclusion was reached:

...the Department of Fisheries and Oceans does not have any Fisheries and Enforcement and Conservation Officers in Alberta. The responsibility to manage the fisheries resources in Alberta was delegated to the Province of Alberta in 1930 by the Natural Resources Transfer Act. The presence of this Department in Alberta is limited to a small staff responsible for the enforcement of the Fish Inspection Act and Regulations.[17]

In my view, this statement reflects an incorrect conclusion in law, as section 9 of the *Constitution Act, 1930, Alberta Memorandum Agreement,* referred to in the letter, expressly transfers rights of fishing to the province "*subject to* the exercise by the Parliament of Canada of its legislative jurisdiction over sea-waste and inland fisheries." However, the perception that the matter has been delegated is significant, and for many federal and provincial administrators, it is the practical reality.

A second federal-provincial agreement was signed on 9 January 1987; it deals more directly with fisheries management.[18] The purpose of the agreement, according to the accompanying news release, is "to strengthen co-operation between the Canada and Alberta governments regarding fisheries issues." From the province's view, the purpose of the agreement is to "make it clear who does what and when in Alberta's fisheries management."[19]

Of particular interest in regard to the issue at hand is the following recital to the agreement:

WHEREAS in order to facilitate proper management of the fisheries resource, the Parties agree to promote the principles of delegation of responsibility and authority to appropriate administrative levels.

In this regard, the parties, in article II, 2 agreed as follows:

> Subject to constitutional and statutory constraints, administrative responsibilities under the *Fisheries Act*, identified in a subsidiary agreement hereunder, shall be delegated by Canada to Alberta or to such agency or official of Alberta as the subsidiary agreement shall provide.

Subsidiary agreements were to be developed on "assignment of administrative responsibilities from Canada to Alberta" as well as six other matters related more directly to fish management issues.[20]

At the time the agreement was reached, it was Alberta's view that the climate for agreements such as this one was excellent. The federal departments of Justice and Fisheries and Oceans were apparently working on a regulatory package under the *Fisheries Act* that would permit explicit delegation of administrative responsibility to some provincial body.[21] Despite these high expectations, no subsidiary agreements under this agreement have been reached, and in fact, negotiations have not taken place for at least a year.[22]

The federal government has shied away from entering into an agreement on the matter of delegation, primarily because of increased public scrutiny of federal-provincial relations in the fisheries area. This has no doubt come about because of EARP litigation[23] and an increasing recognition on the part of governments that the delegation or even transfer of responsibility from the federal to the provincial level on environmental matters will not occur without public controversy.

In summary, in the area of fisheries management, the federal and provincial governments have devised several cooperative mechanisms to avoid conflict between the federal *Fisheries Act* and the various provincial water quality legislative schemes. In Alberta, both informal working arrangements and more formal federal-provincial agreements have evolved to give the province a substantial role in the development and enforcement of rules and regulations under the *Fisheries Act*. At this time, the formal delegation of fisheries management to a provincial body be a very controversial matter which would be opposed by environmentalists. The existing arrangement permits the province to exert considerable control over the management of the fishery while avoiding the divisive issue of which level of government *should* bear the responsibility for ensuring water quality in the province.

SAFE DRINKING WATER

Although both the federal government and the province of Alberta have legislation dealing with matters of water quality, neither has an act in place dealing with "safe drinking water."[24] This is the case in spite of public concern about the quality of the water coming from their taps[25] — in 1989, 95 percent of

Canadians polled said they were concerned with the quality of drinking water in Canada.[26]

As early as 1982, Canadian environmentalists were recommending that something be done to improve the quality of drinking water in Canada. In particular, the Canadian Environmental Law Association (CELA) and Pollution Probe recommended that safe drinking water legislation be enacted at both the federal and provincial level.[27] The proposal was to have enforceable standards incorporated into federal legislation and then adopted under supplemental provincial legislation which would be administered by provincial environmental authorities.[28] The authors' reasoning was based on the conclusion that existing water quality legislation, which controls water pollution at its source, has not proved to be effective in preventing the continuing degradation of Canada's waterways.[29]

The CELA/Pollution Probe position with regard to the establishment of binding, enforceable federal standards has not been universally accepted. For example, the 1985 *Final Report of the Inquiry on Federal Water Policy* [30] takes a different approach. The highly credible panel, which carried on extensive public consultations across Canada received many submissions on the safety of drinking water.[31] It recommended:

> 10.11   The federal government should take the initiative in establishing minimum quality standards for drinking water throughout Canada by:
>
> i)   seeking the cooperation of the provinces in revising and expanding the existing national drinking water guidelines as a matter of urgency;
>
> ii)   inviting the provinces to participate in designing a model safe drinking water act suitable for adaptation and adoption by each jurisdiction;
>
> iii) passing a safe drinking water act to apply to waters under federal jurisdiction.[32]

The report further recommended that a federal drinking water act should apply to federal facilities.[33] It would appear that the limited role suggested for the federal government is based primarily on a perception that the federal government's power to enact such legislation is limited although other reasons are suggested as well. It is interesting to note, however, that the recommendation is qualified in that it is suggested that, if the proposed strategy does not achieve enforceable minimum standards across the country within a reasonable length of time, more direct federal action should be considered.[34]

Currently, standards for drinking water quality are developed by a federal-provincial committee and published by Health and Welfare Canada. The guidelines are not enforceable and do not have the force of law unless they are formally adopted by the relevant federal, provincial or municipal government. The first "Guidelines for Canadian Drinking Water Quality" were published in

1968, and the most recent, the fourth edition, in 1989. In Alberta, the Guidelines have been reverentially incorporated through the "Clean Water (Municipal Plants) Regulations" section 23, which reads as follows:

> The physical, microbiological, chemical and radiological characteristics of the water in a municipal waster supply shall be maintained to meet the health-related concentration limits as contained in the Department of National Health and Welfare (Canada) publication entitled "Guidelines for Canadian Drinking Water Quality 1978."

Canada's "Green Plan"[35] which was released last year contains commitments regarding safe drinking water quality. The Plan promises to enact, in 1991, a Drinking Water Safety Act which will "give the Minister of National Health and Welfare the power to develop regulations *within federal jurisdiction* establishing drinking water quality objectives that would be mandatory."[36] (emphasis added) In my view, those who expect the Act, which is not yet public, to contain legal standards that will be applicable across the country, will be gravely disappointed. It would be my expectation that the regulations will only be applicable within a narrow reading of "federal jurisdiction" — such as Indian lands, airports and military reserves.

Also of note is Alberta's draft "Environmental Protection and Enhancement Act,"[37] which contains a part on potable water,[38] that is new to Alberta's body of statutory environmental law. Pursuant to section 145(6) of the Bill, the Minister of the Environment is authorized to make regulations "prescribing substances for the purposes of this Part, and providing for the establishment of specified concentrations for these substances in potable water." Until draft regulations are available, it is not possible to know whether the Alberta requirements will differ in any way from the national standards. Presumably, they will be at least as stringent as the federal requirements.

In summary, the matter of "safe drinking water" in Canada is currently regulated through voluntary national standards which are given the force of law through provincial legislation. Although both Alberta and the federal government have made a commitment to pass new safe drinking water legislation, it is likely that they will simply formally confirm the current arrangement. This is the case despite long-standing pressure from environmentalists for federal legislation that would ensure a minimum standard of drinking water across the country.

These case examples, being the regulation of "fisheries" and "drinking water standards" in Canada, illustrate some of the mechanisms developed by the federal government and the provinces to deal with complex environmental concerns. The governments have tended to rely on administrative arrangements that are designed to accommodate the concerns of the two levels of government, thereby avoiding conflict.

These arrangements have been frustrating for environmentalists. First, they are confusing; it is difficult for those outside of government to learn about and come to understand informal constitutional working arrangements. Second, in areas subject to cooperative mechanisms, such as the enforcement of the federal *Fisheries Act*, the result is often inaction. Nonetheless, in spite of calls from environmentalists for clear lines of responsibility, and thus accountability, the tone of cooperation and accommodation prevails.

CEPA OR THE BEGINNING OF DISILLUSIONMENT

When the Bill which is now CEPA was introduced into Parliament in 1987, then federal Environment Minister Tom McMillan claimed that the legislation was "the most progressive in the western hemisphere and it's going to be backed up by a compliance and enforcement schedule that will demonstrate to Canadians this government means business when it's going to take on polluters."[39] The minister admitted several months later that he might have oversold the legislation, but that it was still a good act.[40]

Whether the legislation will effectively regulate toxic substances as intended is a matter for assessment by lawyers and technical specialists in the future. The more interesting question, for the purposes of this chapter, is the federal-provincial negotiations that took place during the development of CEPA, and the reaction of the environmental community to those developments. It was these negotiations in particular that contributed to Canadian environmental organizations' disillusionment with the federal government's claims that it intended to work aggressively to protect the environment.

Public consultation is now a standard part of the development of new federal environmental laws and policies. Consultation usually includes a process where the "stakeholders" are given the opportunity to review and comment on drafts. Stakeholder groups commonly include representatives from environmental and industry groups, as well as others with special interest in the topic at hand. Some consultative processes work well and others are unproductive — nonetheless there is an expectation on the part of environmentalists that "the public" will be given an opportunity to have a say in the development of new environmental laws, regulations and policies.

The evolution of CEPA involved a very public process where several consultative mechanisms were used to obtain the public's views on various drafts of the legislation. In retrospect, these processes, along with the supporting materials, enable us to trace the development of the Act, and the role of the provinces in developing the legislative scheme. But the consultative process adopted by the federal government also left environmentalists, and others, with the expectation that they would have an opportunity to shape the new legislation and to ensure that it indeed constituted strong, national "cradle to grave" regulation of toxic substances. The resulting disillusionment with both the substantive provisions in the Act and the processes used to formulate its provisions may have long lasting implications. The following is a description of the evolution of CEPA; the public consultation processes used to review the Act; and the positions of the various parties on the appropriate role for the provinces in the regulation of toxic substances.

The evolution of CEPA started in 1985 with a multi-stakeholder review of the *Environmental Contaminants Act*.[41] The *Environmental Contaminants Act* came into effect in 1976 and dealt mainly with the manufacture and use of toxic substances in Canada. After working with the Act for several years, three federal interdepartmental working groups reviewed the Act and prepared proposals for amendments. A summary discussion paper,[42] released by Environment Canada in February 1985, outlined proposals for amendments to the *Environmental Contaminants Act*. The report was to serve as a basis for public consultation. It contained three main categories of amendment: new chemicals assessment and control; export notification; and upgrading features.

Federal-provincial matters were not raised as a serious concern in the report. The only recommendation relating to the provinces arose from section 5 of the *Environmental Contaminants Act*. That section required that, before the federal ministers of the Environment and Health and Welfare could make a recommendation that a substance or class of substance be added to the schedule pursuant to the Act, the ministers would, within 15 days, consult with any provinces that would likely be materially affected by any such recommendation. The federal discussion paper recommended that the reference to "15 days" be removed because the time period had proved to be too short.[43] The response from both provincial governments and "public opinion groups" on this issue was that "15 days" be replaced by "within a reasonable period" or "as soon as reasonably practical."[44]

The next stage consisted of the formation of two "multi-stakeholder groups," one to work towards a comprehensive approach to the management of toxic chemicals and the other to work on amendments to the *Environmental Contaminants Act*. It is the latter that is of concern here. This "Environmental Contaminants Act Amendments Consultation Committee" followed the "Niagara process"[45] whereby a group made up of representatives of the two levels of government, industry, environmental organizations and organized labour met over a period of time to consider amendments to the Act. Two representatives from environmental organizations sat on the committee and they in turn consulted with a larger group of environmentalists who represented organizations across Canada.

The results of the consultation were published in a final report.[46] Once again, the provincial role in the legislative scheme did not appear to be an area of controversy. However, an interesting recommendation was included with respect to federal-provincial agreements. It was recommended that a provision in the Act (s.3(8)) which authorizes the federal ministers to enter into agreements with the provinces with respect to the collection of data and the conduct of investigations be extended to permit federal-provincial agreements with respect to *any* section in the Act.[47] An appendix to the report (Appendix 6) lists some of the areas that could be addressed by a federal-provincial agreement with the objective of "[ensuring] that the assessment and control of environmental contaminants would be undertaken in a shared and responsible manner that respects jurisdictional mandates and achieves a high level of environmental protection in a cost effective manner."[48] From this, one can assume that there was a high level of support from all participants for cooperative federal-provincial arrangements in dealing with environmental contaminants.

The *Environmental Contaminants Act* was not amended as had been anticipated; instead, on 18 December 1986, a draft "Environmental Protection Act" was released by the federal government for discussion purposes. Members of the "Environmental Contaminants Act Amendments Consultative Committee" knew that Environment Canada was working on a new, comprehensive environmental protection act, but the committee was not formally consulted on the Bill nor were any nongovernmental organizations involved in its drafting.[49] The reason, according to then Environment Minister, Tom McMillan, was that once he became familiar with his portfolio, the need for more comprehensive environmental legislation became clearer.[50] The recommendations of the committee, became, according to the minister, the core of the draft "Environmental Protection Act."[51]

It was at this stage that environmentalists started to become disenchanted with the process. While they were participating on the "Consultative Committee," reviewing the provisions of one act, Environment Canada was working on drafting a completely different one. Nonetheless, a coalition of ten national environmental organizations wrote to Mr. McMillan on 15 December 1986 outlining their views on what should be in new comprehensive environmental legislation.[52] The provincial role was still not a key issue although there were some environmental lawyers who were concerned that Environment Canada, under direction from Justice Canada, would take a narrow view of the federal government's constitutional responsibility for environmental protection.

Following the introduction of the draft "Environmental Protection Act," an extensive public consultation process ensued. Public information meetings and consultation meetings were held across Canada. More than 260 briefs were received by Environment Canada and nearly 40 bilateral meetings were conducted.[53] The process culminated in a national consultation meeting held in Ottawa on 22-24 March 1987.

In the meantime, environmental organizations and others were prepared to respond to the draft act and to enter into important consultation meetings with the federal government. The matter of federal-provincial relations was not yet a central issue, but it was highlighted by some commentators and participants. For example, an editorial in a widely read environmental digest contained the following comment with respect to the draft act:

> There are too many fundamental flaws [in the act] ... assurances that the inevitable conflicts over federal/provincial environmental jurisdiction can be worked out through the Canadian Council of Resource and Environment Ministers (CCREM) don't generate confidence.[54]

In a letter from a representative of the Canadian Environmental Network concerning the consultation process for the Act, the following concern was identified: "a broad concern is expressed with the closed door consultation process with provincial government officials."[55] Further, in a brief prepared in response to the draft act, the Environmental Law Centre criticized the preamble to the draft "Environmental Protection Act" which contained a statement such that it was "necessary and desirable" for the federal government to act "in cooperation" with provincial governments. The organization argued as follows:

> while the current government may believe it to be desirable to cooperate with provincial and territorial governments in fulfilling its role respecting the protection of the life and health of the people of Canada and the environment, it is certainly not always necessary. ... the more politically popular goal of federal-provincial cooperation should not be granted superior or even equal status over responsibility of either level of government to protect human health, life or the environment.[56]

A background paper prepared for the March 1987, National Consultation Meeting, which contained a synthesis of comments on the draft act, noted that many comments were received on the need for greater clarification of the federal and provincial responsibilities.[57]

The overall response by environmental groups to the draft "Environmental Protection Act" was negative. A press release, endorsed by 42 Canadian environmental organizations, described the Act as unacceptable. They recommended that the *Environmental Contaminants Act* be amended, and that a consultation process be started on a new "Environmental Protection Act." Much of the criticism focused on the consultation process, in particular that many recommendations in the *Environmental Contaminants Act* review were missing from the draft act.[58]

CEPA received first reading in the House of Commons on 26 June 1987 and was unanimously adopted on 5 May 1988. In the interim, the Bill underwent extensive scrutiny by a parliamentary committee. When the Act emerged in its final form, it embraced a new concept called "equivalency," meaning where equivalent provincial regulations exist, federal regulations under CEPA would not apply.

The notion of equivalency arose following federal-provincial discussions early in the CEPA bill stage.[59] The equivalency provisions evolved over the course of the debate,[60] but the final requirements found in section 34(5)-(10) are as follows:

- the federal Cabinet can make an order saying that a regulation passed under the section does not apply in a province where there is a written agreement that the province has provisions:
    - that are "equivalent to the regulation, and
    - that are "similar" to requirements in section 108 and 110 in CEPA respecting the investigation of alleged offences
- all agreements under this section must be made public
- the parties may terminate their agreement on six months notice, after which the federal government may revoke its order
- the federal minister must publish an annual report on the administration of these provisions.

(A similar provision respecting international air pollution is found in section 63 of CEPA)

On its face, the notion of equivalency, as expressed in CEPA is attractive. It allows the federal government to establish minimum standards that will apply across the country. If any province has regulations in force that are at least as stringent as the federal requirements, the provincial requirements will apply. Duplication and conflict between regulatory regimes will be avoided; the expensive costs of enforcement will be borne by the provinces; and a dispute with the provinces opposed to CEPA would be avoided.

However, compelling arguments against the equivalency provisions in CEPA also exist. First, it has been suggested that the equivalency section may undermine the constitutional basis for CEPA. If indeed, the federal enactment of CEPA is based on the "peace, order, and good government" authority — that the extra provincial movement of toxic substances is of national concern — as has been argued, then the fact that the provinces are clearly able to legislate in the area may undermine the federal jurisdictional claim.[61] Second, it has been suggested that equivalency does not reduce or avoid duplication of legislative effort as both federal and provincial regulations must exist in one form or other in order for "equivalency" to arise.[62] Doubt has also been expressed as to whether the federal government would ever jeopardize its relations with a province by terminating an equivalency agreement as provided for in CEPA.

Despite the fact that equivalency was a provincial idea, there is a now a provincial cooling towards the mechanism. There is disagreement between the two levels of government on what is meant by "equivalency" — is it "equivalency of results" as suggested by the provinces or something more specific?

Can there be a requirement that provincial governments have "equivalent" enforcement policies in effect as well?[63]

The inclusion of the equivalency provisions has resulted in considerable controversy and criticism of the federal government. For example, it has been said that equivalency provisions in CEPA:

> effectively and deliberately undermine the federal government's ability to implement a comprehensive nationwide toxics program. Clearly, extensive use of the equivalency provisions can only result in a patchwork of inconsistent regulations and enforcement practices across Canada. Different penalties for essentially the same offenses may be established, and this may result in so-called "pollution havens."[64]

Why, then, was the Bill amended to include equivalency? It has been suggested that the reason was the federal government's conservative legal advice which questioned its authority to enact CEPA.[65] It was, undoubtedly, also the pressure exerted by the provinces who saw CEPA as an incursion into areas traditionally falling within the provincial jurisdiction and threatened to challenge its constitutionality in court. The provinces were undoubtedly also motivated by more practical matters such as administrative efficiency and their ability to respond to local concerns.

In my experience, the last minute inclusion of the equivalency provision in CEPA had a devastating effect on Canadian environmental organizations who had participated in the development of the Act. Many environmentalists had given time and resources, without compensation, to assist the federal government to develop effective legislation applicable to toxic substances. They had participated, in good faith, in the review of the *Environmental Contaminants Act* through to the parliamentary hearings on CEPA. As has been demonstrated above, the issue of provincial involvement in CEPA was not a central issue during the consultation process on the Act and was not addressed extensively by the environmental groups. In effect, "equivalency" undermined the efforts of these groups.

The development of the equivalency mechanism at the last moment, in behind-closed-door meetings with the provinces, has also undermined the credibility of Environment Canada. Whether the equivalency provisions will, in fact, weaken CEPA is not the central concern of this chapter. What the changes in the Act showed to environmentalists, was that the federal government was willing to demonstrably soften its own legislation, the "flag ship" of its environmental policy, in order to avoid a dispute with the provinces. In my view, this breakdown will have long-lasting implications.

THE EARP LITIGATION

Despite the fanfare associated with the passage of CEPA and other new environmental legislation, it is likely that the real environmental law story of the 1980s will be the "EARP litigation," that is, the legal efforts by environmentalists to force the federal government to apply its "Environmental Assessment and Review Process Guidelines Order" (EARP).

In order to understand the litigation, it is necessary to briefly review EARP. The EARP "Guidelines Order" contains the rules and procedures for the federal government's environmental impact assessment process. The process is essentially one of self-assessment where an "initiating department" screens upcoming projects to ascertain their potential environmental impact. Most assessments do not proceed beyond this point. However, if any "initiating department" determines that there are potentially adverse environmental effects that are either unknown or important, or if there is significant public concern about the project, the Minister of the Environment will appoint a panel to review the project.

If a project proceeds to the panel review stage, the proponent will prepare an environmental impact statement for review. The review panel will then hold public meetings which are fairly informal and which enable members of the public to state their views on the environmental impact of the proposed project. The final report prepared by the review panel is presented to the federal Minister of the Environment and the minister responsible for the initiating department. The review panel makes recommendations about the proposed project; it does not have any formal decision-making authority.

Controversy about the EARP Guidelines Order has centred on the question of the applicability of the federal assessment process — does it apply to projects that are primarily under the constitutional authority of the provinces? Section 6 of the EARP Guidelines Order states that the EARP process applies to any proposal:

(a) that is to be undertaken directly by an initiating department;
(b) that may have an environmental effect on an area of federal responsibility;
(c) for which the Government of Canada makes a financial commitment; or
(d) that is located on lands, including the offshore, that are administered by the Government of Canada.

Clauses (a), (c) and (d) are straightforward as they clearly invoke matters that come under the purview of the federal government's authority: projects undertaken directly by a federal authority, using federal money or on federal lands.

Clause (b) of section 6 has proved to be much more problematic, particularly when one considers the definition of "proposal" in section 1 of the Guidelines

Order which is "any initiative, undertaking or activity for which the government of Canada has a decision making responsibility." In order for a proposed project to act as a trigger for section 6(c) of the Guidelines Order there must be both a federal decision-making responsibility *and* an environmental effect on an area of federal responsibility.

One might wonder why it took so long — from 1984 to 1987 — for a serious issue to arise as to whether the EARP Guidelines Order applies to provincial projects. Did the federal government, or the Federal Environmental Assessment Review Office (FEARO), which administers EARP, not insist that its process apply to projects meeting the mandatory criteria in the Guidelines Order? The answer is that EARP did not apply to provincial projects mainly because the Guidelines Order was not interpreted by federal officials as binding law. Rather, it was perceived as a voluntary code of practice that was intended primarily to apply to federal departments of government. It was never meant to be a mandatory process that would be applied to all projects that might technically fall within its purview.

In fact, the federal government went so far as to enter into an agreement with the province of Alberta formalizing its cooperative efforts in the area of environmental impact assessments. The agreement,[66] which was reached on 15 May 1986, provided that the jurisdiction that had the prime constitutional responsibility for approval of a development would apply its environmental assessment procedures. Further, it was agreed that the interests and concerns of the other party would be included and addressed in the environmental impact assessment procedures. The agreement facilitated good communication between the governments, but resulted in very few federal assessments in Alberta.[67]

As noted earlier, the EARP process, when invoked, rarely results in a public hearing, and when a review panel is appointed, it is restricted to making recommendations to the relevant ministers. One may reasonably ask: What is the attraction of the EARP process to Canadian environmentalists? What could it possibly offer them? In my view, the attraction of the process is that it offers the potential of a full public hearing before an independent panel appointed by the federal government. In instances where a provincial government has been hasty in authorizing, or indeed undertaking, a project with potentially harmful effects on the environment, EARP may provide the only hope for a full independent public review of the project.

An EARP hearing also offers environmentalists (and others) the opportunity to present their case to the public in an open hearing. In many instances, the chance of altering the course of events may be slight, but at the very least, the parties will be forced to present their side of the issue and subject their reasoning to public scrutiny.

Lastly, there is no doubt that the EARP process can be used as a delaying tactic by environmentalists. Many developers involved in the exploitation of natural resources operate in a volatile market. The delay caused by an unexpected hearing process can change the overall economics of the project and lead to cancellation.

The most important in the series of EARP cases before Canadian courts was the first: the case of *Canadian Wildlife Federation et al. v Minister of the Environment*.[68] In that case, the applicant, a large, national environmental law organization, asked the Federal Court of Canada, Trial Division, to quash a licence already granted to the builders of the Rafferty and Alameda dams in Saskatchewan under the *International River Improvements Act* and to order the federal Minister of the Environment to comply with the EARP Guidelines Order in respect to the project. The applicants were awarded both orders.

In reaching this conclusion, the court had to first decide whether the EARP Guidelines Order was more than a simple description of government policy. It made its decision on the basis of statutory interpretation; pursuant to the *Interpretation Act* a "regulation" includes an "order" established by or under the authority of the Governor in Council and further, the Minister of the Environment has the authority to establish guidelines by order in respect to preservation and enhancement of environmental quality, with the approval of the Governor in Council. Because these requirements were met, the EARP Guidelines Order was found to create rights enforceable by mandamus which is a court order requiring an official to perform a particular act. The court also came to the somewhat easier conclusion that issuance of a licence under the *International River Improvements Act* constitutes a "decision making responsibility" and that the Saskatchewan dams would have an environmental effect on several areas of federal responsibility. This decision was affirmed in a brief decision from the Federal Court of Canada, Appeal Decision.[69]

Reaction in Saskatchewan to the decision of the Trial Division was swift and negative. Deputy Premier Eric Berntson said that the Canadian Wildlife Federation was "fiddling with the very future of this province."[70] Premier Grant Devine said that a lot was at stake — "thousands of jobs, people's lives."[71] Nevertheless, the province agreed to stop work on the dam project until the order was dealt with.[72] For the federal government's part, federal Environment Minister Lucien Bouchard ordered his officials to undertake a complete assessment of the impact of the Rafferty-Alameda dams on the United States, Manitoba, fish, migratory birds and federal lands.[73]

The two-year period since the original court decisions on the Rafferty and Alameda dams have seen a complex series of moves and countermoves by the province of Saskatchewan, the federal government and environmental organizations. The Saskatchewan government is still determined to complete the dams, and the federal government is showing increasing insistence that its

EARP process be applied to the project. The following is a brief chronology of the continuing story of the Rafferty and Alameda dams.

The result of the Environment Canada project review, ordered by Mr. Bouchard, was that more information was required about the project's impact on fish, birds, plants and water in and around the Souris River. In June 1989, Environment Canada sponsored a series of forums in Saskatchewan, Manitoba and North Dakota to examine the environmental impact of the projects. The meetings had a serious flaw in that they were not a part of the prescribed environmental assessment process contained in the EARP Guidelines Order. This should have been obvious.

On 31 August 1989, Mr. Bouchard released his Department's Initial Environmental Assessment of the project. At the same time he reissued a licence for the Rafferty and Alameda dams under the *International River Improvements Act* subject to conditions. Not surprising, this decision was the subject of further litigation before the Federal Court of Canada.

This time, the Canadian Wildlife Federation, with others, asked the court to quash the licence on the basis that the Minister of the Environment had not yet complied with the specific requirements of the EARP Guidelines Order. The court agreed,[74] and in a fairly unusual decision ordered the federal minister to appoint a review panel by 30 January 1990 to assess the environmental impacts of the project. If the Order was not complied with, the licence issued under the *International River Improvements Act* would be quashed. The review panel was duly appointed as required by Mr. Bouchard on 30 January 1990. The Saskatchewan government agreed to halt construction on the project and in return the federal government agreed to pay Saskatchewan $1 million dollars per month to a maximum of $10 million to offset the costs of delays incurred by the stoppage in work. The two governments were accused of making "secret deals" and the provincial NDP called for an inquiry.[75]

Tension increased when construction on the project recommenced in October 1990. The panel appointed to review the project resigned in protest and the new Environment Minister, Robert deCotret, suspended payments to Saskatchewan under the January Agreement. Confusion reigned when Premier Devine of Saskatchewan insisted that he and Mr. deCotret had agreed at a meeting in September 1990 that the project could go ahead. This was denied by Mr. deCotret. Editorial writers suggested that Mr. Devine's actions could only be explained by an expected provincial election and his low standing in the opinion polls; a disagreement with the federal government might divert attention from more local problems.[76]

After receiving considerable pressure to take action to halt construction on the project, Mr. deCotret announced his intention to seek an injunction against Saskatchewan. In the meantime, Saskatchewan initiated a legal action against Mr. deCotret claiming $10 million in damages for a breach of the agreement where he allegedly consented to the completion of the dams.[77] By 23 October 1990, the federal government made application in Saskatchewan for a declaration, damages and mandamus. An application for a temporary injunction was denied on a number of technical grounds based on the law of injunctions.[78] However, one matter was raised in the case which is of interest here, namely the question of the enforceability of the January 1990, federal-provincial agreement. The court concluded that because the agreement did not receive the approval of the Governor in Council as contemplated by section 7 of the *Department of the Environment Act*, the agreement was unenforceable.[79] This decision was appealed unsuccessfully by the federal government.

The last important legal action arising from the construction of the Rafferty and Alameda dams is the case of *Edelbert Tetzlaff and Harold Tetzlaff v. Minister of the Environment and Saskatchewan Water Corporation*[80] which was an appeal of the decision of Mr. Justice Muldoon in *Canadian Wildlife Federation Inc. et al. v. Minister of the Environment.*[81] The Saskatchewan Water Corporation also cross appealed the original decision. The Tetzlaffs argued that Mr. Justice Muldoon did not go far enough and that he should have quashed the federal licence issued in order to allow the EARP review panel to conduct its review. The Saskatchewan Water Corporation argued that the court had gone too far and that the order should be set aside.

The Federal Court of Appeal upheld the decision of the Trial Division. Reading the EARP Guidelines Order strictly, the court found that there was no requirement that the issuance of the licence be delayed until the EARP panel review had been completed. The appeal of the Saskatchewan Water Corporation was also dismissed. Following the decision, the Souris River Basin Authority, who is the builder of the dams, announced that it would expropriate the Tetzlaff's farm for the Alameda dam. Shortly after that, in February 1991, a new EARP review panel was appointed to review the impact of the project in spite of the fact that the Rafferty dam is now virtually completed and work has started on the Alameda dam.

The litigation arising from the Rafferty and Alameda dams, and particularly the decision in *Canadian Wildlife Federation et al. v. Minister of the Environment*[82] spawned environmental actions across Canada. To date, 38 court actions have been initiated with respect to the EARP Guidelines Order.[83] Some, such as *Save The Buckley Society et al. v. Minister of the Environment and Minister of Fisheries and Oceans et al.*[84] have been able to successfully invoke the application of the EARP Guidelines Order and others have not.[85] All of the EARP cases have been controversial, as environmentalists have attempted to legally force the federal government to impose its assessment process on projects that otherwise would have been completed without a federal environmental assessment. The application of EARP to the Oldman dam in southern Alberta has resulted in an especially loud outcry from the province of Alberta, who despite being the proponent of the project, is refusing to participate in the panel hearing process.[86] The Oldman EARP cases [87] have been appealed to the Supreme Court of Canada; the decision, which is expected in the fall of 1991, may finally set the limits on the federal government's authority to conduct environmental assessments on projects falling primarily under the jurisdiction of the provinces.

The confusion caused by the EARP litigation has unquestionably created uncertainty in the business community. Resource developers who have received provincial environmental approvals can never be assured that they will not become a party to litigation requiring them to participate in an EARP review. Pressure has been exerted on all levels of government to bring certainty to the law respecting environmental assessment.

The federal government has responded by preparing new environmental assessment legislation which will replace the EARP Guidelines Order. Bill C-13, the "Canadian Environmental Assessment Act," is now before the House of Commons and only requires clause-by-clause review on third reading before it is passed.[88] The Bill constitutes a comprehensive, legislated federal environmental assessment process. Of interest is section 5 which prescribes the projects that are subject to the process. A federal assessment is required where a federal authority:

- is the proponent and makes a commitment to carry out the project (s.5(a)).
- provides financial assistant to the proponent, except for tax relief unless that tax relief is provided specifically to enable the project to go ahead (s.5(b)).
- has the administration of federal lands and disposes of the lands for the purpose of enabling the project to be carried out (s.5(c)).
- issues a permit, licence or approval to enable the project to be carried out if the statutory provision is "prescribed" pursuant to section 55 (1)(g) (s.5(d)).

Subsection (d) is notable. Rather than using the "decision-making" trigger as was the case in the sections 6(b) and 1 of the EARP Guidelines Order, regulations will be passed by the Governor in Council pursuant to section 55(1)(g) of the new act listing the approval processes that will invoke the federal assessment process. In June 1991, a draft list of regulatory authorities that will trigger the federal assessment process was released for public comment.[89] The draft lists 182 specific statutory provisions in 43 federal statutes and would appear to constitute a fairly comprehensive listing of environmental regulatory processes.

Bill C-13 also contains provisions authorizing joint panel reviews with provinces and others. According to section 37(2), where a referral to a review panel is required or permitted and a province "has a responsibility or an authority to conduct an assessment of the environmental effects of the project or any part of it, the minister may establish a review panel jointly with that jurisdiction." The minister cannot establish a joint review panel unless certain conditions listed in section 38 are met.

The provinces and territories, with the exception of Quebec, jointly made a presentation to the Legislative Committee studying the Bill proposing amendments.[90] Their presentation did not comment on the triggers for the assessment; most comments related to the subject of joint reviews. Interestingly, the provinces proposed a new equivalency section which is exactly analogous to the equivalency provisions in CEPA. In short, it provides that where a province has in place provisions that are equivalent or comparable to the federal Act, the parties would agree that the conduct of an environmental impact assessment or a class of environmental impact assessments would be transferred to the province.

The federal reaction to the provinces' proposal of an environmental assessment "equivalency provision" has not been positive. Federal Environmental Minister Jean Charest has responded as follows:

> By the time a project gets to the panel review stage, it has been confirmed as a major project with significant environmental concerns and significant national interest. In such cases, I believe that a joint panel is in the best interests of the public, the proponent, both orders of government and the environment.[91]

However, Bill C-13 has not been enacted into law, and we cannot be certain whether "equivalency" will form part of the Act until it is finally passed by Parliament.

In summary, the EARP litigation described in this chapter has had a significant effect on the state of federal-provincial relations in the environmental area. Obviously, the court cases have required the federal government to impose its environmental assessment process on projects that otherwise would have been subject to a provincial assessment only. As well, the cases have exposed, and invited public scrutiny of the informal processes used by the governments to sort out their respective roles in environmental impact assessment. Lastly, the cases have directly raised the normative question: where a proposed development has both federal and provincial aspects, which government should conduct the environmental assessment?

CONCLUSION

Until recently, the federal government and the provinces have not disputed the question of who has the constitutional jurisdiction to legislate in relation to the environment. As illustrated in this chapter, the two levels of government have developed cooperative mechanisms that have enabled them to operate in an area of concurrent jurisdiction with little conflict. The regulation of complex technical matters such as "the protection of the fishery" and "safe drinking water," where both the federal and provincial governments have some authority to legislate, has been affected through such arrangements as federal-provincial agreements; federal-provincial working groups on standards; and the delegation of administration to the provinces.

The tradition of cooperation and the infrastructure to support it continues to operate within environment departments across Canada to this day. An objective observer might even conclude that this arrangement has been in the best interests of the environment.

This comfortable working relationship has been challenged by three events: one, the rise of public concern about the environment in the 1980s and the public's insistence that the federal government adopt a strong stance in protecting the environment; the disillusionment of environmental organizations with the federal government, as a result of the manner in which CEPA was developed; and the subsequent court actions, initiated by environmentalists, to force the federal government to apply its environmental assessment process to developments that previously had been regulated exclusively by the provinces. Each of these events has put pressure on the federal government to pass new environmental laws and to take enforcement actions under new and existing statutes. This could not be done, however, without intruding into areas traditionally dealt with either exclusively by or in cooperation with the provinces.

The federal government initially responded to public concerns about the environment by boldly announcing its intention to pass a strong new environmental law that would regulate toxic substances from "cradle to grave." It embraced environmental organizations and engaged them in a discussion about what the legislation should contain. However, at the end of the day, the federal government recanted and adopted an approach that would formally acknowledge the role traditionally played by the provinces in the regulation of toxic substances. This was in response to provincial insistence that the federal government not intrude in areas historically regulated by them; likely, there was also a realization by the federal government of the costs of administering and enforcing CEPA without the assistance of the provinces.

The "wild card" in the process was the environmental organizations who still believed that the federal government had a key part to play in protecting Canada's environment. When the Canadian Wildlife Federation opened the door on a legal mechanism to force the federal government to undertake environmental assessments of provincial projects, environmental organizations across the country followed with their own court actions. The provinces objected, but it was beyond the control of the federal government to put a stop to the court challenges. The only recourse for the federal government, and the one that it has adopted, was to draft new environmental assessment legislation which would bring certainty to the situation and would be drafted in such a way as to prevent court challenges.

An equivalency provision for the "Canadian Environmental Assessment Act" has been openly proposed by the provinces and resisted by the federal government. The federal government's position on equivalency is likely to persist. Although the provinces and industry would unquestionably prefer a regime that would permit the substitution of a provincial environmental assessment for a federal one, joint federal-provincial reviews already provided for in the Act may offer many of the same advantages. The federal government is then able to openly reject the provincial proposal while sacrificing little in terms of relations with the provinces. The clear intention is to avoid the controversy that followed the inclusion of the equivalency provisions in CEPA.

What does this say for federal-provincial relations in the future? On the one hand, it may be that, as a practical reality, the provinces must continue to play the major role in enacting, administering and enforcing environmental laws in Canada. On the other, environmentalists have viewed the cooperative mechanisms that have evolved in this area as a direct cause of the failure of governments to protect the environment. It seems the only possible solution is to increase public confidence in the federal-provincial negotiation process. In my view, increased openness and public involvement in federal-provincial processes is the only way that cooperative mechanisms will become more credible.

The question which naturally follows pertains to the consequences if federal powers over the environment were to be transferred to the provinces. Such a transfer would, in my view, be met with a very negative response from environmental organizations and others as there is still broad support for a federal government that ensures that a minimum standard of environmental quality is met across the country.

NOTES

The author wishes to express her thanks to Shelley Ross and Michelle Spencer who provided invaluable research assistance.

1. A. Lucas, "Natural Resource and Environmental Management: A Jurisdictional Primer," in D. Tingley (ed.), *Environmental Protection and the Canadian Constitution* (Alberta: Environmental Law Centre, 1987), p. 31.

2. For a complete list of the heads of power which pertain to the environment, see Lucas, "Natural Resource and Environmental Management," pp. 32-3.

3. See for example, Alberta *Wildlife Act*, S.A. 1984, c. W-9.1.

4. See for example, Alberta *Clean Air Act*, R.S.A. 1980, c. C-12; Alberta *Clean Water Act*, R.S.A. 1980, c. C-13.

5. See for example, Alberta *Water Resources Act*, R.S.A. 1980, c. W-5.

6. See for example, the *Fisheries Act*, R.S.C. 1985, c. F-14, discussed infra.

7.   For an interesting analysis of the polling data on environmental issues, see K. Neuman, "Public Opinion on the Environment: Trends and Implications for Law and Public Policy in the 1990's" in D. Tingley (ed.), *Into the Future: Environmental Law and Policy for the 1990's* (Alberta: Environmental Law Centre, 1990), p. 3.

8.   Starting with *Canadian Wildlife Federation Inc. et al. v. Minister of the Environment* (1989), 3 C.E.L.R. (N.S.) 288 (F.C.T.D.).

9.   R. Franson and A. Lucas, *Canadian Environmental Law*, vol. 1 (Toronto: Butterworths, 1976), p. 257.

10. Interestingly, however, compliance may not shield a licensee or permittee from a claim by a riparian of reduced water quality. For a discussion of this issue, see E. Swanson and E. Hughes, *The Price of Pollution: Environmental Litigation in Canada* (Alberta: Environmental Law Centre, 1990), pp. 47-9.

11. T. Mill, "Intergovernmental Administrative Coordination and Environmental Accords," in Tingley, *Environmental Protection*, pp. 80-1. Also personal communication, T. Mill, Director, Fisheries Management, Alberta Forestry, Lands and Wildlife, (19 June 1991).

12. Personal communication, T. Mill.

13. The original agreement was extended for a second five year period starting 8 October 1982 by agreement between the parties.

14. "Canada-Alberta Accord for the Protection and Enhancement of Environmental Quality," section 2.

15. See L. Giroux, "Delegation of Administration," in Tingley, *Environmental Protection*, p. 84, n. 29.

16. Ibid., p. 87.

17. Correspondence, Paul Sutherland, Director General, Central and Arctic Region, Fisheries and Oceans to Dr. Martha Kostuch, Vice-President, Friends of the Oldman River, 26 September 1988.

18. "Canada-Alberta Fisheries Agreement."

19. Mill, "Intergovernmental Administrative Coordination," p. 81.

20. These are fish habitat management; aquaculture and fish health; commercial fisheries development; fish inspection; and small craft harbours.

21. Mill, "Intergovernmental Administrative Coordination," p. 82.

22. Mill, personal communication.

23. *Canadian Wildlife Federation Inc. et al. v. Minister of the Environment.*

24. Although both have proposals to do the same, discussed, infra.

25. See for example, *Maclean's* cover, "Danger in the Water," 15 January 1990.

26. M. Nichols and H. Jensen, "Danger in the Water," *Maclean's*, pp. 30-1.

27. T. Vigod and A. Wordsworth, "Water Fit to Drink? The Need for a Safe Drinking Water Act in Canada." Presented to the NDP Environment Task Force on behalf of the Canadian Environmental Law Association and Pollution Probe, February 1982.

28. Ibid., pp. 3-4.

29. Vigod and Wordsworth, "Water Fit to Drink?"

30. Canada, *Final Report: Inquiry on Federal Water Policy: Currents of Change* (Chair: P. Pearce) (Ottawa, September 1985).

31. Ibid., p. 107.

32. Ibid., p. 108.

33. Ibid.

34. Ibid.

35. Canada, *Canada's Green Plan for a Healthy Environment* (Canada: Minister of Supply and Services, 1990).

36. Ibid., p. 35.

37. Alberta, Bill 53, *Environmental Protection and Enhancement Act*, 3rd Session, 22 Legislature, 1991.

38. Ibid., Part 7.

39. "Environment act clears Commons" the *Ottawa Citizen*, 6 May 1988, A 12.

40. Ibid.

41. R.S.C. 1985, c.E-12. (repealed R.S. 1985, c.16 (4th Supp.), s.147)

42. Canada, *Discussion Paper: Proposal to Amend the Environmental Contaminants Act* (Ottawa: Environment Canada, February 1985).

43. Ibid., p. 9.

44. Published by the Commercial Chemicals Branch, Environment Canada, 10 September 1985, pp. 27-8.

45. See The Niagara Institute, *The Environment, Jobs and the Economy—Building a Partnership: Final Project Report* (Ontario: The Niagara Institute, August 1985).

46. Canada, *Final Report of the Environmental Contaminants Act Amendments Consultative Committee* (Ottawa: Minister of the Environment and Minister of National Health and Welfare, October 1986).

47. Ibid., p. 48.

48. Ibid., p. 6-1.

49. R. Lindgren, "Toxic Substances in Canada: The Regulatory Role of the Federal Government" in Tingley, *Environmental Protection*, p. 38.

50. Honourable Tom McMillan, "Notes for an Address to the National Consultation Meeting on the Draft Environmental Protection Act," Ottawa, 23 March 1987, p. 3.

51. Ibid., p. 2.

52. Correspondence, Toby Vigod, Canadian Environmental Law Association and ten others to Honourable Tom McMillan, Minister of the Environment, 15 December 1986.

53. McMillan, "Notes for an Address," p. 6.

54. W. Glenn, "Editorial: The honeymoon is over for McMillan's dream Environmental Protection Act," *Eco/Log Week*, 6 March 1987, 2.

55. Correspondence, Laurie Henderson, Chairperson, National Steering Committee, Canadian Environmental Network to Honourable Tom McMillan, Minister of the Environment, 18 March 1987.

56. "The Environmental Protection Act: Comments and Recommended Amendments," (Alberta: Environmental Law Centre, March 1987) 7.

57. Canada, "A synthesis of public comment received as of March 13, 1987." Background paper for the Workshops on the EPA Policy Preamble, prepared for: National Consultation Meeting on the Draft Environmental Protection Act, 22, 23, 24 March 1987.

58. "Environmentalists tell feds to scrap Environmental Protection Bill, amend Toxics Act," press statement, 23 March 1987.

59. A. Lucas, "Jurisdictional Disputes: Is 'Equivalency' A Workable Solution?" in Tingley, *Into the Future*, p. 32.

60. For a detailed review of the development of the equivalency provisions, see Lucas, ibid.

61. See ibid., pp. 29-30.

62. This argument was raised in the Environmental Law Centre's submission to the Parliamentary Committee on Bill C-74: Canadian Environmental Protection Act, 10 December 1987.

63. See Lucas, "Jurisdictional Disputes," p. 32.

64. Lindgren, "Toxic Substances in Canada," p. 41.

65. Ibid.

66. "Agreement Concerning Environmental Impact Assessments of Projects in Alberta with Implications for Canada and Alberta."

67. The agreement was not renewed by the parties at the end of its three-year term.

68. (1989), 3 C.E.L.R. (N.S.) 287 (F.C.T.D.).

69. *Saskatchewan Water Corporation v. Canadian Wildlife Federation Inc. et al.* (1989), 4 C.E.L.R. (N.S.) 1 (F.C.A.D.).

70. D. Curren, "Rafferty foes irked at Ottawa," the *Leader-Post* (Regina), 13 April 1989.

71. J. Knisley, "Devine warns jobs, lives at stake," the *Leader-Post,* 13 April 1989.

72. "Saskatchewan halts dam work pending appeal of court order," the *Edmonton Journal,* 12 April 1989.

73. J. Coutts, "Ottawa takes cue from court, orders dam study," the *Edmonton Journal*, 13 April 1989, A3.

74. *Canadian Wildlife Federation Inc. et al. v. Minister of the Environment; Saskatchewan Water Corporation* (1989), 4 C.E.L.R. (N.S.) 201 (F.C.T.D.).

75. "NDP wants probe of 'secret deals' on Rafferty dam," the *Edmonton Journal,* 29 January 1990.

76. "Devine's last stand," the *Edmonton Journal,* 13 October 1990.

77. D. Roberts and R. Howard, "Saskatchewan sues over delays to dam," *Globe and Mail,* 20 October 1990.

78. See *Canada (Attorney General) v. Saskatchewan Water Corporation et al.* (1990), 5 C.E.L.R. 252 (Sask. Q.B.).

79. Ibid., p. 283.

80. (21 December 1990), A-48-90 (F.C.A.C.)

81. The Tetzlaff brothers brought an action very similar to that initiated by the Canadian Wildlife Federation and the two were heard together. One set of reasons was issued for both applications.

82. (1989), 3 C.E.L.R. (N.S.) 287 (F.C.T.D.).

83. Official, federal Department of Justice.

84. (14 May 1991), T-2687 (F.C.T.D.)

85. See *Angus et al. v. R. et al.* (1990), 5 C.E.L.R. (N.S.) 157 (F.C.A.D.)

86. R. Helm, "Critics demand Ottawa order draining of Oldman River dam — Horsman says only Superman could stop $325M project," the *Edmonton Journal*, 6 May 1991.

87. See *Friends of the Oldman River Society v. Minister of Transport et al.* (1989), 4 C.E.L.R. (N.S.) 137 (F.C.T.D.); *Friends of the Oldman River Society v. Minister of Transport et al.* (1990), 5 C.E.L.R. (N.S.) 1 (F.C.A.D.)

88. In the last week of May 1991, the federal government passed a motion reviving six bills that had died on the order paper when Parliament prorogued the previous month. Among them was Bill C-78, to "Canadian Environmental Assessment Act." The Bill has been renumbered and is now Bill C-13.

89. FEARO, "Prescribed List of Statutory and Regulatory Authorities that will Trigger the Federal Environmental Assessment Process," (June 1991).

90. A Submission to Bill C-78, An Act to Establish a Federal Environmental Assessment Process: A Submission to The House of Commons Legislative Committee on Bill C-78 by the Ministers of Environment of British Columbia, Alberta, Saskatchewan, Manitoba, Ontario, New Brunswick, Prince Edward Island, Nova Scotia, Newfoundland, Yukon, Northwest Territories, Presented by the Honourable John Reynolds, Minister of Environment for British Columbia (4 December 1990).

91. "Notes for an address by The Honourable Jean J. Charest to the Legislative Committee on Bill C-13," Ottawa, 19 June 1991.

IV

Focus on the Provinces

7

The Search for the Holy Grail:
Maritime Cooperation

Donald J. Savoie

Les efforts pour promouvoir une plus large coopération politique et économique entre les trois provinces maritimes datent d'avant la Confédération. L'histoire nous révèle que le désir intermittent des Maritimes en faveur d'une union politique maximale, sinon d'une coopération régionale accrue, survient généralement en réaction contre tantôt une menace de l'extérieur, tantôt une précarisation de l'unité nationale. Il appert par ailleurs que ces initiatives défensives se fondent pour l'essentiel sur des considérations d'ordre économique et qu'en définitive, l'argument autonomiste ne joue aucunement. Encore aujourd'hui, l'unité canadienne apparaît aléatoire au moment même où la mondialisation de l'économie impose ses règles du jeu aux gouvernements. C'est dans ce contexte que les trois provinces maritimes — et dans une moindre mesure Terre-Neuve — se sont concertées une fois encore afin d'établir une coopération élargie sur divers fronts.

Cet article examine les faits marquants, sur le plan historique, de cette coopération interprovinciale. Par ailleurs, on y découvre qu'à plusieurs moments depuis le siècle dernier, cette idée force trouva peu d'écho auprès des provinces concernées. L'auteur analyse également le rôle du Conseil des premiers ministres des Maritimes en ce qui a trait au récent regain d'intérêt suscité par cette question. Au reste, on y aborde le concours épisodique du gouvernement de Terre-Neuve ainsi que le rôle joué par Ottawa à ce chapitre.

Much of the writing on intergovernmental relations in Canada has been from a federal-provincial perspective. This is quite understandable given the nature of Canadian federalism, our constitutional amending formula, and the importance of federal-provincial cost-shared agreements to the national and regional economies. Still, interprovincial relations are also extensive in Canada and have increased in importance in recent years. All the provincial premiers have been meeting annually for the past 30 years to review, among other things, the state of intergovernmental relations. As well, the four western premiers also now meet regularly to discuss a host of regional and national issues from a western perspective. Nowhere, however, are interprovincial relations pursued more intensively than in the Maritime provinces. There, the three provincial governments joined together to establish the Council of Maritime Premiers and the three premiers now meet on a regular basis to review the issue of interprovincial cooperation. The council has a permanent secretariat and a number of ongoing programs.

There has, however, been a sudden surge in interest in Maritime cooperation in recent months. In the fall of 1990, New Brunswick Premier Frank McKenna, for example, issued a call for greater cooperation that was widely reported and applauded in the national media. Premiers Joe Ghiz of Prince Edward Island and Donald Cameron of Nova Scotia in turn soon voiced their strong support. Newfoundland Premier Clyde Wells then joined in and made a plea for an Atlantic rather than a strictly Maritime perspective to regional cooperation, with press reports suggesting that he favoured full political union of the four Atlantic provinces. Premier Wells subsequently retracted his support, saying that he had been misquoted — and he has since shifted to the more traditional and cooler Newfoundland posture.

Before examining the forces fuelling the most recent call for greater regional cooperation — and the prospects for success — it is important to look back at previous attempts to cooperate. In fact, it is an old idea with a number of historical stopping points. In the past, interprovincial cooperation was often equated with political union, yet the three Maritime provinces have rarely danced the political union or cooperation jig at the same time. As well, the impetus for greater unity has largely been in reaction to threats from outside the region. In particular, interest in greater cooperation is invariably stronger when national unity is in jeopardy, as it now is. In short, the issue always seems to revolve around a question of economics. It is never one of the heart.[1]

LOOKING BACK

Premier McKenna's call for Maritime cooperation can hardly be described as fresh thinking.[2] Similar proposals have been made time and again, going back to, and even preceding, Confederation. Indeed, the Charlottetown conference that led to Confederation was called originally to discuss only Maritime political union. The American Civil War and its threat to Maritime safety, Canada's heavy hand in dealing with New Brunswick and Nova Scotia in negotiating the cost of building an intercolonial railroad, and the perceived smallness of Maritime politics pushed many, including representatives of the colonial office, to look to Maritime political union as the way ahead. Three years before Confederation, Nova Scotia's Charles Tupper had explained the benefits of full union: "uniformity of administration, improvement of the colonies' credit rating, economy in government, removal of tariffs with a consequent improvement in trade, improvement in defence posture and lessening of the purely personal element in political discussion."[3]

At that time, many of the region's newspapers, with the exception of those in Prince Edward Island, were supportive of a Maritime union, at least for a while. One boldly argued that Maritimers should be: "one people in reality. Let the name of Acadia absorb forever the names of New Brunswick, Nova Scotia and Prince Edward Island. Let there be no Upper and Lower, East and West or North and South with us."[4] Initially at least, there was also strong public support for political union. Donald Creighton wrote that support for union "had become a public issue, openly discussed and strongly supported. It even showed some ... signs of becoming a popular movement."[5] It is important to note, however, that the basis for popular support was "largely the negative one of antagonism towards Canada ... swept along ... on a wave of hatred of Canadian duplicity and domination."[6] Accordingly, when Canada decided to proceed with the survey of the intercolonial railway at its own expense, public support for union began to wane, with the result of weakening the prospects for "Maritime union just at the time when it ought to have been at its most vigorous."[7] The press also fell silent on the issue.[8]

Nevertheless, a new lieutenant-governor, Sir Richard Groves MacDonnell, arrived in Halifax on 22 June 1864 with instructions to pursue Maritime union. There were already resolutions before provincial legislative assemblies to hold a conference to pursue the matter. Albeit with varying degrees of enthusiasm, one by one the legislative assemblies agreed to a conference to devise an appropriate blueprint for Maritime union. Unexpectedly, however, Governor-General Viscount Monck asked if the Canadian government could send delegates to the conference to present a case for a larger union. The rest of the story is, of course, well known.

Canadians were not only invited, but the conference organizers went out of their way to welcome them. They delayed discussions on Maritime union for four days to give Canadians an opportunity to air their proposals fully. Later, the delegates put off the question of union altogether and unanimously affirmed "the desirability of a larger union."[9] The reasons why Maritime political union failed at the time were varied. For one thing, delegates saw advantages in a new larger union with "a strong central government [which represented] a necessary buttress against the truculence below the border."[10] As well, a larger federal union meant that the three provinces could each keep their legislative assemblies. It is also important to underline the fact that the main driving force for Maritime union had not come from within the region. It was fuelled by a desire to stand firm against Canada's negotiating position on the building of the intercolonial railway and as a means of resisting American military threats. The idea of a Maritime political union, P.B. Waite explains, "reached the Conference by a power not its own, and there it simply fell to pieces."[11]

There were a number of other attempts to promote Maritime political union from 1867 up to the 1960s. During the 1880s, for example, Nova Scotia raised the idea as a way for the region to leave the Canadian federation. This was because a goodly number of maritime politicians felt betrayed by the terms of Confederation and the unwillingness of the new union to settle the region's outstanding claims. Feelings ran high. One politician argued that "a loyal and contented people had been converted by an act of parliament into a state of serfdom to Canadian greed and spoliation."[12] Another suggested that "The iron-gloved hand of Canadian greed will still be clutching at the tax strings of the Maritime Provinces and meanwhile the stream of emigration will be like the brook as described by Tennyson as running on forever and the cities will be drying up."[13] For some politicians the solution was simply to withdraw from the federation and unite under one government. Some attempts were even made to establish a Maritime union party, but they failed. While not suggesting that the Maritime provinces leave the federation, the Toronto *Globe and Mail* wrote in support of political union, suggesting that "union would enable them to pull together with greatly more effect than at present, would much diminish the cost and labour of governments and above all could lend a vastly increased weight to their voice in the counsels of Canada."[14] Still, there were Maritimers opposed to political union. When the premier of Prince Edward Island declared in 1910 that Maritime union was "so impracticable it could not even be considered," the call for political union was heard less and less.[15]

By the early 1920s, however, one increasingly heard complaints that national economic policies were hurting the Maritime economy. Certainly, the region saw more and more of its youth move elsewhere in the country or to the United States for employment, and many Maritime leaders accused Ottawa and federal policies, which they believed favoured central Canada of being responsible for the region's slow development. This view gave rise to the Maritime rights movement.[16] The movement's energy, however, was directed at misguided federal policies and Maritime union was never an important feature of its agenda. The movement petered out when the Conservative party "appropriated" its agenda and became the political voice for the movement.[17] It did, however, give rise to new cooperative efforts on the part of the three provincial governments and the region's business community.

The provinces launched a series of cooperative efforts, some of which still exist today. For example, they agreed in 1925 to create the Maritime Transportation Commission to attack the freight rate differential between the region and the rest of the country.[18] They decided in 1928 to establish a joint trade commission office in Ontario which operated until 1933.[19] They agreed in 1934 to cooperate in promoting the regional timber industry and to establish the

Timber Commission of Eastern Canada, the forerunner of the Maritime Lumber Bureau.[20] The three Maritime premiers went further in 1956 when, together with the premier of Newfoundland, they decided to establish the Atlantic Premiers' Conference. A leading proponent of the conference, New Brunswick Premier Hugh John Flemming, explained that it would signal "the resumption of a certain order of business which was interrupted in the city of Charlottetown in the year 1864."[21] It was a formal organization in the sense that the four premiers met annually and, though the conference had no staff, the premiers did commission research papers from both government and non-government people. At their first meeting, they agreed to study jointly the following themes:

- the advantages of collaboration in securing better federal-provincial financial agreements;
- the possibility of cooperating to achieve cheaper electric power;
- the desirability of a joint drive to locate defence industries and place defence orders in the Atlantic provinces;
- the means to attack jointly the effects of the tariff on the regional economy;
- the possibilities of cooperation in the marketing of fishing and agricultural products; and
- the possibilities of maintaining joint trade representatives in the United Kingdom and elsewhere.[22]

The Atlantic Premiers' Conference also led to the establishment of numerous coordinating bodies of one kind or another. Interprovincial committees and working groups, bringing together officials from the three provincial governments (or four, whenever Newfoundland agreed to participate), were established to deal with most areas of government activities.[23]

All in all, there is little doubt that some progress was made between the 1920s and the 1960s in promoting interprovincial cooperation in the Maritimes — and in Atlantic Canada from 1949 to 1960. But there were also some serious failures. A proposed Atlantic Institute of Education was discussed many times, but was never established. It had been hoped that the institute would bring together the departments of education and teachers' colleges in the four Atlantic provinces to improve teacher education, promote research in educational planning and establish standards of achievement in teacher education. The Atlantic Provinces Office in London was opened in 1958 and operated until 1969. It sought both to promote trade with the United Kingdom and Europe and to attract European investments to the region. However, Nova Scotia and New Brunswick decided to send their own representative to London in 1969, while Newfoundland and Prince Edward Island opted out of the arrangement altogether. There is more than one story to explain why the office was closed, although everyone appears to agree that when H.W. Jamer, who had directed the office since its establishment, retired in 1968 the provinces began to back away from the agreement. Newfoundland Premier Joey Smallwood reported: "Now that Mr. Jamer has retired, Newfoundland might not be very interested in replacing him. We have been unenthusiastic about it for several years."[24] New Brunswick appointed its provincial deputy minister to represent its interests in London and Nova Scotia soon followed suit. Those familiar with the situation now report that Mr. Jamer had always been in an impossible position trying to serve "four masters," with the four provincial governments often pursuing different interests and different policies.[25] And there were still other failures. A proposed joint industrial commission was one. The New Brunswick industry minister had proposed in 1964 a coordinating agency that would direct industries to specific locations in the region. He had hoped that the agency would be able to balance industrial growth among the four provinces. New Brunswick, he reported, had already stopped negotiations with certain industries, in part because they were trying to play one province off against another.[26] None of the other provinces, however, expressed much interest in the matter and it was soon dropped.

The four Atlantic provinces were soon looking at a much bigger challenge, New Brunswick Premier Louis J. Robichaud used the 1964 federal-provincial constitutional conference in Charlottetown to ask his Atlantic colleagues if there was any interest in moving towards a political union of the four Atlantic provinces. He announced: "Perhaps Premiers Stanfield, Smallwood, Shaw and I may get together today and, on this centennial of the first meeting in Charlottetown, decide to reduce the number of Canadian provinces from ten to seven. Should that occur, the focal point of progress and activity in the nation would unquestionably and rapidly take a marked shift to the east."[27] Robichaud explained why he was issuing such a challenge: "The new pressures of the mid-20th century, the problems of national unity, and the growth in governmental responsibilities, combine in calling for a re-examination of proposals for the union of these four Atlantic provinces."[28] The next step, he suggested, was a "serious" study to look into all facets of the matter since "the subject is too serious to permit the discussion of it to be clouded or subverted by prejudices or petiteness of any nature."[29]

The Robichaud proposal, initially at least, did not meet with much enthusiasm from his Atlantic colleagues. Premier Walter Shaw of Prince Edward Island dismissed the idea and said that the chances for political union "were extremely limited."[30] Premier Stanfield of Nova Scotia did not shut the door on the proposal, but expressed some caution. He reported: "We are prepared to consider it, provided provision is to be made for proper safeguards. On a per capita basis, we have a higher standard of income than the three other provinces and we wouldn't want to have that brought down. We would be only prepared to consider it on a basis of everybody else being pulled up rather than Nova Scotia being pulled down."[31] Premier Smallwood pointed out that Newfoundland was not on the mainland, and so could not be considered a "Maritime" province. In any event, he reported that Newfoundland much preferred dealing directly with Ottawa and not as part of the Maritime Provinces.[32] Perhaps for good measure, Premier Smallwood attended only one more Atlantic Premiers' Conference and it was later disbanded. Despite his reservations, Stanfield obviously saw merit in Robichaud's proposal since he later suggested that Robichaud and he ask their respective legislative assemblies to decide through a free vote whether the two provinces should proceed with a joint study to determine the feasibility of a political union.

THE DEUTSCH STUDY ON POLITICAL UNION

In early 1965, the Nova Scotia and the New Brunswick legislative assemblies unanimously agreed to launch "a study to enquire into the advantages and disadvantages of a union of the Province of Nova Scotia and the Province of New Brunswick to become one province within the nation."[33] A few months later, Fred Drummie, a widely respected senior New Brunswick government official, outlined to the media how the study would proceed. There was little doubt that it would be an ambitious look at a wide array of issues ranging from specific policy areas, to the region's economic circumstances, its history, and issues involving the machinery of government. Fred Drummie was later appointed the study's executive director.

Though the study was slow in getting started, certain developments gave it a major boost. When Alex Campbell was elected premier of Prince Edward Island, he immediately announced that his province would like to join in. John Deutsch, the chairman of the Economic Council of Canada and principal of Queen's University, agreed to head up the study. The media were highly supportive of efforts to promote more cooperation between the Maritime provinces. This was particularly so in central Canada — no surprise in the Maritimes, since "a proposed union of Eastern Canadian provinces had been a creature of the Central Canadian press for a number of years."[34] Newfoundland, however, showed no interest in participating in the study. Not only did its premier stop attending the Atlantic Premiers' Conference, but a pattern emerged in the 1960s in which Newfoundland was less and less willing to develop "a regional" voice in federal-provincial relations or to promote an Atlantic perspective to sectoral issues.[35]

With Prince Edward Island now a full partner in the maritime union study, no one doubted the study's importance and its potential impact. The three premiers issued a joint statement in their respective legislatures reporting their commitment to public consultation and to the "direct participation ... of interested organizations and bodies."[36] The study also received a number of "public briefs" and commissioned some 20 studies.[37]

Not long after the Deutsch Study was formally launched, it became clear that it would shift away from the issue of political union towards identifying ways to promote greater cooperation between the three provinces. This is not to suggest that there was no support among the Maritime population for political union. A public opinion survey sponsored by the study "indicated a favourable attitude to complete union of the three provinces ... on the part of approximately two thirds of the people 16 years of age and over. One quarter of the people are not in favour of such union and the balance, approximately 10 percent, is not sure ... The people of Prince Edward Island are the least in favour while those in New Brunswick are somewhat more in favour than those in Nova Scotia. English respondents favour union more so than do the French."[38] Still, the officials directing the study concluded that to advocate cooperation that would lead to political union would be less threatening than to recommend outright and immediate union. Public opinion polls were one thing, but convincing politicians and the three bureaucracies was quite another. Moreover, for citizens to agree via a public opinion survey on some vague notion of what Maritime political union might be and what it could entail is quite different from agreeing after a full blown debate in which the merits and drawbacks are fully aired.

The Deutsch Study was made public on 27 November 1970 by Premier Campbell and two newly elected premiers, Richard Hatfield of New Brunswick and Gerald Reagan of Nova Scotia. There was little doubt that the study's ultimate objective was political union. However, it urged that the region move only gradually towards this goal by a series of new cooperative arrangements. Still, the study pointed to eventual political union as the preferred option because of the "uncertainties" confronting the region "which ... arise from two dangers — the possible political disintegration of the nation and continued substantial economic disparities in relation to the remainder of the country."[39] The study also made clear why it did not recommend immediate political union despite the favourable response reported in the public opinion surveys: "The historical and traditional loyalties to the individual provincial entities are strong; the attachments to local diversities and interests are more intense than elsewhere in the country. ... The resistance to change in existing political structures is reinforced by the established relationships and interests that are associated with governments, these tend to be particularly intimate and strong. It can be expected that various influential groups, the holders of franchises and concessions, the bureaucratic apparatus, and many who have vested interests in the existing arrangements would be apprehensive of changes that might bring uncertainties. ... There is no question that in the Maritimes many of these forces weigh heavily in the direction of the status quo."[40]

The Deutsch Study looked to new measures involving the machinery of government to encourage greater cooperation and eventually political union. The new machinery would be charged with the responsibility of promoting "regional economic planning, regional negotiations with federal authorities establishing common administrative services, developing uniform legislation, co-ordinating existing provincial policies, preparing a constitution for a single provincial government for the Maritimes and implementing steps leading to political union."[41] Inspired by the European Economic Community, the study recommended three new organizations to undertake the various tasks. It urged the establishment of a Council of Maritime Premiers, a Maritime Provinces Commission and a Joint Legislative Assembly.

The Council of Maritime Premiers would consist of the three premiers, meet at least quarterly, consider recommendations coming from the new Maritime Provinces Commission, approve joint submissions and negotiate with Ottawa on behalf of the region.[42] The Commission, meanwhile, would consist of five members, and be responsible for preparing a long-term development plan for the region, recommending common regional policies, preparing proposals for joint administrative policies and a unification of the three public services, a constitution for a single Maritime province and a timetable for political union.[43] The Joint Legislative Assembly would bring together all members of the three provincial legislatures in a joint session once a year to review the work of the Council and Commission. It would also be charged with determining the method by which the final step of political union would take place.[44] The study urged that a thorough review be undertaken in five years on the progress being realized towards full political union. If, it reported, progress is not being made and "political union cannot be accomplished within a further five years, the entire program should be reconsidered."[45]

The three premiers quickly declared their support for much of the Deutsch Study's findings. Fred Drummie explains: "It was staggering to submit a report on November 21, 1970 in the Confederation Chamber in Charlottetown, and then have it adopted within two months. I do not think there has been a Royal Commission in this country that has ever had that happen. Taken further, within four more months there was a formal and enforceable agreement between the three provinces. Then, lo and behold, we even have it accepted by the Legislatures and formal institutions of regional cooperation were established."[46] Premier Hatfield also reported his support for political union as long as the federal government provided financial assistance to implement it. The other two premiers were much more lukewarm on the issue, with Reagan arguing that cooperation was possible without union and Campbell suggesting that union was not necessary at "this time."[47] Though the premiers took immediate steps to establish the Council of Maritime Premiers, they put off a decision on the Maritime Provinces Commission and the Joint Legislative

Assembly. The power to constitute the Commission was built into the legislation establishing the Council. However, the premiers have never pursued the matter. The power to constitute the assembly remains the prerogative of the three provincial legislative assemblies and this too has not been pursued.

The Council of Maritime Premiers recently celebrated its twentieth anniversary. It can point to a number of initiatives, introduced over this period, that have led to new regional institutions and cooperative measures.[48] There are now a host of regional institutions in place, including the Atlantic Veterinary College, the Maritime Provinces Higher Education Commission and the Land Registration and Information Service, along with a wide array of interprovincial committees that operate joint programs or provide services. The Council reports that it has also successfully promoted a "Maritime" position in dealing with Ottawa.[49] But this is very often relatively easy to do. Indeed, it is scarcely difficult at all to get the three Maritime premiers to gang up on Ottawa, to agree that the federal government should be doing more in, say, regional development and transportation and that it should not be cutting transfer payments to the provinces.

Though the Council can report some success stories, it also has its failures. The attempt to cooperate on trade and investment promotion was stymied by continuing competition and the proposed Maritime Energy Cooperation failed to get off the ground.[50] It will be recalled that in the aftermath of Canada's energy crisis in the 1970s, the three premiers agreed to put in place an energy agency to encourage regional planning, a pooling of capital and the allocation of regional or Maritime energy resources. The reasons for this particular failure have been documented elsewhere and there is no need to go over them here.[51] Suffice to note that in time each province found one reason or another to lose interest in a joint corporation. New Brunswick was able to secure federal financing to construct its own nuclear power plant; a new government in Prince Edward Island declared its firm opposition to nuclear power; and Nova Scotia saw coal generated power as a way to create new jobs in economically-depressed Cape Breton. To further explain their failure to follow through with its establishment, the three provinces also accused the federal government of reneging on its initial commitment to support the Maritime Energy Corporation.

There was also no thorough or public review after five years to assess the progress being made towards full political union, as proposed by the Deutsch Study. Had there been one, the entire program would have been "reconsidered" because there were, of course, no indications that "political union" could have been "accomplished within a further five years." Such a review, however, would have been unfair to the Council for Maritime Premiers, since two key recommendations of the study were never acted upon: the establishment of a Maritime Provinces Commission and a Joint Legislative Assembly.

The Council did, however, commission a review of its own effectiveness in the late 1980s. The report, *Standing Up to the Future*, which was released in 1989, is, unfortunately, largely unfocused, seriously lacking in both clarity and intellectual rigour.[52] It begins by declaring that the "Council of Maritime Premiers has served the provinces of New Brunswick, Nova Scotia and Prince Edward Island well — very well indeed."[53] A few pages later, however, it reports "in no fixed order" that "the current structure and performance [of the council] ... lacks a clear regional agenda on major economic issues facing the Maritime Provinces and a mechanism to develop such an agenda [and] ... it lacks credibility ... as a delivery mechanism for programs within provincial governments and their line departments ... [has] an almost non-existent policy research role conducted internally or funded externally, and no on-line database to strengthen coordinated policy making for the region and a 'wait and see' attitude by Secretariat personnel towards specific agenda items."[54] For good measure, the review adds: "In recent years, various organizational weaknesses have emerged at the Council."[55] The solutions identified are also found wanting, though the review is clear on the issue of political union. It states: "Maritime Union is not a viable option."[56] It does not, however, go into much detail about why this must be so. It then goes on to outline a series of recommendations with which few Maritimers could possibly disagree. It recommends an "emphasis on attainable targets over a fixed time period, say, five years. Assume the overall target is straight forward — to make the Maritimes a have region by the end of the decade, by the start of the 21st century."[57] The review suggests that the way to achieve this target is by "doubling the level of entrepreneurial exports from the Maritimes in five years, double the level of start-ups in each province and develop the technology base of the Maritimes over five years."[58] It is not, however, at all clear on how this can be accomplished. Much like the elephants in the *Jungle Book*, the review "marches from here to there and it doesn't much matter where." It recommends that the Maritimes should "use" the Canadian consulate in Boston more, "should learn from the Scandinavian experience [and explore] what new opportunities are there for new alliances with them to mutual advantage."[59] It suggests that "regional centres of excellence [re science and technology] would help" and that "the principal concern for both public and private sector policy makers in Atlantic Canada should be and must be to improve the macroeconomic performance of the region, i.e. wealth creation, productivity, output and employment."[60] Though the review makes little reference to the Deutsch Study, it appears to borrow from it when it recommends the "establishment of a Maritime Premiers Advisory Board on a three-year basis ... to help the Premiers establish a collective strategic agenda and to serve as a sounding board."[61] The review is not very clear on the precise mandate and operation of such an advisory board, but it seems to have been inspired by Deutsch's recommendation on the establishment of a Maritime commission. Still, the review cautions that "a bold vision of the Maritime Premiers cannot happen by executive fiat — Citizens must be involved."[62] It argues for the establishment of a Maritime Savings Development Fund that would capture the pool of funds available in the region's pension funds to assist local economic development. It also calls for the abolition of all interprovincial trade barriers between the three provinces.[63]

Work on the review was interrupted when it was at "an advanced" stage to "consider the idea of a more strategic relationship between the Maritime governments and the Government of Newfoundland and Labrador."[64] This issue is addressed under the heading "A Digression" — although the first line of the section states: "any analysis of the potential instruments and institutions for the Maritime Provinces can hardly ignore a discussion of the role of the Province of Newfoundland and Labrador in the region's affairs."[65] The review then endorses what it labels an "integration model," meaning that Newfoundland should become a "full partner in the Council and the funding of the Secretariat on an agreed per capita basis."[66]

Despite its drawbacks, however, the review did serve an important purpose in that it placed the issue of maritime cooperation front and centre before the respective policy agendas of both the region and the country at a critical period in Canada's history. Premier McKenna's views on Maritime cooperation were widely reported in the media and, as always, the central Canadian media were enthusiastic, some suggesting that the review did not go far enough and urged the three provinces to agree to full political union. The review also laid out a plan for the three premiers to pursue in order to ensure that any momentum towards greater cooperation would not be lost. It called on them to hold a press conference in early 1990 to outline a specific action plan to promote cooperation and to convene a special assembly of the three Maritime legislatures in mid-1990 for a one-day session on the region's future. It also called for a "master challenge document to the Atlantic media and the public on a series of specific challenges facing the Maritimes."[67]*

LOOKING TO OTTAWA

The federal government appears to favour both Maritime union and cooperation, although it has never said as much publicly. It must, of course, walk a fine line. A former Secretary for Federal-Provincial Relations in Ottawa reports that "asking the federal government for its position on regional cooperation puts it

---

*   It is important to note that Atlantic Canada is the term used when referring to the
    four Atlantic provinces. The "Maritimes" refers only to New Brunswick, Nova
    Scotia, and Prince Edward Island. It is not clear why the review uses both terms in
    this context.

in a no-win position. If the federal government encourages the Maritime provinces to get together, it can be, and is, criticized for applying unnatural and unwanted pressure to force the provinces to act in ways other than those they would prefer. If the federal government does not encourage regional cooperation, it can be, and is, criticized for setting the provinces against each other and for failing to support and encourage what is perceived by many people both inside, and particularly outside, the region as a good thing."[68] Thus, although Ottawa does not wish to be seen publicly to be interfering in the affairs of the three provincial governments, one only needs to spend a few days in Ottawa to hear many politicians of whatever party and senior federal officials report privately their full support for greater cooperation, if not full political union. Indeed, many quite readily admit bewilderment that three such small political entities with the largest — Nova Scotia — having a population base not much greater than the National Capital Commission, are not already united economically and politically.

The federal government has, in fact, made a few tangible efforts to promote Maritime cooperation. For example, it shared the costs of the Deutsch Study and seconded Edgar Gallant, a senior federal bureaucrat, to set up the Council of Maritime Premiers.

Still, such isolated gestures aside and despite the vast number of individuals in Ottawa who favour Maritime cooperation, particularly in economic development, there is precious little evidence to suggest that federal policies are geared to assist this outcome. On the contrary, there is evidence to suggest that they have over the years actually worked against it. Otherwise, how do we explain, for example, Ottawa's change of position with regard to the establishment of the proposed Maritime Energy Corporation? Such second thinkings certainly did not help matters, and probably gave the three provinces a *porte de sortie* to back away from the proposed deal.

There are other examples, but perhaps none more telling than those found in federal regional development efforts that were overhauled in 1972 when the General Development Agreement (GDA) was introduced to implement regional development programs. The GDAs were later replaced by the Economic and Regional Development Agreements (ERDAs), which in turn have been replaced by Cooperation agreements. These agreements have sponsored programs and projects totalling billions of dollars in the three Maritime Provinces since the early 1970s. We have seen new measures sponsored in agriculture, fisheries, transportation, industrial development, energy, minerals development, local development, forestry, ocean-related industries, rural development, pulp and paper, urban development and tourism — among other sectors and specific geographical areas. In some instances the measures have become ongoing, since they continue to be supported by so-called "second," "third" and "fourth" generation agreements. These programs, however, have been almost exclusively provincial in scope. Only in the case of tourism has the federal government recently attempted to introduce a "regional" focus. Ottawa's province-by-province approach to planning economic development in the Maritime provinces has remained consistent over the past 20 years, despite changed portfolios, programs and party in power.[69] There have even been instances where local federal offices were in competition with one another to secure a project for "their" provinces, much as provincial governments have been accused of doing.[70]

In short, the federal government, the one government with the necessary detachment to bring a "Maritime" perspective to economic development, has failed to do so. The bulk of Ottawa's spending for regional development over the past 20 years in the Maritime provinces has been channelled directly to the three provincial governments for provincially designed and implemented programs. This is not to suggest for a moment that Ottawa could easily ignore the fact that provincial governments are the effective agents of political power in the region. Still, it could have promoted a regional perspective in its dealings with them and at least indicated the advantages of signing "regional" rather than strictly "provincial" agreements for a number of sectors.

The impact on the Maritimes of Ottawa's apparent unwillingness to encourage greater regional cooperation has been considerable. For one thing, given the have-not status of the three provinces, the great majority of provincially-designed measures to promote economic development has been, at least in part, federally funded. If the federal government does not follow a regional perspective in its dealings with the provinces, then provincial politicians and officials will naturally pursue provincially-designed programs and seek federal funding for them. Moreover, the pervasive local federal presence — and its ready funding — has encouraged the three provinces to turn to it rather than to one another to promote economic development.

LOOKING AHEAD

The issue of Maritime cooperation has now once again taken centre stage before the regional and, to some extent, the national policy agenda. The forces fuelling it today are not so different from those that provoked a similar interest in earlier times. In 1964, it was the threat to national unity and the pressures of the mid-twentieth century that accounted for Louis Robichaud's call for a "serious" look at political union of the four Atlantic provinces. Once again, Canada's national unity is under stress. The pressures of the global economy are also compelling the three provinces to cooperate more extensively.

Indeed, we now know that the global economy will be imposing its own discipline. New trading patterns are emerging, and Canada's traditional east-west trade may no longer constitute the "ties that bind" that it once did. The impact of the new trade patterns will be considerable on all regions, but probably most noticeable in Ontario. The requirements of the global economy are such that all of Canada's regions will seek to insert themselves into it in different ways. In time, their economic links with the wider world will become more important than those within the country. Thus, New England may become far more significant to the Maritimes than Ontario and Quebec — or certainly the prairies. Similarly, Ontario will look more and more to Michigan, Ohio and New York than to the Maritimes to market its products. Ontario has, in the past, profited immensely from Canada's national policies. That situation is changing now, and Ontario firms will have to compete on a level playing field with American companies, not only in New York, Detroit and Cleveland, but in Halifax and Saint John. The United States, meanwhile, will not be asked to support federal transfer payments to Atlantic Canada — hence the reluctance of Ontario to continue to support slow-growth regions. In any event, the federal coffers are now empty, and the strong pressure for fiscal restraint on Ottawa is here to stay for a long time. These combined factors will result in each of Canada's regions seeking to strengthen its own economy, rather than the national one, in order to compete more successfully in the international marketplace.

There is an important difference today in how the maritimes views interprovincial cooperation from the way it did in 1964. At that time political union was in the air, initially of the four Atlantic provinces, and later of the three Maritime provinces. The Deutsch Study certainly looked to union as the most promising option. Today, this is no longer the case. In a joint release, the three premiers recently stated that: "Political union could threaten the unique culture and identity of our citizens."[71] They are opting instead for economic union.

As with the Deutsch Study, Newfoundland has been on the outside looking in. There are, of course, strong historical reasons why Newfoundland would want to chart its own course. In his report for the Deutsch Study, Richard Leach argued that "Newfoundland has always held itself somewhat aloof, with closer ties to Ottawa and to London than the other provinces."[72] Indeed, until Premier Wells' recent overture, Newfoundland had consistently shunned closer cooperation with the three Maritime provinces — so much so that its government passed an order-in-council in the late 1970s prohibiting any government department from signing a regional agreement with the Maritime provinces without first securing full Cabinet approval. Newfoundland effectively killed the Atlantic Premiers' Conference when it decided in the mid-1960s to no longer attend meetings. The government of Newfoundland also stopped its annual contribution to the operation of the Atlantic Provinces Economic Council in the early 1980s, arguing that its economy was so different that it made no sense to speak of an Atlantic economy. It later established its own Newfoundland and Labrador Economic Council. Patrick O'Flaherty of Memorial University recently explained that "Newfoundland's economy is more tied into that of Central Canada. ... I don't think maritime union represents any real alternative for Newfoundland. It is not a big issue here. I would say that if there is any kind of option that Newfoundlanders would entertain, if Canada does break up, the first one that they will want to explore will be independence. There is still a strong subterranean nationalist feeling in Newfoundland."[73]

It is important to remember that Newfoundland has had a distinct political and economic history. The province was not populated by Loyalists and Acadians and its ties to the rest of Canada are relatively recent. In addition, its economic ties, including trade patterns, to the Maritime provinces are considerably weaker than the links that exist between the three provinces.[74] The current secretary to the Council of Maritime Premiers explains that: "It's hard enough to get three sovereign governments to cooperate on anything and that's in the good times. When you add a fourth, who is further away, whose history is different, whose culture is different and whose aspirations are different, it gets even harder to negotiate anything."[75] Premier Wells, it will be recalled, quickly backtracked on his earlier call for greater cooperation, on the grounds that he does not know quite what "economic cooperation and integration" mean. The St. John's *Evening Telegram* ran an editorial at the height of the discussion entitled "A Boat to Miss?" and argued that "the real reason behind Mr. Wells' reluctance to get involved in the scheme may lie in the simple fact Newfoundland has little to gain by it. ... This may be one boat the province will only be too glad to miss."[76]

In any event, the Maritime premiers are now looking to economic rather than political union. They picked up on some of the recommendations in the report, *Challenge and Opportunity*, recently issued by the Council of Maritime Premiers. This report outlines measures to promote the free movement of goods and services, people and capital across the Maritime provinces. These include proposals to eliminate barriers to the mobility of tradespeople and professionals in the three provinces and initiatives to harmonize government policies and rules for public tendering, business investment incentives and transportation regulation. The report also calls for greater cooperation in fisheries, agriculture, energy, the environment, securities regulation, government bulk purchasing and trade promotion.[77]

The premiers also held a two-day forum of the three provincial cabinets on 17 and 18 June 1991 to review the findings of *Challenge and Opportunity* and to explore new ways to promote regional cooperation. This was the first time ever that the three cabinets met and they agreed to make it an annual event. They also agreed to open most government contracts to bidders from all three provinces, to end barriers to trucking among the provinces, begin bulk purchasing, have one registration for companies, establish a Maritime securities commission and push Ottawa to fund a four-lane highway through the region.[78]

Some observers applauded the meeting, maintaining that the premiers had at least quickened the pace of the tortoise. Others, however, were less optimistic. One observer wrote that the three premiers "didn't always say when or how they'd do it."[79] Premier Joe Ghiz also warned that there could be no economic integration unless Prince Edward Island could secure some form of electric power parity with the other two Maritime provinces.[80] At the moment, Prince Edward Island imports the bulk of its electric power from New Brunswick and pays as much as 30 percent above the cost on the mainland. This explains at least in part why no decision was taken to harmonize the vast array of incentive schemes to the private sector to promote industrial and economic development. Still, Ghiz summed up the outcome of the meeting by acknowledging: "Rome wasn't built in a day. We've gone about as far as we can at this time."[81]

What are the chances for greater interprovincial cooperation this time around? The premiers have essentially two options: they can look cautiously for a sure footing and slowly build up the requirements for greater cooperation. Some, however, argue that only by going at a hare's pace will economic union ever be achieved. As Premier McKenna explains, however, they have decided to proceed slowly — to emulate the tortoise, in fact. There is little doubt that deeply rooted political traditions, strong community attachments and the entrenched self-interest of "provincial" political and bureaucratic machines make cooperation and a move towards economic union difficult. It will be recalled, for example, that residents of Prince Edward Island voted only narrowly in favour in a referendum for a causeway linking their island to the mainland. In addition, there is evidence to suggest that provincial bureaucracies have been dragging their feet on implementing interprovincial cooperation.[82]

As in the past, however, the success of future regional cooperation may well hinge on what happens at the national level. Should the Canadian nation collapse, and the region be left to fend for itself, then we would no doubt see a search for dramatic solutions. Political union would certainly be an option. Should we continue, however, with anything closely resembling the status quo, then Maritime political, or even economic union, would be much more difficult to achieve. For one thing, New Brunswick Acadians — who constitute about 35 percent of the province's population — could well resist political union for fear of losing the gains they have made since the early 1960s in language, education and institution building.

Nor must it be forgotten that full provincial status holds many advantages. Equalization payments and a political and administrative infrastructure are but two examples. Cape Breton could well have today an economy like that found in Prince Edward Island if it had enjoyed provincial status over the years. Provincial status means, at a minimum, having a capital, an elaborate administrative structure with a large number of stable federal and provincial public service jobs, a university and usually a number of consultants. In a have-not region, one does not easily give up these. Moreover, by each having a seat at the First Ministers' Conferences (FMCs), provincial premiers enjoy not only a special status, and high visibility in the national media, but they are given an important say in the future of the country. They can plead, often before a national television audience, for a better economic deal for their regions. Maritime political union would limit them to a single voice, rather than three, in making the case for the region at FMCs. Quite apart from the fact that tigers do not easily part with their stripes, the three Maritime premiers are unlikely to allow the region's voice to be attenuated without some lasting compensation.

The federal government can play an extremely important role in encouraging economic cooperation in the Maritimes. It has not done so over the past 20 years. If Ottawa continues to define its regional development policy strictly on a province-by-province basis, and makes its funding available only through bilateral agreements, then the chances for a Maritime perspective on economic development will diminish. Should the Canadian nation survive our current constitutional crisis, and Ottawa continue with its strictly "provincial" ap- proach, the issue of Maritime cooperation will fade after a few years, only to return when the nation's unity is again uncertain, or when external forces threaten the economy of the region. If interprovincial economic cooperation is to be secured in the Maritime provinces, then all key actors, including the federal government, will have to play their part.

Though the federal government can play an important role, in the end it will be Maritimers themselves — and, in particular, their provincial governments — who will have to provide the political courage. Certainly if anything like the status quo should prevail in Canada, there will be a strong tendency in the region to carry on as before. One can easily foresee, however, that outside forces will increasingly necessitate Maritime cooperation. The large federal deficit, the global economy, the neo-conservative agenda which is holding sway in much of the Western world and the need for all regions to be more competitive, all point to closer economic cooperation and integration. They also point to the challenge laid out for the region several years ago. Given the emerging policy environment, it was argued then that in future the region itself will have to provide the necessary "imagination, the energy and the skills to promote economic development" if it is to prosper.[83] If the region cannot make the decision to cooperate, however politically difficult this may be, it is unlikely that it will be able to provide the imagination, the energy and the skills to do much else.

NOTES

1.   I want to thank David Milne for reading a first draft of this paper and for providing many of the observations found in this paragraph.

2. For an overview of various attempts to promote Maritime union see J. Murray Beck, *The History of Maritime Union: A Study in Frustration* (Fredericton: Maritime Union Study, 1969).

3. Nova Scotia, *Debates and Proceedings of the Nova Scotia House of Assembly*, 1864, p. 184.

4. *Acadian Recorder*, 2 April 1864, p. 1.

5. Donald Creighton, *The Road to Confederation: The Emergence of Canada 1863-67* (Toronto: Macmillan of Canada, 1964), p. 26.

6. W.M. Whitelaw, *The Maritimes and Canada Before Confederation* (Toronto: Oxford University Press, 1934), p. 201.

7. P.B. Waite, *The Life and Times of Confederation 1864-1867* (Toronto: University of Toronto Press, 1962), p. 56.

8. Ibid., p. 59.

9. Beck, *Maritime Union*, p. 16.

10. Waite, *Life and Times of Confederation*, p. 83.

11. Ibid.

12. Nova Scotia, *Debates and Proceedings of the Nova Scotia House of Assembly*, 1885, p. 105.

13. Ibid., p. 110.

14. *Globe and Mail* (Toronto), August 1906, p. 4.

15. Beck, *History of Maritime Union*, p. 37.

16. See Ernest R. Forbes, *The Maritime Rights Movement: A Study in Canadian Regionalism* (Montreal: McGill-Queen's University Press, 1975).

17. Beck, *History of Maritime Union*, p. 44.

18. Richard H. Leach, *Interprovincial Cooperation in the Maritime Provinces* (Fredericton: Maritime Union Study, 1970), p. 30.

19. Ibid., p. 31.

20. Ibid.

21. Fredericton, notes for an opening address by Honorable Hugh John Flemming, premier of New Brunswick at the Atlantic Premiers' Conference held in Fredericton, New Brunswick, 9 July 1956, p. 4.

22. Leach, *Interprovincial Cooperation*, p. 32.

23. Ibid., pp. 28-102.

24. Paul H. Evans, *Report on Atlantic/Maritime Interprovincial Cooperation Between 1950 and 1971* (Halifax: Council of Maritime Premiers, 1985), p. 3.

25. Ibid., p. 55.

26. Ibid., p. 100. It should also be noted that the four provinces agreed to open an Atlantic Pavilion at Expo '67 and to send joint trade missions to New England in the late 1960s.

27. Quoted in "Atlantic Union Suggested," *Chronicle-Herald* (Halifax), 2 September 1964, p. 1.

28. New Brunswick, "Proposal Regarding the Political Union of the Atlantic Provinces submitted to the Atlantic Premiers Conference," September 1964, p. 1.

29. Ibid., p. 3.

30. Quoted in Flemming, p. 95.

31. Evans, *Report*, p. 2.

32. Quoted in Flemming, p. 95.

33. *The Report on Maritime Union Study* (Fredericton: The Queen's Printer, 1970), p. 1.

34. Quoted in Evans, *Report*, p. 94.

35. Ibid., chap. 3.

36. *The Report on Maritime Union*, pp. 2-3.

37. Ibid, see appendix A.

38. Ibid., pp. 108-9.

39. Ibid., p. 9.

40. Ibid., pp. 66-7.

41. Ibid., p. 75.

42. Ibid., p. 76.

43. Ibid., p. 77.

44. Ibid.

45. Ibid., p. 79.

46. Notes for an address by Fred Drummie to the annual meeting of the Institute of Public Administration of Canada, Halifax, 13 September 1976, p. 2.

47. See "Premiers accept three union study proposals," *Chronicle-Herald* (Halifax), 27 January 1971, p. 1.

48. See, for example, Halifax, *The Future of Maritime Cooperation*, Council of Maritime Premiers, 2 June 1981, News Release.

49. See *The Record of Cooperation in the Maritimes*, notes for remarks by Emery M. Fanjoy to the conference on "Regional Cooperation in the Maritime: The Recent Issues and Prospects," 21 April 1981. It is also important to note that there are now over 200 regionally-funded post-secondary programs, including a common medical school, dental school, and forest ranger school among others.

50. See L.F. Kirkpatrick, "Regional Co-operation in the Electrical Generation — A Review," remarks to the conference on "Regional Cooperation in the Maritime: The Recent Issues and Prospects," 21 April 1981.

51. See Donald J. Savoie, "Interprovincial Cooperation in the Maritime Provinces: The Case of Electricity," Canadian Institute for Research in Regional Development, mimeo.

52. Charles J. McMillan, *Standing Up to the Future: The Maritimes in the 1990s* (Halifax: Council of Maritime Premiers, 1989).

53. Ibid., p. 1.

54. Ibid., pp. 10-11.

55. Ibid., p. 11.

56. Ibid., p. 3.

57. Ibid., p. 46.

58. Ibid.

59. Ibid.

60. Ibid., p. 44.

61. Ibid.

62. Ibid., p. 46.

63. Ibid., p. 45.

64. Ibid., foreword.

65. Ibid., p. 38.

66. Ibid., p. 46.

67. Ibid.

68. Michael Kirby, "Regional Cooperation: The View From Ottawa," notes for an address to the Conference on Regional Cooperation in the Maritimes, Halifax, 21-22 April 1981, p. 20.

69. See Donald J. Savoie, *Regional Economic Development: Canada's Search for Solutions* (Toronto: University of Toronto Press, 1986), chap. 9 and appendix A.

70. Donald J. Savoie, *Federal-Provincial Collaboration: The Canada-New Brunswick General Development Agreement* (Montreal: McGill-Queen's University Press, 1981), chap. 3.

71. See "Maritime premiers call for economic union," *Globe and Mail* (Toronto), 24 May 1991, p. 1.

72. Leach, *Interprovincial Cooperation*, p. 30.

73. Quoted in "Is Newfoundland part of Maritime family?" *Chronicle-Herald* (Halifax), 23 May 1991, p. A2.

74. See, among others, David G. Alexander, *Atlantic Canada and Confederation: Essays in Canadian Political Economy* (Toronto: University of Toronto Press, 1983).

75. Quoted in "Newfoundland Role in Maritime Union Key Item for Talks," *Evening Telegram* (St. John's), 22 May 1991, p. 1.

76. "A Boat to Miss?" *Evening Telegram* (St. John's), 26 May 1991, p. 4.

77. *Challenge and Opportunity* (Halifax: Council of Maritime Premiers, May 1991), pp. 25-7.

78. "Maritime Meeting Ends on High-Note," *Ottawa Citizen*, 19 June 1991, p. A11.

79. John Spears, "Maritime Barriers to be Dropped," *Toronto Star*, 19 June 1991, p. A14.

80. "Ghiz Jolts Maritime Meeting by Demanding Cheaper Power," *Toronto Star*, 18 June 1991, p. A9.

81. "Maritime Premiers Agree Some Trade Barriers to go," *Evening Telegram* (St. John's), 19 June 1991, p. 1.

82. See, among others, Fanjoy, *Record of Cooperation,* and Kirby, "Regional Cooperation," p. 20.

83. Quoted in Donald J. Savoie, *Establishing the Atlantic Canada Opportunities Agency* (Ottawa: Office of the Prime Minister, 1987).

8

Pacific Perspectives on the Canadian Confederation: British Columbia's Shadows and Symbols

Norman J. Ruff

Depuis une dizaine d'années, la Colombie-Britannique a subi une transformation à la fois interne et externe de son économie; de fait, cette province privilégie maintenant une diversification de ses échanges sur le plan international ainsi que l'établissement de relations économiques plus étroites avec les Etats riverains du Pacifique et avec ses voisins américains du Nord-Ouest pacifique.

Le credo de l'ex-premier ministre Vander Zalm à l'égard d'Ottawa mettait l'emphase sur le "fédéralisme équitable" et sur les soucis de la Colombie-Britannique face à la tendance fédérale, selon l'auteur, à se décharger de ses responsabilités en matière fiscale. Toujours dans ce domaine, le gouvernement Vander Zalm revendiquait une meilleure répartition des compétences entre les deux paliers de gouvernements.

L'avenir du secteur des ressources naturelles de cette province et la question de la protection environnementale sont aussi intimement reliés à la politique autochtone et à la problématique des revendications territoriales des Amérindiens auprès du gouverne- ment fédéral. Abandonnant sa position initiale relativement à cette question, le gouvernement de la Colombie-Britannique aura finalement accepté de participer au processus visant à règler le contentieux territorial avec les autochtones.

De 1986 à 1991, la Colombie-Britannique a joué un rôle on ne peut plus marginal sur le plan constitutionnel; la proposition de Bill Vander Zalm voulant qu'on recon- naisse le caractère distinct de chaque province resta sans écho ailleurs au pays. Jusqu'en 1991, le dossier de la révision constitutionnelle ne suscita aucune participa- tion du public et peu d'initiatives de la part de la législature britanno-colombienne; or, cette dernière a décidé que toute modification constitutionnelle devra, à l'avenir, être confirmée par référendum par la population de cette province. Malgré l'absence d'une voix officielle cohérente en matière constitutionnelle, la classe politique provinciale semble d'accord, dans son ensemble, sur l'approche à adopter dans le domaine des relations intergouvernementales ainsi que sur la nécessité de faire valoir les préoccupations et l'ordre du jour spécifiques de la Colombie-Britannique.

OVERVIEW

As British Columbia emerges from its troubled 1980s, it seems haunted by many of the same old shadows and displays the same sense of alienation that has always marked its ambivalent relationship with the Canadian Confederation. The propensity to chafe against what it perceives as national indifference, against the constitutional niceties of federalism and, at times, to assume the role of an independent actor as if there were no national government have continued unabated. Since 1984, the growth of what might be termed "market federalism," based on governmental retrenchment, decentralization, and deregulation with an eye to global competitiveness has, however, radically changed the larger national agenda confronting British Columbia's political elites. The early 1980's economic recession also heightened its sensitivity to the federal presence as did still more the subsequent cutbacks and offloadings in the face of national fiscal pressures. In addition, falling provincial revenues added a fresh significance to federal transfer payments and direct expenditures within the province through such regional development initiatives as the ERDA agreements and the post-1988 Western Economic Diversification program. British Columbia now demands a "fair share" and prescribes fiscal disentanglement and fiscal discipline for the federal government. The 1986 change in provincial political leadership and national angst in the aftermath of the Meech Lake constitutional debacle and the need to find an accommodation with aboriginal peoples must also be acknowledged as important determinants of a sea change in intergovernmental relationships with Ottawa and all nine other provinces.

The last decade has been an important period of internal economic and social transition for British Columbia, and there is an acute awareness of global and domestic economic and social change. There has been an acceleration in the realignment of the various sectors of its economy, of the pattern of continuing metropolitan urban growth and metropolitan dominance, and of demographic-immigration driven social change. These trends are in turn informed by a pervasive Pacific Rim outlook on Canada and the World.[1] As a result, the symbols that inform British Columbia's relationships with the Canadian Confederation are undergoing a fundamental redefinition. This chapter attempts to identify some of the major elements in that redefinition through an examination of the recent economic context and social trends, the development of the "fair share" and fiscal disentanglement themes, native affairs policy issues and the province's attitudes and directions in constitutional reform.

THE ECONOMY: A 1990s PACIFIC REGIONAL
AND GLOBAL PERSPECTIVE

Much attention has been directed towards the impact of "globalization" i.e., of nation-blind world trading and investment patterns on the Canadian economy.

Its implications for national sovereignty, domestic decentralization and public expectations raise the possibility for significant political change.[2] Global competition and shifting trade patterns have always been part of the British Columbia economic experience and formed part of the forces that define its relationships within Confederation. While not underestimating the potential of current global trends for national disturbances, these forces are already well-known to an economically vulnerable and politically exposed British Columbia. From a Pacific perspective, their recognition beyond the mountains may have the welcome consequence of engendering a greater appreciation or even appropriation of British Columbia's messages.

The contemporary realities of economic globalization in the 1980s and 1990s re-taught British Columbians what they already knew but had become complacent about over the previous 40 years. As an export-oriented economy dependent on international demand and vulnerable to fluctuations in world commodity prices, it is exposed to any global economic restructuring. Between its peak at the beginning of the recession to the trough towards the end of 1982, the provincial real Gross Domestic Product (GDP) fell by 7.5 percent. In 1981 the unemployment rate was at 6.7 percent, by 1984 it reached a peak of 14.7 percent. Juxtaposed with this were significant reductions in resource-sector employment due to technological change. Where there had been two jobs for each 1,000 cubic metres of timber cut, by the end of the 1980s there was only one. Despite heightened exploitation of the forestry resources, which has seen as much timber cut in the last two decades as the total for the previous 60 years, there is little possibility of ever achieving pre-1980 levels of forestry-sector employment. Provincial government resource revenue fell from $861.9 million in 1980-81 to a low of $542.5 million in 1983-84. The decline in total tax revenues qualified British Columbia as the first province to claim stabilization payments under federal-provincial fiscal arrangements ($80 million for 1983-84 and $94 million for 1984-85). Provincial debt for government purposes grew from $183 million in 1982 to over $5 billion in 1988. Corporate take-overs also introduced a further dimension to decision-making in both the public and private sectors as foreign ownership of the forestry industry rose to 43.2 percent, leaving British Columbia ownership at 29.7 percent and ownership elsewhere in Canada at 27.1 percent.[3] Even if political and business leaders have had few doubts as to the province's future prospects, they certainly have felt obliged to redefine them.

The official readings of the provincial economy and the state of provincial finances that emerged from this period were not only the result of an economic jolt but were designed to startle their audiences. The "New Reality" concept that informed the July 1983 restraint budget and the outlook contained in such government publications as *The Economy in a Changing World* (1985) and *The New Economy* (1986) identified British Columbia's current economic

conditions as structural rather than cyclical in origin and a product of fundamental changes in global demand and patterns of trade. The traditional resource
base was observed to be eclipsed by a faster growing service sector as a future
source of employment for British Columbians. Ordinary British Columbians
were, of course, already living out the harsh realities of their own economy
every day and did not have to be told that new jobs either were "McJobs" for
the young and women in non-unionized, low pay and/or part-time work, or were
highly skilled managerial or professional salaried occupations. Service-sector
growth is not a new phenomenon. The sector contributed 68 percent of provincial GDP in 1989 but had been barely 10 percent below this level throughout
the early 1960s. The growth of the producer-service sector had also already
reinforced metropolitan growth and economic dominance of the province. The
current expansion of the larger urban centres on the Lower Mainland, Vancouver Island and the Okanagan with population declines in the north and other
parts of the interior is all part of a long established pattern of uneven population
growth and increasing regional economic disparities within the province.[4]

From a national perspective, the 1980-81 recession ended with a more
significant shift in the province's already slender trading links with the rest of
the country. Since 1961, British Columbia's international exports have fluctu-
ated between 20-30 percent of its GDP and exports to Canada have remained
at a 7-9 percent level. There has been, however, a marked shift in the origins of
goods purchased by British Columbians. International imports declined during
the recession but since 1983 have grown to 30 year highs. In contrast, purchases
from the rest of Canada have declined to their lowest ever shares of total
imports.[5] The real significance of the "revisionist" picture of the economy was
to force the spokespersons for the province's various policy communities to
reassess and restate their priorities. They are expected to locate themselves in
the context of fresh perspectives on the relative weight of the various sectors
of the economy and global economic competition and investment opportunities.

This situation has muted the old arguments as to why the British Columbia
economy remained truncated, with only limited development of a secondary
manufacturing built on backward linkages from its resource base. Distinctions
between primary resource and manufacturing goods producing sectors and a
service sector are less easily made when white collar job growth and information processing form important components of goods production, and service
sector growth is itself commercially oriented. It is realized that service or goods
producing jobs are found in all sectors as they become increasingly interdepen-
dent.[6] A discussion paper prepared for the British Columbia Round Table on
the Environment and the Economy provided a challenging review of inter-
industry linkages within the British Columbia economy.[7] It was estimated that
a third of all British Columbia jobs in 1989 were related to the export of goods
outside of the province. Less than 10 percent were tied to Canadian trade

compared to 23 percent internationally. From the perspective of recent world trading patterns, there has been little shift in the composition of British Columbia exports. Softwood lumber, pulp, coal, newsprint and copper still compete for top spots by dollar value ranking. Some optimism as to the province's ability to weather new trends may be derived from the diversification of markets for these natural resources in the late 1980s as the United States' share fell from 53 to 39 percent. But whether this could be sustained or merely reflects short-term movements in Japanese, South Korean, Taiwan, other Pacific Rim and European demands remains to be seen. Many jobs within British Columbia depend on the maintenance and growth of those in other sectors. An examination of the "drivers" in the economy estimated, for example, that in 1984 13 percent of the labour force was employed in the retail trade but those jobs were virtually all dependent on demand from other sectors and incomes earned elsewhere.[8] Although the resource sector provides just 15 percent of jobs through direct employment, it produces through indirect means a total of 25 percent of all jobs.

The province had long protested national trade policies which made it "buy in the dearest market and sell in the cheapest"[9] and symbolized economic colonialism from eastern Canada. Given British Columbia's current trading patterns, the unqualified support of the British Columbia government for the Canada-U.S. Free Trade Agreement, tempered by a reminder that multilateral free trade was still more in the province's best economic interest, was entirely expected. Despite the negative impacts on such sectors as the wine and grape industries in the Okanagan Valley and fruit and vegetable processing, support for the free trade initiative carried over from the Bill Bennett to the Vander Zalm regimes.[10] There has been considerably less attention to the prospects arising out of the 1991 trilateral Canada-U.S.-Mexico free trade proposal — save for an unguarded moment when Premier Rita Johnston told a June 1991 Young Social Credit convention that she was "scared stiff" that British Columbia interests would not be adequately protected in the talks by the federal government.[11]

Just prior to the Canada-U.S. Free Trade Agreement, the conduct of the Vander Zalm government during the 1986 softwood lumber dispute can be seen as the first symptom of a new provincial economic agenda. Fifty-two percent of Canadian softwood lumber exports to the United States originated from British Columbia. In 1982-83 the provincial government had been part of a successful collaboration with the forest companies and the federal government in fighting off the U.S. lumber interests' attempt to obtain countervailing duties against British Columbia and other Canadian softwood lumber imports. By contrast, in 1986 British Columbia was instrumental in orchestrating Canada's acceptance of the December 1986 Memorandum of Understanding (MOU), which imposed a 15 percent export tax on softwood exports. One of the first acts of the new Vander Zalm government had been to announce a review of stumpage rates in light of a decline in revenue from $529 million to $187 million from 1979 to 1985. By November 1986, the premier threatened to hold unilateral negotiations with the United States should Ottawa not conclude an agreement. The provincial government subsequently increased revenues under a new timber pricing formula and escaped the export tax. The province's need for increased revenues and the Canadian need for a "clean launch" to the free trade talks were placed above all other considerations, including its former close liaison with the forestry industry.[12] Over the past two years, falling profits due to a high Canadian dollar and weak markets have increased the pressures from the lumber industry to reduce stumpage charges. Recently, B.C. Forestry Minister Claude Richmond sought a renegotiation of the MOU provisions which require United States review of any timber pricing changes in the province. The forestry deputy minister was dispatched to Washington, D. C. in an attempt to hasten the start-up of talks by Canadian trade officials. In any case, on 4 September 1991, the federal government announced that it had given the United States the 30-day notice required in the MOU to withdraw from the controversial agreement.

While the diversification of its markets and closer economic relations with the Pacific Rim are central to the province's contemporary global perspective,[13] the latter is also reinforced by its ever increasing ethno-cultural diversity. Vancouver is becoming part of a global economic network centred on Hong Kong, Tokyo, Taipei and Singapore and, to the chagrin of its residents, a global property market sparking the interest of billionaires.[14] However, it is also home to increasing numbers of Pacific Rim refugees or business immigrants. It is not without some significance that the current lieutenant governor of the province, David Lam, is himself a conspicuous example of the early 1970s inflow of Hong Kong entrepreneurship and capital. In this century, the majority of British Columbia residents have always been from elsewhere, and are either migrants from other provinces or foreign born. Since the 1970s the origins of its immigrants has shifted, however, from being predominately United States and European in origin (62 percent in 1969) to other origins (78 percent in 1989). This has imposed new strains on such public training programs as English as a Second Language (ESL), and other social policies, particularly in Greater Vancouver. Given the province's past history of racial intolerance it would be surprising not to find some negative connotations attached to this trend. A fear of gang lawlessness has, for example, sparked provincial government demands for the deportation of convicted immigrant criminal offenders without rights of appeal.[15] It is the provincial interest in immigration as a source of entrepreneurial skills and investment capital[16] that has been the primary factor in propelling British Columbia to seek a more active role in immigration policy and an agreement with Ottawa along the lines of that contemplated in the Meech Lake

Accord. Thus far B.C. has not been successful (as has Quebec) in reaching such an agreement. Indications are that Ottawa has steadfastly refused to do so.

Without underestimating the importance of the new trans-Pacific linkages, British Columbia's closest Pacific Rim relationships naturally remain those with its most immediate neighbours. British Columbia has always been re-garded as part of a Pacific Northwest geographic region straddling the 49th parallel and its residents maintain direct and personal economic and social links in the neighbouring U.S. states. Since 1989, meetings of political representa-tives from British Columbia, Alberta and five Pacific Northwest states have been directed at development of a regional economic consortium to promote Pacific Northwest regional economic policies which go beyond token political good-neighbourliness. In 1990 the province also signed an economic partner-ship agreement with the state of California covering tourism, transportation and environmental matters, and in July 1991 approved a long-term 13-year natural gas export contract for the California market worth $1.6 billion. The regional and global metropolitan interests shared by Vancouver, Seattle and Portland are also the topic of discussion within their business communities.

Redrawings of the Pacific Northwest map which are blind to existing polit-ical boundaries can perhaps be easily dismissed as fantasy land creations. In the past, each political entity has been shaped by the larger national political and economic ties since the boundaries were settled by the 1846 Treaty of Oregon. As Howay, Sage and Angus observed 50 years ago, the Pacific Coast communities are "friendly rather than intimate."[17] Indeed at times trans-boundary relationships have been even less than friendly as during British Columbia's attempts to increase returns from hydroelectric power and natural gas during Dave Barrett's premiership; in the disputes over fisheries, coastal boundary waters and fish processing; forestry industry clashes over imports of softwood lumber and the 1986 action against British Columbia red cedar shakes and shingles; plus conflicts and concerns for environmental protection such as the 1970s Skagit Valley dispute.[18] The opportunities afforded by the Canada-U.S. Free Trade Agreement and the joint Canada-U.S. market perspectives on Asian investment may, however, promote a new common Pacific Northwest outlook that adds to other reasons for increased cross-border traffic and a sense of Pacific Northwest regionalism.

In summary, the most obvious long-term policy implications of these con-temporary trends suggest the need for close provincial attention to an upgrading of labour force skills and training and to the social planning implications of the continuing metropolitan concentration of new job opportunities. Both carry fresh chances for intergovernmental cooperation and conflict. The continuing debate on a "sustainable development" economic future for the province is also informed by an awareness of diminishing natural resources and trade-offs between quality of life or environmental considerations and job creation which generate their own potential for collisions between intergovernmental policy priorities. The resentment against federal intervention in South Moresby National Park and reactions to the provincial government's own attempt at compromises regarding the Carmanah Valley show that there can be no easy win-win solutions.

FAIR SHARE FEDERALISM

The central hallmark of Premier Vander Zalm's 1986-90 stance towards Ottawa was the pursuit of what can be termed "Fair Share Federalism." A "balance sheet" accounting of British Columbia's financial contributions to Canada and the federal government's financial returns to the province has been a continuous preoccupation of British Columbia's premiers and ministers of finance. The inevitable bottom line indicating a net outflow of funds has always remained an important symbol and confirmation of extortion or at best neglect.[19] Throughout all of its five years in office, the Vander Zalm government doggedly argued for a fair share or a fair deal for British Columbia at every possible opportunity. In this modern version of "Better Terms," the province became a leader in a western chorus of complaints at a failure to secure a "proportionate" share of all forms of federal government contracts, special projects and other regional development expenditures and in national dairy products and chicken, egg and turkey marketing boards. British Columbia rode the wave of western anger in October 1986 at Manitoba's loss of the CF-18 jet aircraft maintenance contract to Montreal, and lobbied hard and long for its own share of major federal awards such as the Polar 8 icebreaker $680 million contract for the Versatile Pacific shipyard in Vancouver and $700,000 support for the Kaon atomic particle project at the University of British Columbia. There is a list of instances that maintained a chill attitude towards the federal government: the "surrender of sovereignty" and land in the establishment of the South Moresby National Park and delays in payments under the $106 million financial compensation package; postponements of federal commitments to the Kaon project; the delayed financial assistance for the Vancouver Island gas pipeline; and the delays and then cancellation of the Polar 8 as part of the 1989-90 budgetary restraint policies (followed in 1991 by assistance to Quebec ship-building while Versatile's Vancouver facilities faced closure). The formation of a joint British Columbia-Ottawa Council of Ministers in 1987 proved only a short lived attempt at effective regional liaison. The premier's statements at first ministers' meetings, convention addresses and speeches from the Throne returned again and again to the fairness theme. They pointed to the inequity in British Columbia receiving only 5 percent of federal contracts when it had 11 percent of the Canadian population. The premier claimed that the province deserved $400 million more in federal contracts and pointed out that the Ottawa River Valley received ten times the level of regional economic expansion and research grants as British Columbia. These arguments reached a peak in 1988 in the contemplation of some kind of a permanent monitoring and evaluation of British Columbia's standing within the federal system.[20] The phantom of federal intrusions that formed part of the Bill Bennett's symbolism also overshadowed the 1980s agenda as challenges were mounted to federal government entry into the regulation of financial securities, and clashes continued in enforcement of federal environmental protection standards for fish and other habitats. In response to the federal Minister of State for Finance, Gilles Loiselle's contemplation of a national securities commission, Mr. Couvelier indicated that he would insist on provincial jurisdiction in easily understood terms: "I'll take my ball and go home. They won't be able to play the game if I've got the ball."[21] The promotion of Vancouver as an international financial centre had received federal acceptance in Mr. Wilson's 1986 budget, which promised to designate both Vancouver and Montreal as such centres. But here too, the province was far from satisfied due to the limited scope of the financial incentives proposed in the federal government's amendments to the Income Tax Act. Ottawa was seen as bowing to opposition from Toronto and Ontario and, after a banking mission in the Pacific Rim, British Columbia presented its own draft International Financial Business Acts which provided for provincial tax refunds and incorporation of international financial business subsidiaries in order to mobilize support to broaden Ottawa's incentives.[22] More cooperation was evident in the 1991 tax changes made by the federal government as the result of recommendations from the Asia Pacific Initiative (API) to encourage Vancouver to also become a International Maritime Centre.

The Vander Zalm and Couvelier initiatives became muted in the face of the 1988-91 domestic controversies surrounding Premier Vander Zalm which, in the wake of the Hughes' conflict of interest inquiry, eventually led to his 2 April 1991 resignation as premier. It is noteworthy that two weeks later, the first pronouncement of his immediate successor, Premier Rita Johnston, on matters of federal-provincial relations was a reassertion of the fair share theme. In her first meeting with Prime Minister Mulroney she requested a list to support the prime minister's claim that the province's share of federal procurements had increased substantially.[23]

FEDERAL OFFLOADING AND FISCAL DISENTANGLEMENT

Closely associated with the "fair share" theme have been relations arising from federal fiscal policy. Federal government retrenchment, deficit reduction through unilateral cut backs in transfer payments, high interest rates, plus the maintenance of a high dollar exchange rate have kept Victoria-Ottawa relationships at a low ebb. The 1984-86 ceilings on the growth of post-secondary

Established Program Financing (EPF) and post-1986 limits on EPF growth at 2 and then 3 percent below the growth in Gross National Product were followed by a 1990 budget freeze, which was in turn extended for three more years in 1991. The protracted renegotiation of the Economic and Regional Development Agreement and reforestation cost-sharing, changes to Unemployment Insurance coverage, other program freezes or reductions such as those for young offenders funding, the freeze in funding increases under the Canada Assistance Plan (CAP) and the 1991 trimming of the provincial-municipal ten-year RCMP agreement can also be added to British Columbia's litany of a federal government offloading its fiscal problems onto the province.

In the 1990 federal budget and the accompanying Bill C-69, the federal government targetted British Columbia (along with Alberta and Ontario) for a 5 percent growth ceiling on CAP expenditures for social welfare and other social assistance programs. This would have resulted in a total loss of $156 million by 1992. Joined by Manitoba, British Columbia successfully argued against this unilateral action in the British Columbia Court of Appeal on the grounds that although Parliament had the power to amend the plan, there was a legitimate expectation that the Government of Canada would only alter it by mutual consent. While the B.C. Court of Appeal agreed with the provincial case, the Supreme Court of Canada overturned the decision on appeal.[24]

Over half of federal transfers to British Columbia come from the EPF arrangements. It was estimated that the federal 1990 and 1991 EPF freezes would cost the province $5,119.6 million by the end of the fiscal year 1994-95. The revisions would accelerate the decline in the federal share of British Columbia's health-care and education costs from 37 percent in 1991-92 to 27 percent by the end of the 1990s with a zero cash transfer and only a tax transfer component within 12 years.[25] British Columbia was even more vociferous in its opposition to the federal government's unilateral extension of its occupancy of the direct taxation field under the Goods and Services Tax (GST) which it labelled as inflationary and a threat to the economy. It joined Alberta's court challenge to the tax and launched its own judicial challenge against the appointment of additional Senators by the Mulroney government to secure passage of its Excise and Income Tax and Unemployment Insurance amendments through the Liberal controlled Senate.

British Columbia's principal influence on the national federal-provincial relations agenda lays in its contribution to the course of discussions of federal-provincial finance ministers and the future of federal transfer payments. In an initiative first pursued at the Western Premiers' 1990 Lloydminister conference and continued in his brief to the Senate Committee considering the GST and again at the finance ministers' Winnipeg December 1990 meeting, British Columbia's finance minister, Mel Couvelier proposed a "disentanglement" of the two jurisdictions. He argued before the committee that the GST was a symptom of a fundamental problem in the fiscal arrangements and that a re-ordering and redefinition of roles and responsibilities was required to address the upward bias in federal spending. This bias was demonstrated, Couvelier contended, in the growth of the federal debt and the continuing expansion of federal programs into provincial jurisdiction, through such initiatives as the proposed day-care plan, national education strategy, environmental regulation, and the creation of the federal Department of Forestry.[26] The suggestion that the federal government reduce its spending in areas of provincial responsibility (including EPF for health care, post-secondary education and social welfare) with a transfer of fully equalized tax room to the provinces attracted the most attention. Three other options for the renewal of fiscal federalism were also supported by all four western provincial finance ministers smarting under the impact of the 1990 federal budget: an independent western Canadian provincial income tax collection; spending limits to eliminate deficits and debt reduction; and reformed policy coordination, including both monetary and fiscal policy.[27]

The disentanglement theme was a little less strongly pursued at the 1991 Western Premiers meeting after Couvelier's 7 May firing by the new premier, Rita Johnston, but provincial spending limits had been introduced by his first successor as finance minister, Mr. Veitch, in a legislative commitment (*Taxpayer Protection Act*) to plan for a "balanced budget" based on a five-year expenditure-revenue budget forecast.[28] Premier Rita Johnston also continued the same theme as part of her policy commitments leading up to the 20 July 1991 Social Credit leadership contest and linked a limitation on the growth of government with a proposal for a constitutional amendment to confirm the property rights of citizens.[29]

ABORIGINAL POLICY ACCOMMODATION

The next major theme in intergovernmental relations concerned British Columbia's aboriginal peoples. The issues in native affairs policy are intimately linked to fundamental concerns for the future of the British Columbia resource sector and environmental protection in the province's own dialectical version of the sustained development debate. No other policy field can match the potential internal and intergovernmental impact of the province's dealings with its aboriginal First Nations. The questions surrounding future relationships between the aboriginal peoples of British Columbia and other British Columbians has become one of the dominant issues and a source of new symbols in the province's policy agenda. The underlying concerns with aboriginal title, rights and forms of self-government are not unique to British Columbia. However, the large number of Native Indian bands (196 made up of some 81,000 status Native Indians) and the political skills of the representatives of British Columbia's First Nations has ensured that they rank high on the public agenda.[30] The ramifications for the province's resource policies has forced the province to abandon its pre-1986 attempt to remain disengaged from the land claim process.

In the passage of these matters through the shoals of first ministers' conferences and in the development of provincial policies down to the end of the 1980s, British Columbia's premiers and attorneys-general had consistently maintained that such matters were outside any provincial responsibility under articles 1 and 13 of the *Terms of Union*, 1871, and sections 91 (24), 92 (5) and 109 of the *Constitution Act, 1867*. At the final session of the series of four first ministers' conferences on aboriginal rights, 26-27 March 1987, Vander Zalm echoed the arguments of former Premier Bill Bennett and former Attorney-General Brian Smith in his opposition to any constitutional recognition of Indian self-government, which they all portrayed as an amorphous concept. In their view, the costs of land claims were entirely a federal matter with compensation to be paid to the province should there be any alienation of provincial lands.

While he had begun his term as premier with gestures of goodwill, such as the visit to a Vancouver Island band at the outset of the 1986 general election campaign, Vander Zalm's constitutional stance, six months later earned him a bitter personal public rebuke from native leaders at the March 1987 conference. Nevertheless there were other more responsive institutional policy developments. A Cabinet Committee on Native Affairs was formed and a full fledged ministry of Native Affairs were created in July 1988. A year later a nine-member advisory Premier's Council on Native Affairs was formed and has played a central role in shaping the government's agenda. Though rejected as a model by most other native groups, a comprehensive self-government agreement had been implemented with the Sechelt Band through a legislated quasi-municipal delegation of powers by the federal and provincial governments.[31]

By the summer of 1990 the provincial government shifted away from its intransigent insistence that land claim issues were a purely federal concern by agreeing to be present at the negotiations.[32] It established its own claims registry and joined the ongoing Nisga'a negotiations. This appeared to be an abrupt break from previous constitutionally based positions, but many of the old symbols, including the vision of native "lock, stock and barrel" ownership of the entire province, were not entirely expunged. In January 1991 Native Affairs Minister Jack Weisgerber spelled out seven guiding principles to be adhered to in a commitment to a "fair and affordable" land claim settlement. Such organizations as the International Woodworkers Association, Council of Forest Industries of British Columbia, Fisheries Council of British Columbia, Canadian Petroleum Association and the British Columbia Wildlife Federation and other groups with a direct interest in land claims were also invited to send representatives to a third-party advisory committee. Premier Vander Zalm still reiterated that the costs of settlement remained a federal responsibility but this has come to sound more like a bargaining position and a little less like the old adamant adversarial stance. The exception to this rule has been attacks on the NDP opposition leader, Mike Harcourt, who has already acknowledged that the province's share would be as much as 25 percent of the costs of a comprehensive land settlement. It was also understood that the land claim process would in some way be made the subject of a referendum under the premier's new referendum legislation.

The legal claims of 35 Gitskan and 13 Wet'suwet'en hereditary chiefs for ownership and governance of their own territories (heard over 374 days of trial in 1987-90) formed an important part of the pressures to ensure that a provincial chair would be placed at the bargaining table. The decision of British Columbia Chief Justice Allan McEachern in this Gitskan-Wet'suwet'en land claims case, *Delgamuukw v A.G.*, March 1991 came as a surprise to the interested parties and most observers. In his judgement, the Chief Justice found that aboriginal rights were intended to be and had been extinguished in colonial times and dismissed the ownership and jurisdictional claims over the 58,000 square kilometres of northern-central British Columbia plus those for aboriginal rights. He left the plaintiffs entitled only to a declaration that they had a continuing legal right (subject to general law) to use unoccupied or vacant crown land for aboriginal subsistence.[33] The decision was most notable in its insistence that the root problems of aboriginal peoples were social and economic, and could not be solved through a legal rights context. They required political accommodation.

Though seemingly caught unprepared for this conclusion and the terms of the judgement, the momentum from a December 1990 tripartite Task Force appeared to continue to carry all parties along in a search for sound land claim settlements with continuing encouragement from the successive provincial Ministers of Native Affairs, Jack Weisgerber and John Savage. In July 1991, the task force released its final set of 19 recommendations regarding negotiations that included the establishment of a coordinating British Columbia Treaty Commission composed of a chairperson, two First Nation appointees and one each for the province and federal governments.[34] Premier Johnston reiterated a year 2000 deadline for their completion, but given past experience this would require a still more radical change in the process. Among the 18 land claims thus far accepted by the federal government, those under active negotiation from the Sechelt and Musqueam bands and the Nisga'a tribal council, for example, had been originally submitted in 1984, 1977 and 1974 respectively.

The issues go far beyond mere institutional or policy tinkering. They impinge on virtually every aspect of resource policy and management in the province including provincial land use, forestry, resource conservation and related environmental questions and still more conspicuously, the intricacies of federal fisheries policies. In its September 1990 policy options paper, the British

Columbia Forest Resources Commission noted that native land claims were creating a high degree of uncertainty over the province's crown lands and a lack of investment in intensive forest management. The successful 1990 challenge of federal fisheries regulations by Musqueam fisherman Ronald Sparrow in the Supreme Court of Canada and its affirmation of "the existing aboriginal right to fish for food and social and ceremonial purposes" has implications extending beyond the length of drift nets to all matters affecting the access to and disposition of Pacific fish stocks.[35] In July 1991, there were quick denunciations from commercial fishermen and Premier Johnston of the federal fisheries minister John Crosbie's suggestion that an interim agreement permitting the actual sale of fish by Native Indians might be considered. The provincial government would prefer that all resource issues be considered together as part of an entire land claim package. The 1990 series of road and rail blockades by British Columbia native peoples, including the four-month Lil'Wat blockade of the Duffey Lake Road, have added to the current sense of urgency. The options finally chosen to address the recognition of distinctive cultural beliefs and values within British Columbia itself will fundamentally reshape both internal provincial policy directions and also the future course of intergovernmental relations.

CONSTITUTIONAL REFORM AND FUTURES

Finally, much of the Vander Zalm premiership was externally dominated by the early promise of the Meech Lake constitutional reform initiative and the subsequent unravelling of the deal between December 1988 and June 1990. In this British Columbia played a relatively insignificant role in comparison to its proactive stance in the shaping of the 1982 *Canada Act*. Perhaps no other area of public policy provides the same opportunity for some degree of independent initiatives and exercise of individual leadership autonomy as does constitutional reform. There were important differences in the manner in which Bill Bennett and Bill Vander Zalm pursued those opportunities. Bill Bennett was thrust into some prominence as chair of the Premiers' Conference during the 1981 constitutional talks and had previously devoted careful attention in the enunciation of intrastate federal solutions to the division of powers impasse. His early 1979 espousal of Senate reform was only later appropriated by Alberta and the Reform Party.

In contrast, Vander Zalm's inexperience and often impatience at first ministers' constitutional dialogue was put to early and critical tests during 1986-87. Only a few days after being sworn in as premier, he attended the August 1986, Annual Premiers' Conference in Edmonton which cleared the way for the April and June 1987 Meech Lake agreement and Langevin Block Accords. A First Ministers' meeting in Vancouver in November 1986, and the unsuccessful March 1987 First Ministers' Conference on aboriginal rights also intervened. Though lacking close experienced advisors, Vander Zalm was perhaps only slightly less prepared than his fellow premiers for the dynamics of the 30 April Meech Lake meeting. He later reported his reluctance to agree to the unanimity requirement for future constitutional amendments since it might impede the prospects of Senate reform. He yielded, however, to pressure from the prime minister not to be the "lone man out."[36] In a single six and a half-hour debate scheduled on the last day of its spring sitting, the British Columbia Legislature approved the Accord on 29 June 1988 with just five opposing votes from the NDP caucus. The latter had attempted to move a package of amendments to the Accord, but were defeated on party lines 17 to 29.[37] The Accord passed with the support of the leader of the opposition, Mike Harcourt, despite his misgivings on aspects of the Accord affecting equality for women, aboriginal self-government and the Yukon and Northwest Territories.

It was not until the dying months of the Meech Lake Accord that the premier attempted to play a constitutional hand of his own after indicating that if he was faced with the Accord again he would not sign it. In a television address, 17 January 1990 to announce his intention to stay on as premier in the wake of a sixth by-election loss, Mr. Vander Zalm mused that the accord was "unacceptable to the people of British Columbia" and that he had a proposal to save it. In a 19 January letter to Prime Minister Mulroney he proposed a five prong approach to the constitutional reform impasse based on a recognition of "our differences while affirming our equality" and a way of addressing the concerns of the opponents of the existing Accord while "allowing the agenda to be balanced in order to deal with the remaining priorities and concerns of other provinces and Canadians." The five elements of his proposal were as follows. First, proclaim those parts of the Accord that already met the seven province-50 percent amending formula requirement by the 23 June 1990 deadline; second, obtain agreement for a "Canada Clause" which would recognize each of the provinces and territories as distinct; third, achieve fundamental and comprehensive Senate reform prior to 23 June 1992; fourth, obtain the subsequent consent of the Manitoba and New Brunswick legislatures for the remaining matters requiring unanimity; and fifth, agreement to pursue discussions on equality rights, property rights, minority language rights, aboriginal rights and other matters with a 23 June 1993 deadline. The argument that there should be an extension of the Accord's recognition of Quebec as constituting a distinct society within Canada to recognition of "the distinctiveness of Canada's national identity, as a product of the distinct and unique characteristics" of each of the provinces and territories drew the immediate attention of critics when the premier released his letter 23 January 1990. The response to the proposal from other first ministers and commentators conveyed the same sense of disbelief and nervous laughter from the prime minister about another "wacky" British

Columbia concept as that evidenced at W.A.C. Bennett's unveiling of a five province map of Canada at the 1969 First Ministers' Conference. Although Vander Zalm's proposal to recognize the distinctiveness of each province might be read in British Columbia as a justifiable recognition of both distinctiveness and provincial equality, outside the province, particularly in Ottawa and Quebec City, it smacked of an ignorance of the full significance and evolution of the concept of Quebec as a distinct society. Whatever the reaction to these proposals, in a 28 May address during the final days of the Meech Lake debacle, Vander Zalm reaffirmed that he would not walk away from a commitment. The nature of his rescue package, however, ensured only a "walk on" role for the premier in the final attempts to rescue the Accord. The lesson for future constitutional talks which all British Columbia politicians appear to have drawn from this experience is not to allow anyone to brow beat or box them in.

Bill Bennett had been a pathmaker in the rise of Senate reform among the range of options for constitutional reform but allowed the initiative to be grasped by the Triple E movement and Alberta. In 1989, on the death of British Columbia Senator Bell, Premier Vander Zalm indicated that Senate reform would be placed on the provincial public agenda. He delayed until July 1990 before simply introducing the *Senatorial Selection Act*, for Senate vacancies to be filled by election held simultaneously with provincial general elections. Had an election been called, this might have been tested, but as the Mulroney government filled the British Columbia vacancy with Pat Carney and proceeded to appoint additional Senators under the never before used section 26 of the *Constitution Act, 1867* to break the blockage of the Goods and Services Tax legislation, the British Columbia government could only assert its opposition through a court challenge to the appointments. The next normal retirement vacancy would not occur until 1996. The province argued that the power to appoint additional senators was intended to be on the advice of the Queen's "Imperial" advisors and since the evolution of the constitution since 1867 made any such advice unconstitutional then the section was inoperative. The British Columbia Court of Appeal rejected this interpretation.[38] The court found that "as a matter of law" section 26 was not inoperative and that the Queen retained an independent discretion to appoint four or eight senators on the recommendation of the Governor General. The court futher declined to answer questions relating to limitations that might be imposed by any constitutional conventions.

While the former regional and economic development minister and attorney general, Bud Smith, evidenced a close interest in constitutional issues and chaired a Cabinet Committee on Confederation, no other cabinet members seemed to be closely involved. Moreover, there had been no attempt to involve the Legislature, not to mention public participation, in the constitutional reform process. Some discussion papers were sponsored by the provincial government but not until 1991, did Bill 81 *Constitutional Amendment Approval Act* belatedly open up the review process by requiring a referendum on amendments to the Constitution of Canada prior to the introduction of any resolution in the Legislative Assembly. Premier Vander Zalm presented it as a clear message to Ottawa that British Columbia must be involved in the constitutional reform process with no unilateral deals between Ottawa and Quebec. At the close of the Spring sitting of the Legislature, the Select Standing Committee on Constitutional Matters and Intergovernmental Relations was also authorized to consult British Columbians on:

1. The social and economic interests and aspirations of British Columbians and other Canadians within the federation; and
2. The form of federation that can most effectively meet the social and economic aspirations of British Columbians and all Canadians.

The Committee made a preliminary report on 15 August 1991, with a series of recommendations for an open process. It was, of course, more than a coincidence that the Annual Premiers' Conference was scheduled to be held at Whistler, British Columbia on 26-27 August 1991.[39] The timing and short period allowed for the Committee's work resulted in just six sparsely attended hearings in Terrace, Prince George, Cranbrook, Nanaimo, Vancouver and Kamloops, 22 July-8 August 1991.

During 1991 and, in particular, the interregnum following the demise of Premier Vander Zalm, the voice of the British Columbia government has been only intermittently heard on the course of the national constitutional debate, including the new options articulated in the Quebec Liberal Party Allaire Report, the Quebec National Assembly Committee, the Spicer Citizens' Forum and the Beaudoin-Edwards joint Senate-House of Commons Committee proposal for a constitutional amending process. Premier Vander Zalm and his finance minister, Couvelier, responded positively to the decentralizing recommendations of the Allaire Report in "me-too" reactions which asserted whatever Quebec got, British Columbia would want the same. The similarities with British Columbia's fiscal policy position and the Report's reference to "institutional limitations on budgetary practice" including limitations on deficits and restricted taxation power also did not go unnoticed.[40] The new premier's reaction to the Beaudoin-Edwards report was, however, that she "couldn't comment as she hadn't read it yet." The spokesperson for the 19 members of the New Democrats' Ottawa caucus, Lynn Hunter, MP had added an addendum to the Beaudoin-Edwards Report in which she protested the revival of the four region amending formula approach of the 1971 Victoria Charter for its failure to recognize British Columbia's distinctive interests as a fifth region separate from the western provinces.[41] The leader of the NDP provincial opposition, Mike Harcourt, similarly asserted that any resurrection of a Victoria Charter style Ontario or Quebec constitutional veto was entirely unacceptable within British Columbia.[42]

During the party leadership contest and, after her convention victory, as chair of the Annual Premiers' Conference, Premier Johnston later assumed a more public stance on federal-provincial matters. She moved away from the "me too" approach of her predecessor in making it known that, as described by Prime Minister Mulroney, "British Columbia is going to write its own ticket." In her convention discussion paper, Johnston argued that there was no point trying to make a deal with Quebec if they "fundamentally don't want to be part of the country," and that Quebec's "make us an offer approach should be dismissed outright." Later, at a pre-Whistler conference trip to meet with Premier Bourassa she personally conceded that "I think we need a bit of educating in British Columbia so that we have a better understanding [of Quebec]."[43]

Two discussion papers sponsored by the Cabinet Committee on Confederation were released in Spring 1991. The first, a technical background paper, argued that any new constitutional arrangements must take account of the global economy, and it briefly summarized views as to whether globalization would result in more decentralization or require a stronger federal role. It identified the principles and values which would have to be balanced in constitutional reform including the need for fiscal responsibility ("sustainability") and the assignment of powers in the interests of legitimacy, accountability and responsiveness versus effectiveness and efficiency ("subsidiarity"). It also set out the range of options open to Canada from five forms of federal relationships to three confederal forms plus complete economic and political separation.[44]

The second paper was a more personal review of directions for constitutional reform by Melvin H. Smith Q.C., former senior provincial public official for constitutional affairs from 1967 to 1987.[45] His recommendations included a restructuring of the central institutions with an elected Senate, a Council of the Federation and constitutionalization of the Supreme Court; maintenance of the existing amending formula; and some decentralization of powers, with delegation and perhaps concurrency with provincial paramountcy. Together with his suspicions of Quebec's agendas (save for the 1980 QLP Beige paper proposals) and the language provisions of the *Charter*, his recommendations stayed within familiar ground and came close to expressing what may be seen as a British Columbia post-1970s consensus on constitutional reform. In early August, while the legislative assembly committee was still on tour, a further collection of opinions from a variety of sources and an analysis of issues related to economic performance were released under the aegis of the cabinet committee.[46] As with the earlier releases, they were published to stimulate discussion and offered a provocative and at times divergent set of perspectives. *La Federation des Franco-Colombiens'* brief to the cabinet committee which argued in favour of a constitutional constituent assembly and a redefinition of federation "in terms of three main national communities, native, anglophone and francophone" was also included in the collection. Pending a report from the all party committee on what they considered to be consensus, there was no attempt to formally define a coherent official approach to constitutional change.

CONCLUSIONS

Current concerns for a fair deal from Ottawa, for fiscal discipline and for effective representation in national institutions have blended with the shadows of the grievances and traditional attitudes that have always defined Ottawa-Victoria relations. The repetition of these concerns by premiers who inevitably assume the same British Columbia persona around the first ministers' table, and who read from the same texts, has at times almost hinted that there might have been be some acquiescence in the perpetuation of such grievances.[47] There are certainly those who refuse to see Ottawa as an adversary and/or seek protection from a central presence in such matters as environmental regulation, the financing of social services and the larger dynamic to aboriginal affairs policies. Notwithstanding these constituencies, federal-provincial relations are one of the few "non-political" items on the provincial policy agenda. Neither the facts nor their solutions undergo significant challenge. The leadership of both major political parties now generally share a consensus as to the sources of the structural problems in intergovernmental relations and their required solutions. In many respects these correspond to a broader western provincial consensus and may even appear to overlap with the concerns of the rapidly growing Reform Party of Canada. This is, however, also a period in which the provincial parties are asserting new symbols for British Columbia's identity in the 1990s. Global economic change has renewed the sense of a Pacific distinctiveness from the Prairie neighbours beyond the Rockies, and has combined with national political changes to breed a determination to give an overriding priority to British Columbia's own agenda.

Fifty years ago in *The Unknown Country* Bruce Hutchinson described many of the trends that are still shaping the province. His view that "Vancouver has always thought of little but Vancouver. Always British Columbia thinks of British Columbia" has been reformulated and restated in various forms many times since.[48] It still applies today as British Columbia's party leaders prepare to assert the province's priorities. In the mid-1990s, there is an opportunity for British Columbia to play a role akin to that played by Alberta in the mid-1970s as the catalyst for the consolidation of a new alignment of intergovernmental political forces. Ottawa-Victoria relations, however, have been long character-ized by misunderstanding and bemusement, by suspicion and anger and, worst of all, by periods of mutual indifference and detachment. Solving the current crisis in Confederation will require better of both.

NOTES

I would like to thank Athanasia Mentzelopoulos for research assistance.

1. British Columbia, Ministry of International Business and Immigration, *British Columbia's Pacific Visions* (December 1990).

2. See Douglas M. Brown and Murray Smith (eds.), *Canadian Federalism: Meeting Global Economic Challenges?* (Kingston: Institute of Intergovernmental Relations, Queen's University, 1991).

3. British Columbia Central Credit Union calculations, *Economic Analysis of British Columbia* (December 1990). See also: British Columbia, Forest Resources Commission, *Background Papers*, volume 5 (April 1991).

4. H. Craig Davis and T.A. Hutton, "The Two Economies of British Columbia," *B.C. Studies*, 82, Summer 1989, pp. 3-15.

5. British Columbia, Intergovernmental Relations, *Confederation for the Twenty-First Century: A Background Discussion Paper* (March 1991), p. 5.

6. See the Economic Council of Canada 1990 study, *Good Jobs, Bad Jobs: Employment in the Service Economy*; and William J. Coffey and James J. McRae, *Service Industries in Regional Development* (Halifax: Institute for Research on Public Policy, 1989).

7. British Columbia, Ministry of Finance and Corporate Relations, Planning and Statistics Division, *The Structure of the British Columbia Economy: A Land Use Perspective* (March 1991).

8. *The Structure of the British Columbia Economy*, Table 6.

9. British Columbia, *British Columbia in the Canadian Confederation*, a submission presented to the Royal Commission on Dominion-Provincial Relations (1938), p. 274.

10. British Columbia, Hon. W.R. Bennett, *Enhancing Canada's Trade Prospects: A British Columbia Perspective* (August 1985); British Columbia, *The Free Trade Agreement: Impact on British Columbia* (1988).

11. In 1989, British Columbia's export trade to Mexico only amounted to $32 million, primarily in wood pulp. Any impact on the provincial economy would be most likely felt in domestic competition for horticultural products and textiles/clothing. There would also be increased competition with Mexico for capital investments seeking easy market access into the United States under a free trade pact. See British Columbia, Ministry of International Business and Immigration, *British Columbia and Mexico: the Trilateral Free Trade Proposal, A Discussion Paper* (November 1990).

12. See M. B. Percy and Christian Yoder, *The Softwood Lumber Dispute and Canada-U.S. Trade in Natural Resources* (Halifax: Institute for Research on Public Policy, 1987); and Russell Uhler (ed.), *Canada-United States Trade in Forest Products* (Vancouver: UBC Press, 1991).

13. *British Columbia's Pacific Visions* (December 1990).

14. See Donald Gutstein, *The New Landlords* (Victoria: Porcepic, 1990).

15. British Columbia, *British Columbia News* (July 1991), p. 5.

16. The investor immigrant program is open to business immigrants investing $250,000 in a government approved project or fund for three years. Entrepreneurial immigrants must establish a business enterprise. Investor immigrants contributed $41.8 million to B.C.in 1987 and $122.9 million in 1988.

17. Howay, Sage and Angus, *British Columbia and the United States* (New York: Russell & Russell, 1942), p. 408.

18. See James P. Groen, "Provincial International Activity: Case Studies of the Barrett and Vander Zalm Administrations in British Columbia," unpublished M.A. thesis Simon Fraser University, 1991.

19. See Robert L. Mansell and Ronald C. Schlenker, "An Analysis of the Regional Distribution of Federal Fiscal Balances: Updated Data," unpublished paper, May 1990.

20. British Columbia, *Speech From the Throne* (18 March 1988). See also account of the preparation of an internal confidential study on the economics of Confederation, related draft legislation and even hints of separatism in Gary Mason and Keith Baldry, *Fantasyland: Inside the Reign of Bill Vander Zalm* (Toronto: McGraw-Hill, Ryerson, 1989), p. 144-45.

21. Peter O'Neil, "Securities Commission Considered," *Vancouver Sun* (26 May 1989), D1.

22. British Columbia, Finance and Corporate Relations, *Budget*, 1987, p.19. The drafts were Bills 49 and 50, *International Financial Business (Tax Refund) Act* and *International Financial Business Act*, 1987.

23. Keith Baldrey, "Johnston's eyebrows sky-high after Mulroney's contract claim," *Vancouver Sun* (24 April 1991), A16. Kim Campbell, federal Minister of Justice and MP for Vancouver Centre responded three days later with a letter outlining new federal procurement policies and some 25,000 contracts in British Columbia.

24. *Reference re Canada Assistance Plan*, 71 D.L.R. (4th), 15 June 1990, pp. 99-140. For the Supreme Court of Canada judgement see *Reference re Canada Assistance Plan* (B.C.) (15 August 1991), (S.C.C.) [unreported]. Bill C-69 received royal assent, 1 February 1991.

25. British Columbia, Honourable John Jansen, Minister of Finance and Corporate Relations, *Budget 1991*, pp. 44-5.

26. The Honourable Mel Couvelier, *Submission to the Standing Senate Committee on Banking, Trade and Commerce*, (1 August 1990). See also British Columbia, Ministry of Finance and Corporate Relations, *British Columbia Statistical and Economic Review, 1990* (November 1990), pp. 132-33.

27. Report of the Western Finance Ministers, *Economic and Fiscal Developments and Federal-Provincial Relations in Canada*, submitted to Western Premiers' Conference, Lloydminister, Saskatchewan, 26-27 July 1990.

28. Bill 92, *Taxpayer Protection Act*, Part 2.

29. Rita Johnston, *Directions for British Columbia's Future: Policies and Priorities* (July 1991), p. 15.

30. See Paul Tennant, *Aboriginal Peoples and Politics* (Vancouver: UBC Press, 1990), chap. 15.

31. Following passage of the federal Bill C-93 *Sechelt Indian Band Self-Government Act*, 1986, British Columbia passed the *Sechelt Indian Government District Enabling Act*, 1987. See discussion of this model in Frank Cassidy and Robert Bish, *Indian Government: Its Meaning in Practice* (Lantzville: Oolichan and Institute for Research on Public Policy, 1989), pp. 135-44

32. This followed the interim recommendations of the Premier's Council on Native Affairs, 25 July 1990.

33. *Delgamuukw v. A.G.*, Reasons for Judgement, No 0843 Smithers Registry, p. 297.

34. *The Report of the British Columbia Claims Task Force*, 28 June 1991.

35. *Regina v. Sparrow* (31 May 1990), 70 D.L.R. (4th) pp. 385-418. The court avoided the commercial aspects of the fishery, but showed an awareness of the potential for increasing conflict between the aboriginal and commercial fisheries.

36. See account in Andrew Cohen, *A Deal Undone: The Making and Breaking of the Meech Lake Accord* (Vancouver: Douglas and McIntyre, 1990), pp. 15-7.

37. British Columbia, *Debates of the Legislative Assembly*, 10, no. 19 (29 June 1988), pp. 5532-68.

38. *Reference re Appointment of Senators Pursuant to the Constitution Act, 1867, s. 26*, 78 D.L.R. (4th), pp. 245-66.

39. British Columbia *Debates* (27 June 1991), pp. 13221-26.

40. Constitutional Committee of the Québec Liberal Party, *A Québec Free to Choose: Report of the Constitutional Committee* (Montreal: Québec Liberal Party, 1991), p. 61.

41. Canada, Joint Parliamentary Committee of the Senate and the House of Commons, on the Process for Amending the Constitution of Canada *Report* (Ottawa: Minister of Supply and Services, 1991), p. 77.

42. "Constitutional expert, Harcourt agree British Columbia should reject 'unfair' proposals," *Times-Colonist* (22 June 1991), A12.

43. Rita Johnston, *Directions for British Columbia's Future: Policies and Priorities* (July 1991), p. 15.

44. Borrowing from Ron Watts, the options were status quo, "modernized" federalism, decentralized federalism, "asymmetrical" federalism, bipolar federalism, confederation of regions, sovereignty-association, common market, and separation. See *Confederation for the Twenty-First Century: A Background Discussion Paper.*

45. Melvin H. Smith, *The Renewal of the Federation: A British Columbia Perspective* (Victoria: Ministry of the Provincial Secretary, May 1991).

46. British Columbia, *Confederation for the Twenty-First Century;* and Donald J. Wright, *The Economy and Constitutional Change* (Victoria: July 1991).

47. Premier Barrett's apparently pragmatic attitude to matters of federal-provincial policy 1972-75, including provincial natural resources ownership, is at least one notable exception to this, but in doing so he lived up to another government attribute — a reputation for "eccentricity."

48. Bruce Hutchinson, *The Unknown Country* (Toronto: McClelland and Stewart, 1948), p. 275.

V

Chronology

9

Chronology of Events July 1990 – June 1991

Darrel R. Reid

An index of these events begins on page 239

6 July 1990
Social Assistance –
Intergovernmental
Aspects

The Federal Court of Appeal rules that Manitoba cannot legally deduct overpayments from monthly social assistance cheques. The court ruled that federal transfer payments to Manitoba are illegal as long as the province's Social Assistance Act continues to allow collection of overpayments by reducing welfare cheques. The decision upheld a 1989 ruling that threatened $5 billion in annual transfer payments to the provinces.

10 July 1990
Regulation –
Environment –
Alberta

Federal Justice Minister Kim Campbell announces that the Alberta government will not face federal prosecution over construction of the Oldman River dam in southern Alberta. The decision followed a RCMP investigation under Fisheries Act charges that construction of river diversion tunnels would disrupt and destroy fish habitat. In reaching her decision, Campbell said she took into consideration that Alberta has a program to address environmental consequences of the project. The impact study was ordered by the Federal Court of Appeal in March, but the Alberta government has asked the Supreme Court to hear arguments against the ruling.

11 July 1990
Aboriginal Peoples
– Land Claims

Quebec provincial police (Sûreté) and Oka Mohawks clash over the latter's barricades to prevent a proposed golf course on land claimed by the Mohawks. A Sûreté officer is killed. The incident provokes a tense standoff involving armed Mohawks and 1000 police officers. The siege prompts the nearby Kanewake Mohawks to close off the Mercier Bridge, causing massive traffic problems for thousands of commuters on the south shore of the St. Lawrence River.

16 July 1990
Western Premiers –
Western Governors

Saskatchewan Premier Grant Devine, Manitoba Premier Gary Filmon and a delegation of officials from Alberta meet with the United States' western governors in Fargo, ND. The meeting, a first, is described as an opportunity for the premiers to become better aquainted with the governors and some of the issues the two have in common. Discussions in a session entitled "Beyond the Free Trade Agreement" are held on trade, tourism, the environment, energy and regional development.

18 July 1990
Aboriginal Peoples
– Land Claims
– Northwest
Territories

In a joint assembly after days of debate the Dene and Métis of the Mackenzie River Delta of the Northwest Territories vote to send a major $500 million land claim agreement back to Ottawa for sweeping revisions. The agreement, which was to be ratified by 31 March 1991, would give the natives 180,000 sq. kilometres of land, subsurface mineral rights to another 10,000 sq. kilometres and special hunting and fishing rights as recognized in the constitution. The key concern is what is known as the "extinguishment clause," which cedes all Dene rights to the lands and water they now have under treaties 8 and 11 to the federal government.

25 July 1990
Bloc Québécois

A group of independent MPs led by former environment minister Lucien Bouchard announce the formation of the Bloc Québécois, the goal of which is to act in Parliament in the interests of a sovereign Quebec. According to its policy statement, the group will not form a party and individual members will be free to speak and vote according to their consciences. The Bloc Québécois declares that its "national allegiance is to Quebec," and they consider the Quebec National Assembly to be the "supreme democratic institution of the people of Quebec."

27 July 1990
Western Premiers'
Conference

Canada's western premiers meet for two days in Lloydminster to discuss the "new realities" of Confederation after the failure of the Meech Lake Accord. The premiers conclude that it may be time to draft a new fiscal federalism for the country and radically curtail Ottawa's spending powers. In a series of communiqués the premiers agree that the west's concerns continue to be given short shrift by a federal government preoccupied with Ontario and Quebec. They agree to set up a permanent western premiers' council that will consult the public on constitutional and other issues affecting western Canada. They also release a report by western finance ministers that recommends establishing a regional income tax to eliminate the need for federal transfer payments and to stop money flowing to central Canada. Other issues examined were the need for the establishment of provincial income tax systems to replace federal ones and the need to establish environmental guidelines and to press Ottawa for more provincial control.

9 August 1990
Aboriginal Peoples
Land Claims –
British Columbia

British Columbia Premier Bill Vander Zalm announces that his government will reverse its 117-year old policy of refusing to negotiate native land claims. According to the premier, the province will join the federal government in trying to find a "just settlement of Indian land claims."

13-14 August 1990
Annual Premiers'
Conference

Canada's premiers meet for their annual meeting in Winnipeg. Quebec Premier Robert Bourassa, however, does not attend. The main achievement of the two-day meeting is a tentative agreement to reduce interprovincial trade barriers by allowing companies to bid freely for government contracts in other provinces. The agreement, to take effect 31 October, does not include Quebec, although Quebec Intergovernmental Affairs Minister Gil Rémillard indicates 15 August that the province endorses the pact in principle and will likely sign it. The premiers also urge Ottawa to push ahead with a first ministers' conference on the economy in November. Senator Lowell Murray states on 15 August that there are no plans for such a meeting and, with Meech Lake dead, all such conferences must be reevaluated.

15 August 1990
Regulation –
Environment –
Prince Edward
Island

A federal panel examining the environmental risks involved in building a fixed link between Prince Edward Island and the mainland reports that the $600 million project would cause unacceptable environmental damage to the fisheries in the Northumberland Strait.

20 August 1990
Aboriginal Peoples
– Land Claims

At the request of Quebec Premier Bourassa, the Canadian Armed Forces move in to replace the police at the barricades at both Oka and Kanewake.

22 August 1990
Constitutional
Committees –
Quebec

Quebec Premier Bourassa and Parti Québécois Leader Jacques Parizeau announce the appointment of Jean Campeau, former chairman of the Caisse de Dépôt et de Placement du Québec, and Michel Bélanger, president of the National Bank of Canada, as co-chairmen of the special parliamentary commission on the constitutional and political future of Quebec in the aftermath of the demise of the Meech Lake accord.

22 August 1990
Constitutional
Committees –
Alberta

Alberta acting Premier Jim Horsman announces the creation of a ten-member constitutional committee drawn from government members, to hold hearings in Alberta beginning in the fall of 1990 and to consult with other governments. The committee is to be chaired by Mr. Horsman, who serves as Alberta's Minister of Federal and Intergovernmental Affairs.

27 August 1990
Aboriginal Peoples
– Land Claims

After suspending formal negotiations between federal and provincial representatives and Mohawk representatives, Quebec Premier Robert Bourassa requests that the army move in and destroy barricades at both Oka and the Mercier bridge. The next day armed forces troops begin dismantling the barricades at Oka and Kanewake.

30 August 1990
Senate –
Appointments

Prime Minister Brian Mulroney announces the appointment of five new Progressive Conservative senators. Called to the Senate are: Pat Carney of Vancouver, a former federal energy minister; Mario Beaulieu, a Montreal businessman; Nancy Teed, a former New Brunswick cabinet minister; Gerald Comeau, a one-time Tory MP from Nova Scotia and Consiglio di Nino of Toronto, president of Cabot Trust. The appointments boost Conservative seats to 36 compared to the Liberals' 52, four Independents, one Liberal-Independent and one Reform Party member.

30 August 1990
Taxation – Quebec;
Goods and Services
Tax

Quebec Finance Minister Gérard D. Lévesque announces in the Quebec legislature that Quebec will become the first province to harmonize its taxation policy
with the federal government's Goods and Services Tax
(GST). Quebec will replace its current provincial sales
tax with a GST-type tax similar to the federal one and
will also collect the federal GST for Ottawa. According
to Mr. Lévesque, the province was forced into changing
its fiscal policy by the federal government's determination to put the GST into place on 1 January.

6 September 1990
Elections – Ontario

In a stunning upset, the Ontario New Democratic Party
wins the Ontario provincial election, giving the province
its first New Democratic government and the first east
of Manitoba. The NDP captures 74 seats to the Liberals'
36 and the Conservatives' 20. On 30 July when Liberal
Premier David Peterson called the election just three
years into his second term, the Liberals held a massive
majority of 93 seats to 18 for the NDP and 17 for the
Tories.

11 September 1990
Constitutional
Committees –
New Brunswick

New Brunswick Premier Frank McKenna announces the
creation of a nine-member commission to examine his
province's interests in a reformed federal system. The
commission will include two cabinet ministers, two
MLAs, one native chief and several community activ-
ists.

11 September 1990
Regional
Development –
New Brunswick

The federal and New Brunswick governments sign three
long-term agreements totalling $66 million aimed at
assisting in the revitalization of urban, industrial and
mineral development in the province.

11 September 1990
Elections –
Manitoba

Manitoba Premier Gary Filmon leads his Progressive
Conservatives to a slim majority victory in today's provincial election. The Tories, who had 24 members before, capture 30 seats and 42 percent of the popular vote.
The New Democratic Party becomes the official opposition with 20 seats, and the Liberals are reduced to seven.

12 September 1990
Senate –
Appointments

Prime Minister Brian Mulroney appoints John Buchanan, premier of Nova Scotia, to the Senate. Also
named to the Senate is Noel A. Kinsella, a public servant
and academic, raising to ten the number of Progressive
Conservatives appointed to the Senate in recent weeks.

In Nova Scotia, Roger Bacon, former deputy premier and housing minister in Mr. Buchanan's Progressive Conservative government is sworn in as premier until a new Conservative leader can be chosen at a party convention.

14 September 1990
Megaprojects –
Hibernia

Federal Energy Minister Jake Epp, International Trade Minister John Crosby and Newfoundland Premier Clyde Wells sign an agreement on the $5.2 billion Hibernia offshore oil project. The agreement between Ottawa, Newfoundland and a consortium of four companies led by Mobil Oil Canada will not be final until Parliament passes legislation authorizing the federal contribution of $2.7 billion. The project is expected to create up to 6,000 jobs during construction and about 1,100 during production. About $3 billion worth of construction work will go to Canadian firms, with $1.6 billion in Newfoundland alone. Companies in Quebec and the Maritimes will also get contracts.

17 September 1990
Supreme Court –
Appointments

Prime Minister Mulroney names William A. Stevenson, formerly a judge of the Alberta Court of Appeal, to the Supreme Court of Canada. Mr. Stevenson's appointment fills the vacancy created when former chief justice Brian Dickson resigned 30 June and was succeeded by Antonio Lamer. He is the seventh judge named by Mr. Mulroney to the nine-member court since 1984.

23 September 1990
Senate –
Appointments

Prime Minister Mulroney brings the Senate to full strength by appointing five new members. Appointed to the Senate are: former federal solicitor-general James Kelleher; Brascan president Trevor Eyton; former Quebec Liberal cabinet minister Claude Castonguay; John Lynch-Staunton, chairman of de Kuyper Canada Inc.; and Mabel DeWare, a former New Brunswick cabinet minister.

25-27 September 1990
Senate; Goods and
Services Tax

The Liberal-dominated Senate Banking Committee recommends that the Conservative government's Goods and Services legislation be scrapped. Despite a Tory filibuster, the report is tabled in the Senate on 26 September. In response, the Mulroney Cabinet passes an order noting that three important financial measures passed by the Commons — unemployment insurance reform, tax changes and the GST — have been stalled in the Senate for at least five months. The government then asks the Queen for permission under section 26 of the constitution to invoke a never-before used clause to expand the Senate to get the bills passed.

Having received royal assent on 27 September Mr. Mulroney appoints eight new members to the Senate, claiming that Liberal Senators were undermining the principle of responsible government by blocking the GST and other legislation. The move raises the number of Senators to 112, giving the Conservatives a plurality in the Senate. With the latest appointments there are 54 Conservatives in the upper house, 52 Liberals, one Reform Party member, four independents and one Independent-Liberal. The eight new Senators are: Ontario heart surgeon Wilbert Keon; Michael Meighen, former national president of the Conservative party; Michael Forrestall, a former Nova Scotia Conservative MP; Normand Grimard, a Quebec lawyer; Thérèse Lavoie-Roux, a former Quebec Liberal cabinet minister; James Ross, a Fredericton lawyer; Janis Johnston, a Winnipeg consultant; and Eric Berntson, former deputy premier of Saskatchewan.

26 September 1990
Aboriginal Peoples – Land Claims

The standoff between Oka Mohawks and army troops at Oka comes to an end when about 50 Mohawks lay down their arms and surrender to military custody.

27 September 1990
Regulation – Financial Institutions

Gilles Loiselle, federal Minister of State for Finance, introduces long-delayed legislation in the Commons to revise the Trust and Loan Companies Act. The bill is to serve as a model for two more bills to be tabled later to complete the restructuring, to introduce changes to the Bank Act and a new insurance companies act. Under the new rules, the big banks will be able to own insurance and trust companies, but trusts and insurers may not own big banks. Most of the key proposals are virtually identical to those of a 1986 policy paper and draft bill that died in June 1988 amid bickering that pitted Ottawa against the provinces and much of the financial sector.

27 September 1990
Regulation – Energy

The National Energy Board rules that Hydro-Québec may proceed with two major export contracts to Vermont and New York. According to the ruling, however, Hydro-

Québec is required to submit plans for new dams or generating stations to fulfil the U.S. contracts to "appropriate environmental reviews." The conditions take into account concerns of Quebec Cree and environmentalists that new dams in the North will flood large areas of land and destroy native habitat.

28 September 1990
Senate –
Appointments

Federal New Democratic Party leader Audrey McLaughlin observes that the Mulroney government's appointment of eight new Senators leaves New Brunswick with one more senator than members of Parliament — a situation she claims violates the constitution. At a news conference the next day Justice Minister Kim Campbell states that the eight new Senators represent regions, not provinces, and therefore there are "no implications for the number of seats in the House of Commons."

4 October 1990
Megaprojects –
Hibernia

Legislation for the Hibernia oil megaproject is approved by the House of Commons.

4 October 1990
Taxation –
Saskatchewan

Saskatchewan Premier Grant Devine announces that his government will take steps to harmonize its sales tax with the federal government's Goods and Services Tax, but will not piggyback its tax on GST-inclusive prices.

12 October 1990
Regulation –
Environment –
Saskatchewan

Saskatchewan Premier Devine announces that construction of the controversial Rafferty-Alameda dam projects would proceed "full steam ahead" after members of a federal environmental review panel quit in frustration over continued work on the project. Ottawa and the province had agreed in January to halt work on the half-built Rafferty dam until a court-ordered federal review was completed. On 15 October federal Environment Minister Robert de Cotret announces his intention to force Saskatchewan to stop construction of the dams either by cancelling the project's federal licence or by taking court action. The same day, Saskatchewan Environment Minister Grant Hodgins indicates that his province is prepared to defy Ottawa over the project.

17 October 1990
Taxation –
Federal-Provincial
Relations

Ontario Premier Bob Rae announces that his province will intervene in cases launched by both British Columbia and Alberta challenging both the federal government's controversial Senate legislation and the GST.

18 October 1990
Supreme Court;
Justice,
Administration of

In a Supreme Court of Canada ruling the court stays extortion charges against four Ontario men because of the "unreasonable and intolerable" case backlog at the Peel Region courthouse in Brampton, Ontario. The ruling prompts hundreds of cases to be dismissed on similar grounds across the province. On 31 October Ontario Attorney-General Howard Hampton announces that the province will appeal the dismissal of some of the more serious charges thrown out of the courts.

25 October 1990
Language Policy

Charging that the Conservative government is dealing a blow to bilingualism and risking more damage to national unity by its inaction, Official Languages Commissioner D'Iberville Fortier tables a special report in Parliament urging the Conservative government to speed implementation of the *Official Languages Act.*

25 October 1990
Regulation –
Environment –
Quebec

Quebec Energy Minister Lise Bacon announces that Quebec will go to the Federal Court of Appeal to overturn a National Energy Board ruling of 27 September which made the construction or upgrading of hydro generating facilities subject to federal environmental review. According to Ms. Bacon, "The federal government's intervention in the management of natural resources is a serious and intolerable encroachment upon Quebec's constitutional jurisdiction."

30 October 1990
Council of
Maritime Premiers

The Council of Maritime Premiers meets in Charlottetown to discuss greater economic integration between the three provinces and the reduction of interprovincial barriers. According to Prince Edward Island Premier Joe Ghiz, the Council accepted in principle the recommendations of a report by Charles McMillan of York University that recommends removing interprovincial trade barriers, opening up government procurement programs and making professional service guidelines in medicine and law portable.

1 November 1990 *Spicer Commission*	Prime Minister Mulroney announces the creation of a "Forum on Canada's Future," headed by Mr. Keith Spicer, former chairman of the Canadian Radio-Television and Telecommunications Commission. The Forum, which is to be composed of eminent Canadians from all walks of life, is to travel across Canada to seek a consensus on what people want from their country, reporting back to the government by Canada Day, 1 July.
6 November 1990 *Bélanger-Campeau Commission – Quebec*	Hearings for the Bélanger-Campeau Commission begin in Quebec City. According to Premier Robert Bourassa he is counting on a strong consensus from the Commission looking into the future of Quebec to ensure that the province's demands for change are heard in the rest of Canada.
6 November 1990 *Taxation – Federal-Provincial Relations*	Yukon Government leader Tony Penikett announces that the Yukon government has joined British Columbia's court challenge of the Conservative government's enlargement of the Senate. The B.C.-Yukon challenge will argue that the appointment of eight extra senators to ensure passage of the GST would upset regional balance in the Senate.
7 November 1990 *Aboriginal Peoples – Land Claims*	Federal Indian Affairs Minister Tom Siddon announces that Ottawa's $500 million land claim agreement reached in April with the Dene and Métis of the Western Arctic is dead. Instead, Ottawa has decided to negotiate with each region in the area to divide up more than 180,000 sq. kilometres of land. The decision means Ottawa will no longer formally negotiate with the Métis Association of the Northwest Territories and the Dene Nation.
8 November 1990 *Aboriginal Peoples – Land Claims*	In a report to the federal government made public by Secretary of State Gerry Weiner, Quebec Public Security Minister Claude Ryan declares that calling out soldiers to deal with armed Mohawk warriors at Oka was the only way to establish law and order. Ryan states that the Sûreté du Québec did not have the manpower and equipment to end the 77-day disturbance.
15 November 1990 *Regulation – Environment*	Saskatchewan wins the first round of its court battle with Ottawa over the Rafferty-Alameda dams when Chief Justice Donald K. MacPherson of the Saskatchewan

Court of Queen's Bench turns down Ottawa's application for an injunction halting work on the project. Mr. MacPherson rules that a temporary stop-work order would hurt the province by causing costly delays, more than the project would harm the environment. On 19 November federal Environment Minister Robert de Cotret announces that his department will appeal the ruling.

15 November 1990
Regulation – Energy

The National Energy Board approves a TransCanada Pipeline's plan to build the $546 million initial phase of a $2.6 billion expansion of its cross-country natural gas pipeline. The board agrees with TransCanada that increased capacity is needed to deliver 155 million cubic feet of gas daily from Alberta gas fields to Ontario, Quebec and the New England States beginning late next year. The TransCanada expansion is designed to meet growing demand for natural gas in Ontario and Quebec, but its primary function will be to serve markets in the northeastern United States.

16 November 1990
Regulation –
Environment

Federal Environment Minister Robert de Cotret announces the appointment of a six-member panel to review the Oldman River dam project in southern Alberta. The committee is to conduct an independent examination of the environmental and socio-economic effects of the controversial $350 million project. The Federal Court of Appeal had ruled 13 March that Ottawa must apply its environmental assessment and review process to the Oldman project.

28 November 1990
Regulation –
Environment

Federal-provincial meetings are held in Victoria aimed at harmonizing federal and provincial environmental assessment procedures. Provincial environment ministers express their concern to federal Environment Minister Robert de Cotret that Ottawa is using new environmental legislation to expand its jurisdiction over provincial projects. The ministers are also briefed on a final draft of Ottawa's long-awaited Green Plan, the federal government's environmental strategy.

3 December 1990
Aboriginal Peoples
– Land Claims

The federal and British Columbia governments, as well as the First Nations Congress, announce the formation of a committee to study negotiating all British

Columbia's aboriginal land claims at the same time. According to Indian Affairs Minister Tom Siddon, it is hoped that the negotiation process will be in effect by June 1991.

4 December 1990
Regulation –
Environment

In a joint submission to a Commons committee the provincial governments demand major changes in the federal government's proposed environmental assessment legislation. The provinces put forward a series of amendments which would allow Ottawa to turn over its authority over environmental assessment to provincial governments, provided they have in place comparable assessment standards. The provinces also want additional guarantees that they be consulted at various points in the assessment process.

5-6 December 1990
Federal-Provincial
Fiscal Relations

Provincial finance ministers meet in Winnipeg to seek ways to support social programs such as medicare in the face of declining federal support. The provinces agree that the biggest threat to social programs is the federal government debt, and called on Finance Minister Michael Wilson to meet with them soon to discuss bringing spending under control.

6 December 1990
Constitutional
Committees –
Manitoba

Manitoba Premier Gary Filmon announces the establishment of an all-party Manitoba Constitutional Task Force to be chaired by University of Manitoba Professor Wally Fox-Decent. According to the premier, the Task Force is to follow up on the work of the province's Meech Lake Task Force and provide advice on priorities for future constitutional negotiations.

7 December 1990
Health Policy –
Quebec

Quebec Health Minister Marc-Yvan Coté announces sweeping changes to that province's health system. The reforms, in the making since 1985, are aimed at streamlining Quebec's health-care system, which consumes almost one-third of the province's budget. In addition to the introduction of user fees for medical service in some cases, the new proposals would also tax such supplementary services as medication for the elderly, dental work and eye care, and encourage doctors to set up practice in underserviced regions. According to Mr. Coté, the Quebec government is prepared to lead a fight against

Canada Health Act provisions aimed at deterring medical user fees in the provinces.

11 December 1990
Regulation –
Environment

Federal Environment Minister Robert de Cotret announces details of the federal government's long-awaited $3 billion Green Plan, promising more than 100 measures to protect Canada's land, water, soil, forests and wildlife over the next five years.

13 December 1990
Constitutional
Change

Prime Minister Mulroney announces the establishment of a special joint committee of MPs and senators to examine the processes of constitutional amendment in Canada. The 17-member committee, which is to be headed by Quebec Senator Gerald Beaudoin and Alberta Conservative MP Jim Edwards, is to hold public hearings and report back to Parliament by 1 July.

13 December 1990
Manpower Training
– Federal-Provincial
Relations

In a statement to the Quebec legislature, Quebec Manpower Minister André Bourbeau announces that Quebec will ask Ottawa to give up all control it has in the province over manpower training programs. According to Mr. Bourbeau, having two governments active in the same domain has created competing and contradictory programs. For this reason, the Quebec Cabinet decided to ask for full jurisdiction after consulting labour and business groups.

17 December 1990
Taxation – Goods
and Services Tax

After months of bitter wrangling, federal legislation to implement the Goods and Services Tax is given royal assent in the Senate. Liberal senators and MPs boycott the ceremony.

17 December 1990
Interprovincial
Trade Barriers –
Quebec

In a letter to the other premiers and Prime Minister Mulroney, Quebec Premier Robert Bourassa announces his willingness to go along with an agreement reached by the other provinces in August to bring down some interprovincial barriers, but on the condition that a dispute settlement panel is established. As well, Quebec will also participate only through signing bilateral agreements with each of the other provinces and Ottawa, not the multilateral accord set to come into effect on 1 January.

17 December 1990
*Industrial
Development –
Nova Scotia*

The federal and Nova Scotia governments sign a $63 million agreement to foster industrial development in Nova Scotia. The agreement, funded equally by the two governments, will be used primarily to establish new manufacturing and secondary processing plants in the province.

19 December 1990
*Regulation –
Financial
Institutions*

The federal government introduces legislation to revise the Bank Act, as part of its overhaul of regulations governing all financial institutions. The new bank law is designed to help meet the government's objective of letting banks, trust and insurance companies cross more freely into each others' turf in a less-regulated environment. The bill dovetails with changes already introduced 27 September in a new trust and loan companies bill. Still to come is an overhaul of legislation governing insurance companies and credit cooperatives.

19 December 1990
*Constitutional
Change – Ontario*

Ontario Premier Bob Rae announces the creation of an all-party committee chaired by New Democratic MPP Tony Silipo that will tour the province in February to gauge public opinion on the province's role and future in a renewed federalism. Rae wants Ontarians to voice what economic, social and political expectations they have of all levels of government, to help the province negotiate change that makes the country more responsive to their needs.

19 December 1990
*Aboriginal Peoples
– Land Claims*

The federal and Alberta governments announce that they have reached a land claim agreement worth up to $56 million with a northern Indian band known as the Woodland Cree. The band was formed 18 months ago when a small group of natives sent a petition to Ottawa after talks broke off between the federal government and the Lubicon band over a long-standing land claim.

The same day the Stoney Indian band, located near Calgary, accepts Ottawa's offer of $19.6 million to compensate for land taken from the band 60 years ago to build a hydroelectric dam.

20 December 1990
*Constitutional
Change – Quebec*

Quebec's Bélanger-Campeau Commission completes a six-week, province-wide tour in Quebec City after hearing more than 200 briefs, the majority of them endorsing sovereignty as the province's best option.

21 December 1990 *Federal-Provincial Energy Disputes*	Finance Minister Michael Wilson and Alberta Treasurer Dick Johnston announce that their two governments have partially settled the province's claim of compensation for energy revenues lost following the collapse of world oil prices in 1986. According to the agreement, Ottawa will pay the province $148.5 million in addition to $75 million Alberta has already received. The remainder of Alberta's $418 million claim will be decided by arbitration. Alberta's claim was made in 1987 under the federal-provincial oil-price stabilization fund created to cushion oil-producing provinces from rapid industry downturns.
21 December 1990 *Supreme Court*	Prime Minister Mulroney appoints Frank Iacobucci, Chief Justice of the Federal Court of Canada and a former deputy minister of justice, to the Supreme Court of Canada to replace retiring Justice Bertha Wilson.
27 December 1990 *Immigration Policy*	Federal Immigration Minister Barbara McDougall announces a five-year agreement with Quebec which is to give that province exclusive responsibility for the selection of independent immigrants. The agreement also gives Quebec responsibility for both the linguistic and cultural integration of immigrants, as well as economic integration services available to permanent residents. The agreement, based on the 1978 Cullen-Couture agreement, is designed to enable Quebec to recruit francophone immigrants and to provide more money for French-language training for non-francophones. Ottawa will contribute $332 million over the life of the deal as compensation for Quebec's taking over some of its responsibilities for immigration.
11 January 1991 *Agriculture*	Federal Agriculture Minister Don Mazankowski announces two new federal "safety net" programs to help farmers through tough times. The Gross Revenue Insurance Program, expected to be the more popular, will guarantee farmers a certain return per hectare despite low prices; its costs will be shared between farmers, each province and the federal government. The Net Stabilization Account will see government and farmers setting aside money that can be used when farmers' incomes fall. Each province will have the opportunity to opt into either or both programs.

28 January 1991
*Federal-Provincial
Relations – Canada
Pension Plan*

Canada's federal and provincial finance ministers meet in Toronto. After discussions the ministers agree to double worker and employer contributions to the Canada Pension Plan over the next 20 years. Without the changes, the CPP would run low by 2011 because more people than expected are taking early retirement and productivity is rising more slowly than anticipated.

29 January 1991
*Quebec Liberal
Party –
Allaire Report*

The Quebec Liberal Party releases a report written by a committee headed by Quebec City lawyer Jean Allaire, which recommends a radically different form for Canada. The report proposes that Quebec should be given exclusive control over a wide range of areas, including communications, energy, environment, agriculture and regional development. Ottawa would retain sole jurisdiction over defence, customs and currency, while there would be shared powers in such fields as foreign and native affairs, taxation, justice, fisheries and transport. Quebec and the rest-of-Canada would retain a common Parliament, but the Senate would be abolished and the Bank of Canada reorganized to add regional input. A new constitution would be drafted, with an amending formula including a veto for Quebec. The report is to be debated at a Liberal convention in March after which negotiations would begin with Ottawa. If the rest of Canada rejects these proposals, Quebecers would be asked to vote on political sovereignty in the fall of 1992, along with an offer of economic union with the rest-of-Canada.

29 January 1991
*Regulation –
Telecommunications*

Manitoba Tel becomes the last provincially-owned telecommunications firm to come under the regulation of the Canadian Radio-Television and Telecommunications Commission. Although in 1989 the Supreme Court of Canada ruled that Ottawa had the power to regulate all phone companies in Canada, Manitoba and other provinces had vowed to fight the loss of provincial control. Manitoba Minister responsible for Manitoba Tel Glen Findlay and Federal Communications Minister Marcel Masse sign an agreement under which Manitoba Tel will be regulated by the CRTC. In return, the provincial government will be consulted on policy matters by the federal regulatory body and will receive an improved voice on the CRTC through a Manitoba-based commissioner and an expanded regional office.

5 February 1991
Regulation –
Environment

Federal Environment Minister Robert de Cotret names a new three-member panel to review the environmental impact of the controversial Rafferty-Alameda dams project in Saskatchewan. The panel, chaired by provincial historian John Archer, replaces a five-member panel that resigned last October to protest Saskatchewan's continued construction of the project.

6 February 1991
Senate

The British Columbia Court of Appeal rules that Ottawa had the constitutional authority to appoint eight new senators last September. In a 5-0 decision the court rejects arguments by British Columbia, joined by Ontario and Yukon, that the obscure section of the constitution used to enlarge the Senate by eight members is no longer valid. The court rules that section 26 of the constitution gives the Queen independent discretion to direct the appointment of additional senators on the recommendation of the Governor-General.

7 February 1991
Constitutional
Committees –
Alberta

Alberta Minister of Federal and Intergovernmental Affairs Jim Horsman announces the creation of a new all-party legislative committee to hold public hearings across the province to determine what Albertans see as Canada's future. As part of the process, a 20-page discussion paper which outlines possible courses for Canada's future is released. The Alberta committee is to submit its recommendations by 1 July.

12 February 1991
Constitutional
Committees –
Manitoba

Manitoba's constitutional task force completes its hearings. According to chairman Wally Fox-Decent, Manitobans want Quebec to stay in Confederation, but not at the cost of dismantling the central government. The all-party task force, set up by Premier Gary Filmon to help Manitoba develop a position for future constitutional negotiations, held hearings in five communities.

12 February 1991
Regulation –
Environment

Federal Environment Minister Robert de Cotret and his Quebec counterpart Pierre Paradis sign an agreement for a joint environmental study of the James Bay 2 hydroelectric project. The agreement sets out the participation of Ottawa, Quebec, Cree Indians and Inuit in the environmental assessment of the $8 billion Great Whale project, which is to include joint public hearings. The agreement applies to the Great Whale complex only; the two governments remain in disagreement over federal participation in the assessment of roads, airports and other infrastructures needed to build the complex.

12-13 February 1991
Constitutional
Change

In speeches in Toronto and Quebec Prime Minister Mulroney outlines what he believes to be the basic principles that must be respected in any upcoming constitutional change. According to Mr. Mulroney, any constitutional changes must:

• lead to a more prosperous Canada;

• reduce overlapping jurisdictions between the federal and provincial governments and barriers to trade between provinces;

• respect the diversity and equality of Canadians;

• be practical and achievable;

• maintain standards so that, for example, pensions are portable and health care is accessible to all;

• move decision-making "closer to the people"; and

• preserve the Charter of Rights and Freedoms.

13 February 1991
Federal-Provincial
Fiscal Relations

Maritime finance ministers meet to discuss the state of federal-provincial fiscal relations. According to the ministers, the economic gap between their region and the rest-of-Canada is widening and Ottawa must do something about it. Nova Scotia, New Brunswick and Prince Edward Island are getting poorer and their ability to deliver services is deteriorating. The ministers urge Ottawa to lift the limit on equalization payments to the region, which they maintain has so far cost the Maritimes $400 million in lost revenue.

19 February 1991
Regulation –
Environment;
Supreme Court

In a case prompted by the Alberta government in its disagreement with Ottawa over the construction of the Oldman dam, seven of the ten provinces open arguments in the Supreme Court of Canada over the legality of Ottawa's environmental assessment guidelines. The provinces argue that Ottawa has improperly delayed provincial projects that are suspected of having only minor impacts on such federal jurisdictions as fisheries, wildlife, transportation or Indian affairs. A ruling on the case is expected to take six months.

19 February 1991
Regulation – Energy

New Brunswick Premier Frank McKenna, in an appearance before the National Energy Board, argues the need for a $1 billion natural gas pipeline extension that would cut Atlantic Canada's dependence upon imported oil. According to Mr. McKenna, new licences to export natural gas to the United States should be limited until the Atlantic provinces are connected to the pipeline system. Until that time, he argues, New Brunswick will oppose all future gas export applications presented before the NEB.

20 February 1991
Taxation –
Saskatchewan;
Goods and Services
Tax

On the occasion of presenting a mini-budget to the Saskatchewan legislature Finance Minister Lorne Hepworth announces that the province will merge its provincial sales tax with the federal Goods and Services Tax, a move which is expected to raise an additional $126 million for the province. Saskatchewan joins Quebec as the second province to fully harmonize its sales tax with the GST.

26 February 1991
Budgets

Federal Finance Minister Michael Wilson introduces a tough budget of spending cuts and wage restraints designed to fight the recession and to hold the federal deficit in check. The budget cuts $1.2 billion in government spending, restrains public servant wages, raises cigarette taxes and increases unemployment insurance premiums. The most controversial elements of the budget are a series of cuts to federal transfer payments to the provinces for welfare, education and health costs that are estimated to save the federal government $4.48 billion over a five-year period. This will be accomplished in two ways:

• a two-year freeze on all health and post-secondary education payments under the Established Programs Financing scheme imposed last year will continue for another three years, saving the federal treasury at least $2.14 billion over five years;

• similarly, the cap of five percent on increased welfare payments to the three richest provinces, Ontario, British Columbia and Alberta, will be extended for another three years, costing those provinces at least $2.3 billion over five years.

26 February 1991
Premiers –
Nova Scotia

Following his election as leader of the governing Nova Scotia Conservatives on 9 February, Donald Cameron is sworn in as the province's twenty-first premier.

1 March 1991
Constitutional
Committees –
Ontario

Ontario's Confederation Committee ends its month-long series of hearings. According to Chairman Tony Silipo the need for leadership was a recurring theme during the legislative committee's 20-city tour. Other themes included a demand for public consultation in any future constitutional changes, the need to address native issues and self-government and a desire to keep Quebec within Canada, although not at the expense of dismantling Canada's central government.

On 21 March the committee tables its report in the Ontario legislature. While it finds that Quebec's separation would be especially damaging to Ontario, constitutional renewal cannot focus solely on the demands of Quebec.

2 March 1991
Agriculture

At a meeting of federal and provincial agriculture ministers in Regina, Federal Agriculture Minister Don Mazankowski signs a statement of principle on a so-called "third line of defence" payment to farmers. The payments would be temporary supplements to two recently-announced income support programs. The "safety net" programs will be paid for by Ottawa, the provinces and individual farmers.

3 March 1991
Federal-Provincial
Fiscal Relations

Federal Finance Minister Michael Wilson and his provincial counterparts meet in Montreal to review the federal government's recent budget. High on the agenda is Mr. Wilson's move to save $4.5 billion over three years in federal payments to the provinces for health, education and welfare, a move which the provinces believe will sharply cut services in the poorer provinces. For his part, Mr. Wilson urges the provincial ministers to follow Ottawa's lead in restricting wage increases for public servants and warns them that taxpayers cannot afford to pay the rising bill for medicare and there will have to be changes.

4 March 1991 *Forestry*	Newfoundland and the federal government sign a $64.3 million deal to develop forests and increase the number of private woodlot owners in the province. The money will be spent over four years to prepare and plant about 20,000 hectares of forest. Ottawa will contribute $45 million to the program, while Newfoundland will provide $19.3 million.
5 March 1991 *Regulation – Environment*	Federal Environment Minister Robert de Cotret announces a $25 million plan called the Pollution Prevention Initiative designed to sharply reduce toxic discharges into the Great Lakes and the St. Lawrence River within 10 years. The plan — the first under Ottawa's $3 billion Green Plan — provides for the establishment of pollution prevention program and an information centre.
9 March 1991 *Quebec Liberal Party – Allaire Report*	At its party convention the Quebec Liberal Party endorses the constitutional proposals of the Allaire committee with only minor modifications. The next day Premier Robert Bourassa, in a speech designed to placate party federalists, stresses that federalism is still the party's first choice. According to Mr. Bourassa, Quebec does not want "to cut the bridges" with the rest-of-Canada but there must be major changes to federalism to make the country more "functional."
13 March 1991 *Regulation – Environment*	U.S. President George Bush and Prime Minister Mulroney sign an agreement in Ottawa committing the two countries to curb emissions that cause acid rain and to reduce other air pollutants. It is aimed at airborne pollution drifting north from the United States to damage Canadian lakes and forests and Canadian-caused damage to New York state. Under the agreement, U.S. industry is to pay an estimated $4 billion annually to cut in half its emissions of sulphur dioxide by the year 2000, while Canadian industry will pay $500 million annually under Canadian acid-rain control programs.
18 March 1991 *Aboriginal Peoples – New Brunswick*	New Brunswick Premier Frank McKenna announces that his province is to become the first in Canada to set aside at least one seat in the legislature for aboriginal people. Mr. McKenna appoints an electoral reform committee to "consider and propose the best approach to

ensure that New Brunswick's aboriginal people are given the best representation in the Legislative Assembly." According to Mr. McKenna, the seat or seats would be non-voting, but would give native people a voice in the legislature, which now consists of 58 Liberals and no opposition members.

20 March 1991
Spicer Commission

The Citizens' Forum on the Future releases an interim report of its findings entitled *What We Have Heard So Far*, which identifies seven major areas of concern expressed by more than 75,000 Canadians in discussion groups, written briefs and on the Forum's toll-free hot line. These include: national identity; the economy; native peoples; Quebec; provincial equality; multiculturalism and political leadership. According to chairman Keith Spicer, the value most cherished by those interviewed was "the notion of individual equality, with no special treatment for any group."

25 March 1991
Constitutional Committees – Alberta

A federal-Alberta task force on native justice issues its report in Edmonton. The task force, headed by Mr. Justice Robert Cawsey of the Alberta Court of Queen's Bench, was established to examine why natives make up such a high proportion of Alberta's prison population. Among its findings the committee suggests that the present judicial system is racist and unfair to Indians and should be replaced by native courts and police. White judges should also get to know more about native culture.

25 March 1991
Language Policy

Commissioner of Official Languages D'Iberville Fortier releases his annual report to Parliament. According to the report, Canada has made substantial progress in the area of linguistic rights. However, Mr. Fortier warns, those rights could be threatened in future constitutional negotiations. However, the report, entitled *A Partial Thaw*, is uncharacteristically optimistic in its observation that equality of English and French in federal institutions has been achieved beyond expectations.

25 March 1991
Council of Maritime Premiers

The Council of Maritime Premiers meets in Woodstock, New Brunswick to discuss the development of an integrated, regional economy for the region. The three premiers agree to draw up a white paper on economic integration to present to their legislatures late this spring. Then the cabinets of Nova Scotia, New Brunswick and Prince Edward Island are to meet in Moncton in June to discuss the issue. Economic integration would include the gradual elimination of interprovincial trade barriers including more open government procurement and greater mobility for business and workers. The premiers agree initially to a year-long moratorium on new regulations that would inhibit the free flow of goods, services and people among the provinces.

27 March 1991
*Constitutional
Committees –
Quebec*

Quebec's Bélanger-Campeau Commission on Canada's future releases its final report. Among its findings, the Commission recommends that the Quebec legislature should adopt a law this spring making provision for a referendum on sovereignty no later than October 1992, if a suitable proposal for renewed federalism is not offered by the rest-of-Canada. The Commission also recommends the establishment of two legislative committees: one to examine the mechanics of sovereignty, and the other to evaluate new constitutional offers from the rest-of-Canada.

27 March 1991
*Constitutional
Change – Ontario*

After a four-day discussion of the Silipo committee's interim report and only hours after the report of Quebec's Bélanger-Campeau Commission, Ontario Premier Bob Rae sets out for the first time his broad ideas for renewed federalism. According to Mr. Rae, Ontario is ready to discuss a new division of roles between Ottawa and the provinces but is not in favour of slicing away so many federal powers that the Canadian government ceases to exist. He calls for a convention of federal and provincial legislators and territorial and native leaders which would seek to find common ground from which new rules for Confederation would be drafted. A new constitution should recognize Quebec's unique character, strengthen the Charter of Rights concerning native people and women and include an amending formula that would not require the unanimous consent of the provinces. He also indicates his willingness to discuss Senate reform, a key demand of the western and Maritime premiers.

29 March 1991 *Premiers –* *British Columbia*	British Columbia Premier Bill Vander Zalm announces that he will step down as soon as the Social Credit Party can choose a new leader. Mr. Vander Zalm had been dogged by allegations of mixing private business with government affairs in the sale of his family's Fantasy Gardens theme park.
2 April 1991 *Constitutional* *Change*	Liberal Party leader Jean Chrétien unveils his proposals for resolving Canada's constitutional crisis. Mr. Chrétien urges the prime minister to present a "detailed and concrete" package of reform proposals by 1 June. This would then be referred to a joint Commons-Senate committee that would hold public hearings, with the results of its deliberations to be submitted to a national referendum early next year. The referendum would not be binding but, if the public agreed to the changes, it would provide a strong moral impetus to governments to push the reforms through their legislatures. Other components would include:

- a reformed, elected Senate;

- the reduction of interprovincial trade barriers;

- the right of aboriginal peoples to self-government;

- allocation of federal-provincial powers to whichever government "can handle the matter best"; and

- a new amending formula that would give a veto to four regions of the country — Atlantic Canada, Quebec, Ontario and the west.

2 April 1991 *Premiers –* *British Columbia*	British Columbia Premier Bill Vander Zalm resigns as premier of British Columbia and is succeeded by Rita Johnston, Canada's first woman premier. Ms. Johnston, former Deputy Premier and Minister of Transportation and Highways is sworn in several hours after the release of a report that found Mr. Vander Zalm guilty of conflict of interest in the sale of his Fantasy Garden theme park.
6 April 1991 *Reform Party of* *Canada*	At a party convention in Saskatoon the Reform Party of Canada votes overwhelmingly to amend its constitution to allow the party to field candidates east of Manitoba. The party hopes to capitalize on the discontent of English-speaking voters in Ontario and the Atlantic

provinces. Reform Party leader Preston Manning expects the move east will put to rest the party's image as a narrow-minded fringe group — a notion the convention took pains to dispel. In a speech to the convention Mr. Manning stressed that the party wants Quebec to stay in Canada, but not at any cost. Rather, a new Canada must be more than a reaction to Quebec demands and aspirations.

7 April 1991
Bloc Québécois;
Parti Québécois

At a Parti Québécois policy convention in Montreal the party votes overwhelmingly to throw its support behind the sovereignist Bloc Québécois in future federal elections. The Bloc Québécois hopes to win at least 60 of Quebec's 75 seats in the next federal election.

18 April 1991
Agriculture

Federal officials in eight cities announce another $400-million infusion of cash for farmers. The aid package is a complicated mix of interest-free loans, income insurance, soil conservation and cash. Much of the new money is aimed at supplementing two new national "safety-net" programs announced in January which farmers and provinces have been slow to join. About one-quarter of the aid will go toward a 25 percent reduction in farmers' premiums for the Gross Revenue Insurance Plan. Costs for provincial governments will also be cut by about 10 percent.

21 April 1991
Constitutional
Change

Prime Minister Mulroney announces the appointment of Joe Clark, former Secretary of State for External Affairs, as Minister Responsible for Constitutional Affairs. Mr. Clark is to be responsible for the development of the government's constitutional position and for the consultative processes to be followed in seeking a new national consensus. As well, Mr. Clark is to chair a new Cabinet Committee on Canadian Unity and Constitutional Negotiations, which replaces the Cabinet Committees on Federal-Provincial Relations and on Cultural Affairs and National Identity.

23 April 1991
Aboriginal Peoples
– Land Claims

Speaking to the First Nations Congress in Victoria, Prime Minister Mulroney announces plans to establish a royal commission on aboriginal affairs as the first step in his government's program for addressing aboriginal concerns. Mr. Mulroney also promises to have native participation in the constitutional process and to put more federal effort and money towards resolving hundreds of land-claim issues. Acting mainly on the recommendations of a committee headed by aboriginal leaders, he promises a five-part solution:

- a commitment to spend $355 million on resolving land claims over the next five years;

- the establishment of a land-claims commission that will act as an arbiter of disputes between the government and native people;

- a fast track process for dealing with land claims under $500,000;

- a decision to increase the authority of the Indian Affairs department by allowing it to approve settlements of up to $7 million without reference to the Treasury Board; and

- the establishment of a joint native-government working group on land claims.

7 May 1991
*Aboriginal Peoples
– Land Claims*

A Commons committee publishes its report on the Oka crisis, which it calls an avoidable tragedy for which natives, governments and everybody else involved should take more blame. The committee recommends that Ottawa establish an independent judicial inquiry into events at Oka, inviting Quebec to participate. The inquiry would also look at native justice and policing issues in the province and other sources of possible conflict.

9 May 1991
*Regulation –
Environment*

The federal and provincial governments release the main elements of a $100 million plan to combat ground-level ozone — the most dangerous ingredient of city smog. The five-year plan is to be modelled on the existing program to combat acid rain. It provides for the negotiation of bilateral agreements between Ottawa and the provinces to cap emissions of the pollution that causes ground-level ozone.

10 May 1991 *Constitutional* *Change –* *British Columbia*	The British Columbia government releases a report *The Renewal of the Federation — a British Columbia Perspective*, prepared by longtime civil servant Mel Smith. According to the report, half the senators from each province should be chosen as part of provincial elections and provinces should have six, eight or ten senators, depending on size. The Supreme Court of Canada should be increased to ten members drawn from all regions, but Quebec should no longer be guaranteed three representatives. Court appointments should be made by what Smith calls a council of the federation, a permanent body to broker "federal-provincial issues" on which provinces and Ottawa would have an equal vote.
13-14 May 1991 *Western Premiers'* *Conference*	The western premiers and territorial leaders meet in Nipawin, Saskatchewan. High on the agenda is national unity. The premiers outline four vague principles that any new national arrangement must meet, demanding that it reflect the federal nature of Canada, address the practical problems and be flexible and fair in the process. According to the premiers, the west will not take a back seat on constitutional change or free trade talks with Mexico. According to Saskatchewan Premier Grant Devine, the west will not be pushed around by Quebec. "We are not going to be intimidated by some province's ultimatum." The leaders also issue a communiqué calling for reaffirmation of a 1985 agreement giving provinces a role in continental free trade talks. The premiers also call for more provincial control over immigration and chastise Ottawa for cutting back funding for health, post-secondary education and social services.
14 May 1991 *Regulation – Energy*	The National Energy Board turns down a major electricity export application by Ontario Hydro. The utility had applied for a permit to export electricity to a group of seven U.S. utilities over a 15-year period. The board instead issues a permit for only three years, saying it does not have enough information to assess the environmental impacts of the exports beyond that time.
15 May 1991 *Constitutional* *Change – Quebec*	Quebec's Liberal government tables a bill establishing the mechanism for a referendum on sovereignty for Quebec by October 1992. The body of the bill says Quebec will hold a referendum in either June or October

1992. But a lengthy preamble states the legislature "continues to hold the sovereign power to decide any power pertaining to the referendum and to pass appropriate legislation." The bill also creates two legislative committees — one to study the impact of sovereignty and the other to assess constitutional offers from the rest-of-Canada.

16 May 1991
Regulation –
Environment

In a ruling a Federal Court of Canada judge orders a full environmental review of Alcan Aluminum Ltd.'s half-built, $800-million hydroelectric project in northern British Columbia, saying the federal cabinet erred in exempting the controversial project from the legally-required assessment process. Ottawa approved the project in September 1987 and exempted it from independent review last October. The court case was launched by the Carrier-Sekani Tribal Council and other groups opposed to Alcan's expansion of existing hydroelectric facilities on the Nechako River.

16 May 1991
Education,
Post-Secondary

Federal Employment and Immigration Minister Bernard Valcourt is appointed to head a federal initiative on education aimed at exploring ways in which the federal and provincial governments can cooperate in encouraging more students to undertake scientific, technological and engineering education. He calls for a new "national learning culture" which will make Canada's education system more effective. The announcement is criticized by several provinces, who see this as another federal intrusion into what is a field of provincial jurisdiction.

17 May 1991
Mayors of Great
Lakes

Mayors of Great Lakes cities sign a maritime agreement entitled the "Declaration of Indiana" at the close of the fifth annual international Great Lakes-St. Lawrence Mayors Conference in Merrillville, Indiana, calling on the Canadian and United States governments to keep the Great Lakes-St. Lawrence Seaway "strong and healthy" into the next century. Among resolutions passed at the conference are calls for a binational strategy and adequate funding to reduce the discharge of industrial pollutants, an education program to stop the spread of dangerous exotic species, and better reaction and clean-up programs for toxic spills.

29 May 1991
Regional
Development –
Quebec

Federal Health Minister Benoît Bouchard announces that the federal government plans to create a department of regional development exclusively for Quebec. The department, which is to be headed by Mr. Bouchard, is to operate along the lines of the Western Diversification Office and the Atlantic Canada Opportunities Agency.

30 May 1991
Law Enforcement

Solicitor-General Doug Lewis agrees to extend the current contract for RCMP services to the provinces for one more year. In return, he expects authorities in eight provinces and two territories to return to the bargaining table to negotiate a longer-term contract that will see them assume a greater share of the estimated $761-million annual policing cost. When the last agreement expired 31 March without a new agreement, former federal Solicitor-General Pierre Cadieux had threatened to impose a deal unilaterally upon the provinces.

31 May 1991
Atlantic Premiers'
Conference

The Atlantic premiers meet in Sydney, Nova Scotia to discuss the prospects for economic integration between their provincial economies. Newfoundland Premier Clyde Wells announces that he will ask his cabinet whether Newfoundland should sign a year-old agreement that lets any Maritime business bid on procurement contracts offered by the three governments. A discussion paper released by the Maritime premiers called for removal of a wide range of trade barriers. The premiers have rejected the idea of a political union, but they want economic changes because of the uncertainty of federal transfer payments and regional economic development money. The premiers also meet with federal Constitutional Affairs Minister Joe Clark to discuss the best process for bringing about constitutional changes.

6 June 1991
Supreme Court

The Supreme Court of Canada upholds Saskatchewan's electoral map, ruling that boundaries for the 66 provincial ridings, drawn up two years ago, do not violate the Charter of Rights and Freedoms, but fall within reasonable limits. The 6-3 judgement overturns a March Saskatchewan Court of Appeal decision that the boundaries were unconstitutional because they were weighted too heavily in favour of rural voters and strayed too far from the principle of one person, one vote. The ruling has implications for several provinces and the federal government, which might have had to redraw electoral boundaries had the Supreme Court upheld the earlier ruling.

7 June 1991
Constitutional
Committees –
Nova Scotia

Nova Scotia Premier Don Cameron announces the creation of a committee to develop a constitutional position for the province. Led by former federal Liberal cabinet minister Eric Kierans, the 12-member non-partisan committee is to begin public hearings in September.

7 June 1991
Regulation –
Environment

The federal and Manitoba governments announce that they will conduct a joint environmental review of the massive Conawapa hydroelectric project in a move designed to alleviate Canada's "chaotic assessment system." An independent six-member panel has been given a broad mandate to study the proposed $5.7 billion hydroelectric generating station and dam on the Nelson River about 800 kilometres north of Winnipeg.

9-10 June 1991
Federal-Provincial
Tax Relations

Canada's federal and provincial finance ministers meet in Charlottetown, where discussions centre upon a federal plan that would give provinces more control over how their income tax is collected. Under the scheme, Revenue Canada would continue to collect income tax for all provinces except Quebec, which collects its own. But each province would have more flexibility to decide how much individual taxpayers would pay. Currently, the provinces' tax cut is based on a percentage of the federal tax owed when Canadians fill out their combined federal and provincial tax returns. The provinces also receive a commitment from federal Finance Minister Don Mazankowski to renew the system of equalization payments to the poorest provinces.

12 June 1991
Constitutional
Change

A group of prominent Canadians calling themselves the Group of 22 releases a report entitled *Some Practical Suggestions for Canada*, which proposes a significant adjustment of federal and provincial powers. According to the group — which includes former premiers William Davis and Allan Blakeney, among others — the federal government should withdraw totally from contributing to health care, education and other social programs delivered by the provinces. Aboriginal people should be given the right to self-government, and Ottawa would withdraw from most areas involving energy, natural resources and the environment. To strengthen the economic union, the provinces would be forced to eliminate barriers to the free movement of people, goods, services and capital within the country.

19 June 1991
Language Policy

Parliamentarians choose Mr. Victor Goldbloom, a former Quebec cabinet minister, as Canada's new Commissioner of Official Languages. He replaces D'Iberville Fortier, who retired recently after a seven-year term.

20 June 1991
Constitutional
Committees –
Beaudoin-Edwards

The Beaudoin-Edwards committee on constitutional amendment issues its report. The committee recommends a new amending formula, similar to the "Victoria formula" agreed to by the premiers in 1972. Under this plan the new amending formula would give a veto over constitutional change to Quebec, Ontario, and two Atlantic or two western provinces containing more than 50 percent of the region's population. Other recommendations by the committee include:

- only three areas require unanimous consent in order to be changed: the status of official languages, Canada's relationship to the monarchy and provincial control over natural resources;

- that the government hold a referendum on proposed constitutional amendments, which would have to be approved by a majority in all four regions to carry;

- that aboriginal Canadians be given a permanent seat at the constitutional negotiating table;

- that a constituent assembly not be held at this time. Instead, the report suggests another parliamentary committee be sent across the country to search for a consensus.

27 June 1991
Spicer Commission

The Citizen's Forum on Canada's Future, otherwise known as the Spicer Commission, makes public its report, which calls for new thinking about Canada's national institutions and symbols. The committee's recommendations include:

- urging the government to review and coordinate its thinking on national institutions and symbols to "give them more evident importance and to avoid the impression among Canadians that they are losing their sense of Country";

• suggesting that people outside Quebec could accept that the province "should have the freedom and the means" to be its own unique self with a distinctive place in a "renewed Canadian family";

• calling on federal and provincial governments and the private sector to tell Canadians of the economic, political, social and international consequences of an independent Quebec;

• an independent review of the application of official languages policy;

• "prompt, fair settlement of the aboriginal land and self-government claims";

• elimination by the federal government of overlapping jurisdictions;

• a relaxation of overly rigid party discipline; and

• the need for a constituent assembly to address the country's constitutional problems.

28 June 1991
Aboriginal Peoples
– Land Claims

Representatives from Inuit groups and the government of Quebec sign an agreement on self-government which lays out a framework for negotiations leading to the establishment of an autonomous regional government. The body would govern residents — both Inuit and non-native — who live north of Quebec's 55th parallel.

Chronology: Index

Industrial Development 17 December 1990

Interprovincial Trade Barriers 17 December 1990

Justice, Administration of 18 October 1990

Language Policy 25 October 1990, 25 March 1991, 19 June 1991

Law Enforcement 30 May 1991

Manpower Training 13 December 1990

Mayors, Great Lakes Region 17 May 1991

Megaprojects – Hibernia 14 September 1990, 4 October 1990

Parti Québécois 7 April 1991

Premiers 26 February 1991, 29 March 1991, 2 April 1991

Quebec Liberal Party – Allaire Report 29 January 1991, 9 March 1991

Reform Party of Canada 6 April 1991

Regional Development 11 September 1990, 29 May 1991

Regulation – Energy 27 September 1990, 15 November 1990, 19 February 1991, 14 May 1991

Regulation – Environment 10 July 1990, 15 August 1990, 12 October 1990, 25 October 1990, 15 November 1990, 16 November 1990, 28 November 1990, 4 December 1990, 11 December 1990, 5 February 1991, 12 February 1991, 19 February 1991, 5 March 1991, 13 March 1991, 9 May 1991, 16 May 1991, 7 June 1991

Regulation – Financial Institutions 27 September 1990, 19 December 1990

Regulation – Telecommunications 29 January 1991

Senate 25-27 September 1990, 6 February 1991

Senate – Appointments 30 August 1990, 12 September 1990, 23 September 1990, 28 September 1990

Social Assistance – Intergovernmental Aspects 6 July 1990

Spicer Commission 1 November 1990, 20 March 1991, 27 June 1991

Supreme Court 17 September 1990, 18 October 1990, 21 December 1990, 19 February 1991, 6 June 1991

Taxation 30 August 1990, 4 October 1990, 17 October 1990, 6 November 1990, 17 December 1990, 20 February 1991

Western Premiers' Conference 27 July 1990, 13-14 May 1991

Western Premiers – Western Governors 16 July 1990

Appendix

Constitutional Reform in the Post-Meech Era:
A Select Bibliography*

compiled by Dwight Herperger

Abele, Frances. "The Politics of Fragmentation." in idem, ed. *How Ottawa Spends: The Politics of Fragmentation 1991-92*. Carleton Public Policy Series, No. 6. Ottawa: Carleton University Press, 1991, p. 1-32.

Alberta. Constitutional Reform Task Force. *An Overview of Federalism (Roundtable I)*. Edmonton, 26 October 1990.

———. *Dynamics of Federalism (Roundtable II)*. Edmonton, 2 November 1990.

———. *Restructuring Federalism (Roundtable III)*. Edmonton, 23 November 1990.

———. *'The Amending Process' and 'The Economics of Federalism' (Roundtable III)*. Edmonton, 30 November 1990.

———. *Alberta in a New Canada: A Discussion Paper from the Constitutional Reform Task Force of Alberta*. Edmonton, 1990.

Alberta. Select Special Committee on Constitutional Reform. *Transcript of Public Hearings (Subcommittee A)*. Vol. 1. Edmonton, 24 May to 1 June 1991.

———. *Transcript of Public Hearings (Subcommittee B)*. Vol. 1. Edmonton, 24 May to 1 June 1991.

Baines, Beverly. "After Meech Lake: The Ms/Representation of Gender in Scholarly Spaces." in Smith, David E., Peter MacKinnon and John C. Courtney, eds. *After Meech Lake: Lessons for the Future*. Saskatoon: Fifth House Publishers, 1991, p. 205-18.

Bear Robe, Andrew. "First Nations and Aboriginal Rights." *Constitutional Forum*, 2, 2 (1991 Winter): 46-9.

---

* This select bibliography is comprised of writings on constitutional reform that have appeared in the last year. For an earlier, comprehensive bibliography of writings on the Meech Lake Accord, see the 1990 edition of this volume.

Bercuson, David J. and Barry Cooper. *Deconfederation: Canada Without Quebec.* Toronto: Key Porter, 1991.

Bickerton, James. "Waiting for the Future: Atlantic Canada after Meech Lake." in Abele, Frances, ed. *How Ottawa Spends: The Politics of Fragmentation 1991-92.* Carleton Public Policy Series, No. 6. Ottawa: Carleton University Press, 1991, p. 127-55.

Bissonnette, Lise. "Québec After Meech: On the Threshold." *Constitutional Forum, 2,* 2 (1991 Winter): 58-61.

Blais, André. "The Constitutional Game in Quebec: Options, Interests, Strategies, Outcomes." in Young, Robert, ed. *Confederation in Crisis.* Toronto: James Lorimer & Company, 1991, p. 65-74.

Boadway, Robin. "Constitutional Design in a Federation." in Watts, Ronald L. and Douglas M. Brown, eds. *Options for a New Canada.* Toronto: University of Toronto Press, 1991, p. 237-57.

Boadway, Robin W., Thomas J. Courchene and Douglas D. Purvis, eds. *Economic Dimensions of Constitutional Change.* Vols. I and II. Kingston: John Deutsch Institute for the Study of Economic Policy, 1991.

Boadway, Robin W., Douglas D. Purvis and Jean-François Wen. "Economic Dimensions of Constitutional Change: A Survey of the Issues." in Boadway, Robin W., Thomas J. Courchene and Douglas D. Purvis, eds. *Economic Dimensions of Constitutional Change.* Vol. I. Kingston: John Deutsch Institute for the Study of Economic Policy, 1991, p. 11-44.

Boothe, Paul and Richard Harris. "Alternative Divisions of Federal Assets and Liabilities." in Boadway, Robin W., Thomas J. Courchene and Douglas D. Purvis, eds. *Economic Dimensions of Constitutional Change.* Vol. II. Kingston: John Deutsch Institute for the Study of Economic Policy, 1991, p. 453-74.

Bourgault, Pierre. *Now or Never: Manifesto for an Independent Quebec.* Translated by David Homel. Toronto: Key Porter Books, 1991.

British Columbia. Cabinet Committee on Confederation. *Confederation for the Twenty-First Century: A Background Discussion Paper.* Victoria: Department of Intergovernmental Relations, 1991 March.

Brock, Kathy L. *A Mandate Fulfilled: Constitutional Reform and the Manitoba Task Force on Meech Lake.* Winnipeg, 1990 December.

Business Council on National Issues. *Canada's Constitutional Options.* Ottawa, 18 September 1990.

——. *Canada and the 21st Century.* Ottawa, 1991 April.

Cairns, Alan C. "Constitutional Minoritarianism in Canada." in Watts, Ronald L. and Douglas M. Brown, eds. *Canada: The State of the Federation 1990.* Kingston: Institute of Intergovernmental Relations, 1990, p. 71-96.

——. "Constitutional Change and the Three Equalities." in Watts, Ronald L. and Douglas M. Brown, eds. *Options for a New Canada.* Toronto: University of Toronto Press, 1991, p. 77-100.

——. "Passing Judgement on Meech Lake." in Williams, Douglas E., ed. *Disruptions: Constitutional Struggles, from the Charter to Meech Lake*. Toronto: McClelland and Stewart, 1991, p. 223-63.

——. "Roadblocks in the Way of Constitutional Change." *Constitutional Forum*, 2, 2 (1991 Winter): 54-8.

——. "The Charter, Interest Groups, Executive Federalism, and Constitutional Reform." in Smith, David E., Peter MacKinnon and John C. Courtney, eds. *After Meech Lake: Lessons for the Future*. Saskatoon: Fifth House Publishers, 1991, p. 13-31.

——. *Disruptions: Constitutional Struggles, from the Charter to Meech Lake*. Edited by Douglas E. Williams. Toronto: McClelland and Stewart, 1991.

Campbell, Robert M. and Leslie A. Pal. *The Real Worlds of Canadian Politics: Cases in Process and Policy*. 2nd ed. Peterborough: Broadview Press, 1991.

Canada. Citizens' Forum on Canada's Future. *Report to the People and Government of Canada*. [Spicer Report]. Ottawa: Supply and Services, 1991 June.

Canada. Federal-Provincial Relations Office. *Amending the Constitution of Canada: A Discussion Paper*. Ottawa: Supply and Services, 1990 December.

Canada. New Democratic Party. *Canadian Constitution Discussion Paper*. Ottawa, 1991 March.

Canada. Special Joint Committee of the Senate and the House of Commons. *The Process for Amending the Constitution of Canada*. [Beaudoin-Edwards Report]. Ottawa, 1991 June.

Canadian Study of Parliament Group. *The Future of Canadian Federalism*. Ottawa, November 1990.

Chant, John F. "Financial Regulation under Alternative Constitutional Arrangements." in Boadway, Robin W., Thomas J. Courchene and Douglas D. Purvis, eds. *Economic Dimensions of Constitutional Change*. Vol. II. Kingston: John Deutsch Institute for the Study of Economic Policy, 1991, p. 409-24.

Chodos, Robert, Rae Murphy and Eric Hamovitch. *The Unmaking of Canada*. Toronto: James Lorimer & Company, 1991 June.

Cloutier, Édouard. "We the People: Public Opinion, Sovereignty and the Constitution." in Young, Robert, ed. *Confederation in Crisis*. Toronto: James Lorimer & Company, 1991, p. 9-18.

Cohen, Andrew. *A Deal Undone: The Making and Breaking of the Meech Lake Accord*. Vancouver: Douglas & McIntyre, 1990.

Cooper, Mary H. "The Deepening Canadian Crisis Over Quebec." *Editorial Research Reports* [a publication of Congressional Quarterly], 14 (12 April 1991): 206-19.

Courchene, Thomas J. *Forever Amber: The Legacy of the 1980s for the Ongoing Constitutional Impasse*. Reflections, No. 6. Kingston: Institute of Intergovernmental Relations, 1990.

——. "Canada 1992: Political Denouement or Economic Renaissance?" in Boadway, Robin W., Thomas J. Courchene and Douglas D. Purvis, eds. *Economic Dimensions of Constitutional Change.* Vol. I. Kingston: John Deutsch Institute for the Study of Economic Policy, 1991, p. 45-69.

———. "Forever Amber." in Smith, David E., Peter MacKinnon and John C. Courtney, eds. *After Meech Lake: Lessons for the Future.* Saskatoon: Fifth House Publishers, 1991, p. 33-60.

———. *In Praise of Renewed Federalism.* The Canada Round: A Series on the Economics of Constitutional Renewal, No. 2. Toronto: C.D. Howe Institute, 1991 July.

———. *The Community of the Canadas.* Reflections, No. 8. Kingston: Institute of Intergovernmental Relations, 1991.

Courchene, Thomas J. and John N. McDougall. "The Context for Future Constitutional Options." in Watts, Ronald L. and Douglas M. Brown, eds. *Options for a New Canada.* Toronto: University of Toronto Press, 1991, p. 33-51.

Craven, Greg. "Canada and Québec Playing Constitutional Chicken: The View from an Australian Pedestrian." *Constitutional Forum,* 2, 2 (1991 Winter): 61-3.

Dufresne, Jacques. *Le courage et la lucidité: Essai sur la constitution d'un Québec souverain.* Sillery, Quebec: Septentrion, 1990.

Elman, Bruce P. and A. Anne McLellan. "Canada After Meech." *Constitutional Forum,* 2, 2 (1991 Winter): 63-7.

Farrow, Maureen. *Reshaping Canada to Compete.* Toronto: Coopers & Lybrand, 1991.

Fortin, Pierre. "How Economics is Shaping the Constitutional Debate in Quebec." in Young, Robert, ed. *Confederation in Crisis.* Toronto: James Lorimer & Company, 1991, p. 35-44.

———. "The Threat of Quebec Sovereignty: Meaning, Likelihood and Economic Consequences." in Boadway, Robin W., Thomas J. Courchene and Douglas D. Purvis, eds. *Economic Dimensions of Constitutional Change.* Vol. II. Kingston: John Deutsch Institute for the Study of Economic Policy, 1991, p. 335-44.

Fournier, Pierre. "L'échec du Lac Meech: un point de vue québécois." in Watts, Ronald L. and Douglas M. Brown, eds. *Canada: The State of the Federation 1990.* Kingston: Institute of Intergovernmental Relations, 1990, p. 41-68.

———. *A Meech Lake Post-mortem: Is Quebec Sovereignty Inevitable?.* Montreal and Kingston: McGill-Queen's University Press, 1991.

Gagnon, Alain-G. "Other Federal and Nonfederal Countries: Lessons for Canada." in Watts, Ronald L. and Douglas M. Brown, eds. *Options for a New Canada.* Toronto: University of Toronto Press, 1991, p. 207-33.

———. "Everything Old Is New Again: Canada, Quebec and Constitutional Impasse." in Abele, Frances, ed. *How Ottawa Spends: The Politics of Fragmentation 1991-92.* Carleton Public Policy Series, No. 6. Ottawa: Carleton University Press, 1991, p. 63-105.

Gibbins, Roger. "Constitutional Politics in the West and the Rest." in Young, Robert, ed. *Confederation in Crisis.* Toronto: James Lorimer & Company, 1991, p. 19-27.

Gotlieb, Allan. "The Changing Structure of the World Community." in Boadway, Robin W., Thomas J. Courchene and Douglas D. Purvis, eds. *Economic Dimensions of*

Constitutional Change. Vol. II. Kingston: John Deutsch Institute for the Study of Economic Policy, 1991, p. 515-24.

Group of 22. *Some Practical Suggestions for Canada.* Montreal: le Groupe Columbia, 1991 June.

Harris, Richard G. and Douglas D. Purvis. "Some Economic Aspects of Political Restructuring." in Boadway, Robin W., Thomas J. Courchene and Douglas D. Purvis, eds. *Economic Dimensions of Constitutional Change.* Vol. I. Kingston: John Deutsch Institute for the Study of Economic Policy, 1991, p. 189-211.

Hawkes, David C. and Marina Devine. "Meech Lake and Elijah Harper: Native-State Relations in the 1990s." in Abele, Frances, ed. *How Ottawa Spends: The Politics of Fragmentation 1991-92.* Carleton Public Policy Series, No. 6. Ottawa: Carleton University Press, 1991, p. 33-62.

Hawkes, David C. and Bradford W. Morse. "Alternative Methods for Aboriginal Participation in Processes of Constitutional Reform." in Watts, Ronald L. and Douglas M. Brown, eds. *Options for a New Canada.* Toronto: University of Toronto Press, 1991, p. 163-87.

Helliwell, John F. and Alan Chung. "Are Bigger Countries Better Off?" in Boadway, Robin W., Thomas J. Courchene and Douglas D. Purvis, eds. *Economic Dimensions of Constitutional Change.* Vol. II. Kingston: John Deutsch Institute for the Study of Economic Policy, 1991, p. 345-67.

Herperger, Dwight and R. L. Watts. *Looking Forward, Looking Back: Constitutional Proposals of the Past and their Relevance in the Post-Meech Era.* Montreal: Council for Canadian Unity, 1990.

Howitt, Peter. "Constitutional Reform and the Bank of Canada." in Boadway, Robin W., Thomas J. Courchene and Douglas D. Purvis, eds. *Economic Dimensions of Constitutional Change.* Vol. II. Kingston: John Deutsch Institute for the Study of Economic Policy, 1991, p. 383-408.

Institute of Intergovernmental Relations. *Approaches to National Standards in Federal Systems.* [Research report prepared for the Government of Ontario]. Toronto, 1991 September.

"In the Aftermath of Meech Lake: Looking Ahead ..." *Constitutional Forum,* [special issue of the journal of the Centre for Constitutional Studies, Edmonton], 2, 2 (1991 Winter): 1-68.

Jackel, Susan. "Women in the Aftermath of Meech Lake." *Constitutional Forum,* 2, 2 (1991 Winter): 43-6.

Laforest, Guy. "Quebec Beyond the Federal Regime of 1867-1982: From Distinct Society to National Community." in Watts, Ronald L. and Douglas M. Brown, eds. *Options for a New Canada.* Toronto: University of Toronto Press, 1991, p. 103-22.

——. "Interpreting the Political Heritage of André Laurendeau." in Smith, David E., Peter MacKinnon and John C. Courtney, eds. *After Meech Lake: Lessons for the Future.* Saskatoon: Fifth House Publishers, 1991, p. 99-107.

Lallier, Adalbert. *Sovereignty Association: Economic Realism or Utopia?.* Oakville: Mosaic Press, 1991.

Latouche, Daniel and Alain-G Gagnon, eds. *Allaire, Bélanger, Campeau et les autres: Les Québécois s'interrogent sur leur avenir.* Montreal: Québec-Amérique, 1991.

Lederman, W. R. "Charter Influences on Future Constitutional Reform." in Smith, David E., Peter MacKinnon and John C. Courtney, eds. *After Meech Lake: Lessons for the Future.* Saskatoon: Fifth House Publishers, 1991, p. 115-19.

Leslie, Peter M. "Options for the Future of Canada: the Good, the Bad and the Fantastic." in Watts, Ronald L. and Douglas M. Brown, eds. *Options for a New Canada.* Toronto: University of Toronto Press, 1991, p. 123-40.

Martin, Robert. "The Charter and the Crisis in Canada." in Smith, David E., Peter MacKinnon and John C. Courtney, eds. *After Meech Lake: Lessons for the Future.* Saskatoon: Fifth House Publishers, 1991, p. 121-37.

McLellan, A. Anne. "The Constitutional Politics of Language." *Constitutional Forum,* 2, 2 (1991 Winter): 49-53.

Meekison, J. Peter. "Distribution of Functions and Jurisdiction: A Political Scientist's Analysis." in Watts, Ronald L. and Douglas M. Brown, eds. *Options for a New Canada.* Toronto: University of Toronto Press, 1991, p. 259-84.

———. "The Amending Formula and the Agenda for Change." *Constitutional Forum,* 2, 4 (1991 Summer): 93-8.

Meisel, John. "Mirror? Searchlight? Interloper?: The Media and Meech." in Smith, David E., Peter MacKinnon and John C. Courtney, eds. *After Meech Lake: Lessons for the Future.* Saskatoon: Fifth House Publishers, 1991, p. 147-68.

Mercredi, Ovide. "Aboriginal Peoples and the Constitution." in Smith, David E., Peter MacKinnon and John C. Courtney, eds. *After Meech Lake: Lessons for the Future.* Saskatoon: Fifth House Publishers, 1991, p. 219-22.

Milne, David. "Equality or Asymmetry: Why Choose?" in Watts, Ronald L. and Douglas M. Brown, eds. *Options for a New Canada.* Toronto: University of Toronto Press, 1991, p. 285-307.

———. *The Canadian Constitution.* 2nd ed. Canadian Issues Series. Toronto: James Lorimer & Company, 1991.

Mintz, Jack M. and Thomas A. Wilson. "The Allocation of Tax Authority in the Canadian Federation." in Boadway, Robin W., Thomas J. Courchene and Douglas D. Purvis, eds. *Economic Dimensions of Constitutional Change.* Vol. I. Kingston: John Deutsch Institute for the Study of Economic Policy, 1991, p. 169-88.

Monahan, Patrick J. *After Meech Lake: An Insider's View.* Reflections, No. 5. Kingston: Institute of Intergovernmental Relations, 1990.

———. "Riding the Constitutional Rollercoaster: A Commentary." in Watts, Ronald L. and Douglas M. Brown, eds. *Options for a New Canada.* Toronto: University of Toronto Press, 1991, p. 157-62.

———. *Meech Lake: The Inside Story.* Toronto: University of Toronto Press, 1991.

Network on the Constitution. *The Network.* University of Ottawa. [a new periodical first appearing in January 1991].

———. *Taking Stock: The Network Seminars on Canadian Federalism.* Edited by Donald G. Lenihan. Ottawa, 1991 July.

Norrie, Kenneth, Robin Boadway and Lars Osberg. "The Constitution and the Social Contract." in Boadway, Robin W., Thomas J. Courchene and Douglas D. Purvis, eds. *Economic Dimensions of Constitutional Change.* Vol. I. Kingston: John Deutsch Institute for the Study of Economic Policy, 1991, p. 225-54.

Ontario. *Changing for the Better: An Invitation to Talk About a New Canada.* Toronto, 1991 January.

Ontario. Ministry of the Attorney General. Constitutional Law and Policy Division. *The Protection of Social and Economic Rights: A Comparative Study.* [Staff Paper]. Toronto, 19 September 1991.

Ontario. Select Committee on Ontario in Confederation. *Interim Report.* [Silipo Committee]. Toronto, 21 March 1991.

Orban, Edmond. "Constitution and Regional Cleavages: A View from Québec." in Smith, David E., Peter MacKinnon and John C. Courtney, eds. *After Meech Lake: Lessons for the Future.* Saskatoon: Fifth House Publishers, 1991, p. 83-97.

Owram, Doug. "The Historical Context of Meech Lake." *Constitutional Forum*, 2, 2 (1991 Winter): 23-6.

Percy, Mike. "The Aftermath of Meech Lake: Implications for the Western Canadian Economy." *Constitutional Forum*, 2, 2 (1991 Winter): 35-8.

Pocklington, T. C. "Some Drawbacks of the Politics of Constitutional Rights." *Constitutional Forum*, 2, 2 (1991 Winter): 42-3.

Quebec Liberal Party. Constitutional Committee. *A Québec Free to Choose.* [Allaire Report]. Montreal, 28 January 1991.

Quebec. Commission on the Political and Constitutional Future of Québec. *Report.* [Bélanger-Campeau Report]. Quebec, 1991 March.

———. *Eléments d'analyse économique pertinents à la révision du statut politique et constitutionnel du Québec.* Quebec, 1991.

———. *Eléments d'analyse institutionnelle, juridique et démolinguistique pertinents à la révision du statut politique et constitutionnel du Québec.* Quebec, 1991.

———. *Les préoccupations et les perceptions se dégageant de la consultation populaire.* Quebec, 1991.

———. *Les avis des spécialistes invités à répondre aux huit questions posées par la Commission.* Quebec, 1991.

Quebec. Equality Party. *Quebec in Canada: One Nation — One Future.* Montreal, 1991 March.

Raboy, Marc. "Canadian Broadcasting, Canadian Nationhood: Two Concepts, Two Solitudes, and Great Expectations." in Smith, David E., Peter MacKinnon and John C. Courtney, eds. *After Meech Lake: Lessons for the Future.* Saskatoon: Fifth House Publishers, 1991, p. 181-97.

Resnick, Philip. *Toward a Canada-Quebec Union.* Montreal and Kingston: McGill-Queen's University Press, 1991.

Reuber, Grant L. "Federalism and Negative-Sum Games." in Young, Robert, ed. *Confederation in Crisis.* Toronto: James Lorimer & Company, 1991, p. 45-56.

Robertson, Gordon. *Does Canada Matter?.* Reflections, No. 7. Kingston: Institute of Intergovernmental Relations, 1991.

——. "What Future for Canada?" in Smith, David E., Peter MacKinnon and John C. Courtney, eds. *After Meech Lake: Lessons for the Future.* Saskatoon: Fifth House Publishers, 1991, p. 227-35.

Russell, Peter. "The Future Process of Canadian Constitutional Politics." in Young, Robert, ed. *Confederation in Crisis.* Toronto: James Lorimer & Company, 1991, p. 75-87.

——. "Towards a New Constitutional Process." in Watts, Ronald L. and Douglas M. Brown, eds. *Options for a New Canada.* Toronto: University of Toronto Press, 1991, p. 141-56.

Scott, Anthony. "Piecemeal Decentralization: The Environment." in Boadway, Robin W., Thomas J. Courchene and Douglas D. Purvis, eds. *Economic Dimensions of Constitutional Change.* Vol. I. Kingston: John Deutsch Institute for the Study of Economic Policy, 1991, p. 273-97.

Scott, Ian. "After Meech Lake." in Smith, David E., Peter MacKinnon and John C. Courtney, eds. *After Meech Lake: Lessons for the Future.* Saskatoon: Fifth House Publishers, 1991, p. 251-7.

Simeon, Richard. "Why Did the Meech Lake Accord Fail?" in Watts, Ronald L. and Douglas M. Brown, eds. *Canada: The State of the Federation 1990.* Kingston: Institute of Intergovernmental Relations, 1990, p. 15-40.

Simeon, Richard and Mary Janigan, eds. *Toolkits and Building Blocks: Constructing a New Canada.* Policy Study, No. 14. Toronto: C.D. Howe Institute, 1991 April.

Smith, David E., Peter MacKinnon and John C. Courtney, eds. *After Meech Lake: Lessons for the Future.* Saskatoon: Fifth House Publishers, 1991.

Smith, Jennifer. "Representation and Constitutional Reform in Canada." in Smith, David E., Peter MacKinnon and John C. Courtney, eds. *After Meech Lake: Lessons for the Future.* Saskatoon: Fifth House Publishers, 1991, p. 69-82.

Smith, Melvin H. *The Renewal of the Federation: A British Columbia Perspective.* [Study commissioned by the Government of British Columbia]. Victoria: Queen's Printer for British Columbia, 1991 May.

Smith, Murray G. "The Quebec Sovereignty Scenario: Implications for Canadian Trade Policies." in Boadway, Robin W., Thomas J. Courchene and Douglas D. Purvis, eds. *Economic Dimensions of Constitutional Change.* Vol. II. Kingston: John Deutsch Institute for the Study of Economic Policy, 1991, p. 475-88.

Smith, Roger S. "Constitutional Reform: Does Economic Efficiency Fit In?" *Constitutional Forum,* 2, 2 (1991 Winter): 38-41.

Soberman, Dan. "European Integration: Are There Lessons for Canada?" in Watts, Ronald L. and Douglas M. Brown, eds. *Options for a New Canada.* Toronto: University of Toronto Press, 1991, p. 191-205.

Taras, David. "How Television Transformed the Meech Lake Negotiations." in Smith, David E., Peter MacKinnon and John C. Courtney, eds. *After Meech Lake: Lessons for the Future.* Saskatoon: Fifth House Publishers, 1991, p. 169-80.

Taylor, Charles. "Shared and Divergent Values." in Watts, Ronald L. and Douglas M. Brown, eds. *Options for a New Canada.* Toronto: University of Toronto Press, 1991, p. 53-76.

Trimble, Linda. "The Meech Lake Accord and the Future of the Welfare State." *Constitutional Forum*, 2, 2 (1991 Winter): 32-4.

Tupper, Alan. "Meech Lake and Democratic Politics: Some Observations." *Constitutional Forum*, 2, 2 (1991 Winter): 26-31.

Usher, Dan. "The Design of a Government for an English Canadian Country." in Boadway, Robin W., Thomas J. Courchene and Douglas D. Purvis, eds. *Economic Dimensions of Constitutional Change.* Vol. I. Kingston: John Deutsch Institute for the Study of Economic Policy, 1991, p. 91-116.

Vaillancourt, François. "The Division of Powers in Canada: Theory, Evidence and Proposals for Quebec." in Boadway, Robin W., Thomas J. Courchene and Douglas D. Purvis, eds. *Economic Dimensions of Constitutional Change.* Vol. I. Kingston: John Deutsch Institute for the Study of Economic Policy, 1991, p. 255-72.

Vipond, Robert C. *Liberty and Community: Canadian Federalism and the Failure of the Constitution.* Albany: State University of New York Press, 1991.

Watts, Ronald L. "Canada's Constitutional Options: An Outline." in Watts, Ronald L. and Douglas M. Brown, eds. *Options for a New Canada.* Toronto: University of Toronto Press, 1991, p. 15-30.

——. "Canadian Federalism in the 1990s: Once More in Question." *Publius: The Journal of Federalism*, 21, 3 (1991 Summer): 169-90.

——. "The Federative Superstructure." in Watts, Ronald L. and Douglas M. Brown, eds. *Options for a New Canada.* Toronto: University of Toronto Press, 1991, p. 309-36.

Watts, Ronald L. and Douglas M. Brown, eds. *Options for a New Canada.* Toronto: University of Toronto Press, 1991.

Wells, Clyde K. "Reforming the Amending Formula: The Case for a Constitutional Convention." *Constitutional Forum*, 2, 3 (1991 Spring): 69-73.

Whyte, John D. "The Future of Canada's Constitutional Reform Process." in Smith, David E., Peter MacKinnon and John C. Courtney, eds. *After Meech Lake: Lessons for the Future.* Saskatoon: Fifth House Publishers, 1991, p. 237-49.

Young, Robert, ed. *Confederation in Crisis.* Canadian Issues Series, Toronto: James Lorimer & Company, 1991.

Yukon. Executive Council. *Green Paper on Constitutional Development.* Whitehorse, 1990.

List of Titles in Print

Institute of Intergovernmental Relations, *Annual Report to the Advisory Council, May 1, 1990*/Institut des relations intergouvernementales, *Rapport annuel au conseil consultatif, 1er mai 1990.* (charge for postage only)

Institute of Intergovernmental Relations, *Annual Report to the Advisory Council, July 1, 1989*/Institut des relations intergouvernementales, *Rapport annuel au conseil consultatif, 1er juillet 1989.* (charge for postage only)

William M. Chandler and Christian W. Zöllner, *Challenges to Federalism: Policy-Making in Canada and the Federal Republic of Germany*, 1989. ($25)

Peter M. Leslie, *Rebuilding the Relationship: Quebec and its Confederation Partners/Une collaboration renouvelée: le Québec et ses partenaires dans la confédération*, 1987. ($8)

A. Paul Pross and Susan McCorquodale, *Economic Resurgence and the Constitutional Agenda: The Case of the East Coast Fisheries*, 1987. ($10)

Bruce G. Pollard, *Managing the Interface: Intergovernmental Affairs Agencies in Canada*, 1986. ($12)

Catherine A. Murray, *Managing Diversity: Federal-Provincial Collaboration and the Committee on Extension of Services to Northern and Remote Communities*, 1984. ($15)

Peter Russell et al, *The Court and the Constitution: Comments on the Supreme Court Reference on Constitutional Amendment*, 1982. (Paper $5, Cloth $10)

Allan Tupper, *Public Money in the Private Sector: Industrial Assistance Policy and Canadian Federalism*, 1982. ($12)

William P. Irvine, *Does Canada Need a New Electoral System?* 1979. ($8)

Canada: The State of the Federation

Ronald L. Watts and Douglas M. Brown, editors, *Canada: The State of the Federation, 1990.* ($17)

Ronald L. Watts and Douglas M. Brown, editors, *Canada: The State of the Federation, 1989.* ($16)

Peter M. Leslie and Ronald L. Watts, editors, *Canada: The State of the Federation, 1987-88.* ($15)

Peter M. Leslie, editor, *Canada: The State of the Federation 1986.* ($15)

Peter M. Leslie, editor, *Canada: The State of the Federation 1985.* ($14)

Canada: L'état de la fédération 1985. ($14)

The Year in Review

Bruce G. Pollard, *The Year in Review 1983: Intergovernmental Relations in Canada.* ($16)

Revue de l'année 1983: les relations intergouvernementales au Canada. ($16)

S.M. Dunn, *The Year in Review 1982: Intergovernmental Relations in Canada.* ($12)

Revue de l'année 1982: les relations intergouvernementales au Canada. ($12)

S.M. Dunn, *The Year in Review 1981: Intergovernmental Relations in Canada.* ($10)

R.J. Zukowsky, *Intergovernmental Relations in Canada: The Year in Review 1980, Volume I: Policy and Politics.* ($8) (*Volume II not available*)

Research Papers/Notes de Recherche (formerly Discussion Papers)

29. Thomas O. Hueglin, *A Political Economy of Federalism: In Search of a New Comparative Perspective With Critical Intent Throughout,* 1990. ($10.00)

28. Ronald L. Watts, Darrel R. Reid and Dwight Herperger, *Parallel Accords: The American Precedent,* 1990. ($6)

27. Michael B. Stein, *Canadian Constitutional Renewal, 1968-1981: A Case Study in Integrative Bargaining,* 1989. ($12)

26. Ronald L. Watts, *Executive Federalism: A Comparative Analysis,* 1989. ($6)

25. Denis Robert, *L'ajustement structurel et le fédéralisme canadien: le cas de l'industrie du textile et du vêtement,* 1989. ($7.50)

24. Peter M. Leslie, *Ethnonationalism in a Federal State: The Case of Canada,* 1988. ($4)

23. Peter M. Leslie, *National Citizenship and Provincial Communities: A Review of Canadian Fiscal Federalism,* 1988. ($4)

22. Robert L. Stanfield, *National Political Parties and Regional Diversity,* 1985. (Postage Only)

21. Donald Smiley, *An Elected Senate for Canada? Clues from the Australian Experience,* 1985. ($8)

20. Nicholas R. Sidor, *Consumer Policy in the Canadian Federal State,* 1984. ($8)

19. Thomas O. Hueglin, *Federalism and Fragmentation: A Comparative View of Political Accommodation in Canada,* 1984. ($8)

18. Allan Tupper, *Bill S-31 and the Federalism of State Capitalism,* 1983. ($7)

17. Reginald Whitaker, *Federalism and Democratic Theory,* 1983. ($7)

16. Roger Gibbins, *Senate Reform: Moving Towards the Slippery Slope,* 1983. ($7)

14. John Whyte, *The Constitution and Natural Resource Revenues,* 1982. ($7)

Reflections/Réflexions

9. Donald J. Savoie, *The Politics of Language*, 1991. ($4.00)

8. Thomas J. Courchene, *The Community of the Canadas*, 1991. ($5)

7. Gordon Robertson, *Does Canada Matter?* 1991. ($3)

6. Thomas J. Courchene, *Forever Amber: The Legacy of the 1980s for the Ongoing Constitutional Impasse*, 1990. ($5)

5. Patrick J. Monahan, *After Meech: An Insider's View*, 1990. ($6)

4. Albert Breton, *Centralization, Decentralization and Intergovernmental Competition*, 1990. ($3)

3. Peter M. Leslie, *Federal Leadership in Economic and Social Policy*, 1988. ($3)

2. Clive Thomson, editor, *Navigating Meech Lake: The 1987 Constitutional Accord*, 1988. ($4)

1. Allan E. Blakeney, *Canada: Its Framework, Its Foibles, Its Future*, 1988. ($3)

Dean's Conference on Law and Policy

2. John D. Whyte and Christopher N. Kendall (eds.), *The Death and Life of Constitutional Reform in Canada*, 1991. ($8)

Bibliographies

Aboriginal Self-Government in Canada: A Bibliography 1987-90. ($10)

Aboriginal Self-Government in Canada: A Bibliography 1986. ($7)

Bibliography of Canadian and Comparative Federalism, 1986. ($20)

Bibliography of Canadian and Comparative Federalism, 1980-1985. ($39)

A Supplementary Bibliography, 1979. ($5)

A Supplementary Bibliography, 1975. ($10)

Federalism and Intergovernmental Relations in Australia, Canada, the United States and Other Countries: A Bibliography, 1967. ($9)

Aboriginal Peoples and Constitutional Reform

Background Papers

16. Bradford W. Morse, *Providing Land and Resources for Aboriginal Peoples*, 1987. ($10)

15. Evelyn J. Peters, *Aboriginal Self-Government Arrangements in Canada*, 1987. ($7)

14. Delia Opekokew, *The Political and Legal Inequities Among Aboriginal Peoples in Canada*, 1987. ($7)

13. Ian B. Cowie, *Future Issues of Jurisdiction and Coordination Between Aboriginal and Non-Aboriginal Governments*, 1987. ($7)

12. C.E.S. Franks, *Public Administration Questions Relating to Aboriginal Self-Government*, 1987. ($10)

11. Richard H. Bartlett, *Subjugation, Self-Management and Self-Government of Aboriginal Lands and Resources in Canada*, 1986. ($10)

10. Jerry Paquette, *Aboriginal Self-Government and Education in Canada*, 1986. ($10)

9. Marc Malone, *Financing Aboriginal Self-Government in Canada*, 1986. ($7)

8. John Weinstein, *Aboriginal Self-Determination Off a Land Base*, 1986. ($7)

7. David C. Hawkes, *Negotiating Aboriginal Self-Government: Developments Surrounding the 1985 First Ministers' Conference*, 1985. ($5)

6. Bryan P. Schwartz, *First Principles: Constitutional Reform with Respect to the Aboriginal Peoples of Canada 1982-1984*, 1985. ($20)

5. Douglas E. Sanders, *Aboriginal Self-Government in the United States*, 1985. ($12)

4. Bradford Morse, *Aboriginal Self-Government in Australia and Canada*, 1985. ($12)

2. David A. Boisvert, *Forms of Aboriginal Self-Government*, 1985. ($12)

1. Noel Lyon, *Aboriginal Self-Government: Rights of Citizenship and Access to Governmental Services*, 1984. ($12)

Discussion Papers

David C. Hawkes, *The Search for Accommodation*, 1987. ($7)
David C. Hawkes, *Aboriginal Self-Government: What Does It Mean?* 1985. ($12)

Position Papers

Inuit Committee on National Issues, *Completing Canada: Inuit Approaches to Self-Government*, 1987. ($7)

Martin Dunn, *Access to Survival, A Perspective on Aboriginal Self-Government for the Constituency of the Native Council of Canada*, 1986. ($7)